Congressional Reform

Congressional Reform
The Changing Modern Congress

Leroy N. Rieselbach
Indiana University

A Division of Congressional Quarterly Inc.
Washington, D.C.

Library of Congress Cataloging-in-Publication Data

Rieselbach, Leroy N.
    Congressional reform : the changing modern Congress / Leroy N. Rieselbach
        p.   cm.
    Includes bibliographical references and index.
    ISBN   0-87187-838-0
    1. United States. Congress—Reform.   I. Title.
JK1061.R495   1993
328.73'09'045—dc20   93-40455
                                                                        CIP

Contents

Preface

A s the saying goes: the more things change, the more they stay the same. Although much has changed in America's national legislature in nearly three decades of agitation for reform, at least one thing remains the same: "Congress is a much maligned institution." So I wrote in the preface to the 1977 edition of this book. Senators and representatives come and go, policy questions gain or lose prominence, and critics continue to assault Congress and propose to reform it. The 1960s and 1970s constituted a significant reform era, but as the 1990s unfold Congress remains the object of much scorn and derision. To many, it still seems unable to perform effectively its basic chores—making policy, overseeing the executive branch, and representing the citizenry.

The legislature is an easy target in many respects. Its members often seem to behave idiosyncratically. They seem more interested in promoting their own personal political interests—reelection or attaining higher office—than in crafting effective legislation. As a group, they frequently appear to defer excessively to the president, especially in foreign policy, but the chief executive castigates them as uncooperative and parochial in their outlook. The complicated congressional process baffles all but the most dedicated observers. Constituents may appreciate their own senators and representatives, who cater to their concerns, but most of the time they hold Congress, the institution, in "minimum high regard."

During the 1960s and 1970s, members of Congress recognized the institution's shortcomings. They acknowledged that the oft-quoted aphorism "the president proposes and Congress disposes" had a ring of truth. Congress was often slow to act, and when its members did take action, they did not always effectively resolve the nation's policy problems. They admitted that their job performance did not always allay fears about their ethics and integrity. As a result, they launched a major campaign, which began formally with passage of the Legislative

Reorganization Act of 1970, to reform and revitalize their institution. This book addresses the causes and character of these reforms and their consequences from the 1970s to the early 1990s. Emphasizing the uncertainties of change and reform, it examines the continuing effort to devise new and presumably better ways to conduct legislative business.

Assessing reform is a tricky matter. First, reform implies change for the better, but what one person sees as improvement may appear deleterious to another. Second, to put it bluntly, Americans have spent little time thinking about, much less deciding, what ideally Congress should be, what it should do in national politics. Matters of the moment color evaluations deeply: when Congress behaves "properly"— whether that means supporting or opposing the president, passing or rejecting favored legislation, or focusing on constituency service and oversight rather than on policy making—the observer approves; when its acts seem inappropriate, the same observer finds Congress wanting. In the absence of widely shared standards of judgment, definitive conclusions about reform and its consequences are virtually impossible.

Despite the subjectivity of reform evaluations, a close look at the institutional changes discussed and implemented since the mid-1960s may sharpen our thinking and enable us to face up to the real-world and normative implications of congressional reform. Can the nation afford to permit the executive branch and the administrative apparatus to dominate the formulation of public policy? Are there reasonable ways to harness administrative expertise to the "public good" or to equip Congress to assert more forcefully its own conception of the "national interest"? Are there clear channels through which legislators can hear the voices of individuals, alone or in organized groups? Are there structural mechanisms that can permit Congress, representing the citizenry, to exert policy influence? Can the public be motivated to hold its elected lawmakers to strict account for the ways they conduct the country's business? Finally, is there some way to create a governmental system capable of both solving problems efficiently and responding to the needs and preferences of the people?

Authors obviously incur numerous obligations in the course of their work, and I record mine with pleasure. Roderick Bell first offered me the opportunity to write about congressional reform. Bruce Oppenheimer provided an enormously insightful and valuable reading of this manuscript and a previous version, offering suggestions that required rethinking and rewriting many portions of the text. Over the years, I have learned a great deal (much of which is contained in these pages) from discussions of Congress in general and legislative change in particular with colleagues and students too numerous to name here. The Department of Political Science at Indiana University has offered a congenial environment and has given me the time and material support needed to continue my research and writing. A succession of department chairs and the department's administrative assistant, Doris-Jean Burton, have made my life easier for more than two decades, allowing important matters to drive out the trivial. Numerous departmental staff members—most recently, Joanne Day—produced a manuscript from my longhand scrawls and incompetent word processing with good humor and dispatch. Finally, Brenda Carter and Lydia Jeanne Duncan of CQ Press greatly facilitated the production of the book. I am more than grateful to these people for their invaluable help.

The book draws on four essays: "Assessing Congressional Change, or What Hath Reform Wrought (or Wreaked)?" in *The United States Congress: Proceedings of the Thomas P. O'Neill, Jr., Symposium*, ed. Dennis Hale (Chestnut Hill, Mass.: Boston College, 1982), 167-207; "Reforming Congress: Philosophy, Politics, Problems, Prospects," in *Reforming Government and Bureaucracy*, ed. Donald J. Calista, vol. 9 of *Public Policy Studies: A Multivolume Treatise* (Greenwood, Conn.: Jai Press, 1986), 129-153; "Legislative Change, Reform, and Public Policy," in *Encyclopedia of Policy Studies*, 2d ed., ed. Stuart S. Nagel (New York: Marcel Dekker, 1993); and "Congressional Reform," in *Encyclopedia of the American Legislative System*, ed., Joel H. Silbey (New York: Scribner's, forthcoming). The selected bibliography is an updated version of that included in "Legislative Change, Reform, and Public Policy," *Policy Studies Review* 2 (1983): 813-821.

Always last but never least comes one's family, and as the family grows, so too does the joy it provides. The affection, encouragement, and forbearance of Helen Rieselbach has been an inspiration. Our children and their families—Erik; Kurt, Joanne, Jurgen, and Maya; Alice and Brian; and Karen—have enriched my life immeasurably. To them goes love and appreciation far deeper than any words can convey.

Introduction: Congress under Fire

The years of the Bush administration (1989-1993) were not a happy time for the United States Congress; it was continually attacked from all sides for sins of omission and commission. In this era of "divided government," the Democrats held legislative majorities in both the House and the Senate, while the Republican commander in chief sat in the Oval Office, armed with a powerful veto pen. Many observers, both inside government and out, thought Congress lacked the capacity to address the fundamental policy questions confronting the nation. Individual lawmakers in both chambers, engaged in electoral combat to retain their positions in the legislature, drew flak for having ethical failings that critics charged prevented them from serving the broader national interest. Thus both policy-making incapacity and member malfeasance had made Congress an inviting target of popular protest. The onslaught received considerable media attention and provoked a barrage of self-criticism by the incumbent legislators as well as heavy shelling by their electoral challengers. But such public criticism of Congress is hardly unprecedented; citizen discontent dates, in the modern era, at least from the mid-1960s.

Although contemporary dissatisfaction with congressional performance antedates the Vietnam War and the Watergate crisis, those two singular events were the catalyst for the first major reform movement in Congress since the 1940s and produced the most far-reaching set of changes in congressional procedures and practices since the second decade of this century.[1] These events demonstrated with finality that the modern liberals' faith in the ultimate benevolence of the American president was misplaced: the chief executive did not automatically become an engine of progress and sound policy. Vietnam and Watergate, symbolic of the dominant "imperial presidency" of that era,[2] created both the climate and the commitment for a complete reexamination of the relationship between the two elected branches of the national government, a reassessment that led many observers

1

to conclude that Congress should operate as a more effective check on the executive.

The Indochina conflict revealed congressional impotence in foreign affairs. American involvement, as John Kennedy and Lyndon Johnson engineered it, and disengagement, as Richard Nixon conducted it, were managed almost exclusively by presidential decision. Only after the Watergate burglary and cover-up swamped Nixon did Congress act to cut off funds for military involvement in Vietnam. In most other areas, especially military strategy and defense posture, the nation's foreign policy was formulated beyond the purview of Congress; critics of Congress charged that the president and the Pentagon had restricted it to a minor role in world politics.

In domestic affairs, the events surrounding Watergate told a similar tale of presidential dominance. A president, without hindrance from Congress (even one controlled by his political opposition), engaged in or condoned numerous illegal activities: obstructing justice by concealing evidence of the break-in at Democratic National Committee headquarters; using federal agencies—the Federal Bureau of Investigation, the Central Intelligence Agency, and the Internal Revenue Service— for political purposes; employing campaign "dirty tricks"; trying to influence the judge in the case of Daniel Ellsberg, the author of the *Pentagon Papers*; and temporarily accepting a surveillance plan that infringed on the civil rights of citizens. Moreover, with regard to the federal budget, Nixon challenged Congress directly: he tried to force it to limit spending, and in an unprecedented action, he began to impound (refuse to spend) money that Congress had duly appropriated.

A more general criticism, which predated Watergate, was that Congress did not respond to national needs. Vested interests within the legislature remained firmly in support of the status quo: the environmental crisis continued unabated, crime escalated, poverty and unemployment worsened, and inflation eroded the purchasing power of those who did have jobs. Congress did not respond adequately to these crises, its antagonists asserted, because it was not organized to deal effectively with contemporary policy problems. It had abdicated its responsibility, enabling the executive to play the role of prime mover in public affairs.[3] The aim of the reform movement that gained momentum in the Vietnam-Watergate era was to remedy these deficiencies, to make Congress a better, more efficient legislature.

Congress adopted numerous reforms in the 1970s (see Chapter 3). The 1980s were a period of relative quiescence on the reform front; the newly adopted procedures evolved and were allowed to run their course. The changes that were made in legislative practice and performance were more pragmatic and piecemeal, less the product of a self-conscious effort to alter the ways Congress conducted its business.

Many observers of the legislature professed to see little difference between the two decades in terms of congressional capacity and performance. Critics charged that Congress continued to defer excessively to the president and was unable to put its own stamp on the affairs of state. They found the institution incapable of giving sustained attention to pressing matters of public policy—such as the swelling federal budget deficit, crime, drugs, health care, and educational shortcomings—that were eroding the quality of American life.

Some attributed these failings to an increasing tendency of individual members to turn inward, seeking to protect their own political and electoral interests, and the interests of their constituents, at the expense of national concerns. According to the darkest view of senators and representatives, they were all too often beholden to special interests, more concerned with securing campaign contributions from powerful interest groups and political action committees (PACs) than with finding solutions to the problems that increasingly plagued ordinary citizens, with whom they were out of touch. They voted themselves large salary increases and accepted honoraria, travel reimbursement, and other compensation from interest groups that asked them to give speeches, write articles, or attend group meetings and conventions. In addition, they provided themselves numerous perquisites of office that helped incumbents ensure their reelection.[4] In the view of many citizens, they constituted an arrogant elite, unwilling to run the political risks of confronting difficult policy issues and an opposition president who challenged them. Congress, in short, was in a state of crisis, caught in a crossfire between frustrated executive branch personnel (especially the president) and irate citizens who were, as the public had in the 1970s, demanding reforms to improve congressional performance.[5]

Events of the 1980s lent credence to these manifold dissatisfactions and provided ammunition for a new round of reforms. Presidents Ronald Reagan and George Bush commanded the foreign policy terrain, as had their predecessors; substantial numbers of legislators opposed executive initiatives but could not find ways to impose their preferences on the commander in chief. Under President Reagan a secret operation was begun to trade arms to Iran in exchange for the release of American hostages held by pro-Iranian forces in Lebanon: the profits from these arms sales were diverted to support the Nicaraguan contras, a rebel faction seeking to overthrow the duly elected government of that nation. Congress had expressly prohibited use of American funds for military activities to depose the Nicaraguan regime. The staff of the National Security Council, working out of the White House, managed the Iran-contra operation and took great pains to keep Congress in the dark. House and Senate investigations, and a special commission that the president subsequently appointed, eventually confirmed that the executive effectively, and improperly, bypassed Congress. Independent prosecutor Lawrence Walsh obtained convictions or guilty pleas from nine persons for obstructing the actions of Congress or deliberately withholding information from it.[6]

Fearful of Iranian domination of the Middle East, the Reagan and Bush administrations undertook secret dealings with Iraq, again largely beyond the purview of Congress. By offering intelligence and material support, the White House hoped to shore up Iraq as a counterweight to Iran in the Middle East. The Bush administration continued to assist Iraq despite substantial evidence that Saddam Hussein, the Iraqi leader, was using U.S. aid to develop chemical, biological, and even nuclear weapons of mass destruction. These matters took on significance in light of the Persian Gulf War of 1990-1991. In August 1990, Iraq seized neighboring Kuwait, threatening Saudi Arabia and the free flow of oil from the Middle East. With United Nations concurrence, President Bush orchestrated the formation of a coalition, including Arab and western nations, to evict the invading Iraqis. Confronted with a fait accompli, both the House (in a 380-29 vote) and the Senate (96-3) passed resolutions backing the president. Neither chamber was prepared to invoke the War Powers Act of 1973, which was intended to give Congress the ability to prevent presidential commitment of American forces to real or imminent combat without legislative approval. By the end of 1990, more than 400,000 troops were poised on the border between Saudi Arabia and Kuwait. The administration set a deadline of January 15, 1991, for Iraq to comply with UN resolutions and withdraw from Kuwait. Congress debated inconclusively about what to do; the president had asserted full authority to act as he saw fit. When the deadline passed, unheeded, the president sought congressional approval of a military ouster of the Iraqi forces. Many in Congress, remembering the lessons of Vietnam, preferred to use economic sanctions to force Iraq to withdraw. But unwilling to challenge the administration directly, the legislators grudgingly passed (by a vote of 250-183 in the House and 52-47 in the Senate) a resolution authorizing war with Iraq.

The Middle East was not the only region of the world where troubles erupted in the 1980s. Without consulting Congress, President Reagan dispatched American troops to Grenada in 1983 after a left-wing coup had been staged in that small Caribbean island republic. President Bush sent the marines to capture Panamanian dictator General Manuel Noriega in 1986, again without first securing congressional approval. He also resolutely resisted legislative efforts to impose limitations on China's "most favored nation" trading status as well as other sanctions, as punishment for China's brutal suppression of the people's "democracy movement," particularly the massacre of student protesters in Tiananmen Square in June 1989. In addition, American foreign trade policy reflected the administration's free trade perspective rather than the protectionist preferences of many members of Congress. Congress ceded to the president the authority to negotiate a North American Free Trade Agreement with Canada and Mexico under a "fast track" procedure that required the lawmakers to vote for or against the agreement in toto, with no possibility of amendment. Overall, U.S. foreign policy followed presidential initiatives; Congress found itself on the periphery, forced to respond to executive actions and unwilling or unable to assert its own priorities.[7]

On the domestic front, the record of Congress was somewhat better, but even here the widespread perception was that social problems were of such magnitude that the legislature could not cope with them. On a few occasions, when the president was prepared to negotiate and compromise, significant measures became law. Passage of the Clean Air Act of 1990 and the Americans with Disabilities Act were some major accomplishments of the Bush years. But when the administration dug in, even heavy congressional pressure could not deter it. Legislative proposals to protect abortion rights, to grant employees leave to care for ill family members without jeopardizing their jobs, and to fight crime were casualties of the president's mighty veto pen.[8] In all, President Bush vetoed forty-six bills and Congress mustered the two-thirds vote needed to override only one, a bill to regulate the cable television industry. At the end of the Bush administration, issues of deficit reduction, health care, educational reform, and aid to urban areas and the homeless were still unresolved.[9]

In part, policy inaction was caused by a series of congressional scandals that diverted attention from programmatic concerns and brought the legislature into popular disrepute. The Senate Ethics Committee found that five senators—the so-called Keating Five—had used poor judgment in attempting to influence regulators' treatment of a troubled savings and loan association. Alan Cranston (D-Calif.) was disciplined and subsequently retired from office. The ethics panel also chastised David Durenberger (R-Minn.) and Mark Hatfield (R-Ore.) for financial improprieties and launched investigations of sexual harassment charges that had been filed against Brock Adams (D-Wash.) and Bob Packwood (R-Ore.). In the House, allegations of ethical lapses forced the resignations of the Speaker, Jim Wright (D-Texas), and majority whip Tony Coehlo (D-Calif.). More than 300 members were found to have written overdrafts on their accounts at the chamber's "bank," perhaps more accurately described as a check-cashing service. Employees of the House Post Office pleaded guilty or were convicted of embezzlement and drug dealing. In addition, juries returned indictments for various corrupt practices against Harold Ford (D-Tenn.), Nicholas Mavroules (D-Mass.), and Joseph McDade (R-Pa.).

The House seemed singularly reluctant to take these allegations seriously, and the feeling grew that members of Congress considered themselves above the law. The mass media covered these matters in detail and displayed them prominently. They also dealt extensively with the questionable Senate conduct of a series of confirmation hearings. President Reagan's nomination of Robert Bork to the Supreme Court generated more partisan wrangling and ideological posturing than reasoned analysis. The all-male Judiciary Committee's probing of the sexual harassment charges that had been leveled against Judge Clarence Thomas, Bush's choice for the high court, was sensationalist and unseemly. The Intelligence Committee's examination of Robert Gates, nominated for promotion to director of the Central Intelligence Agency, skirted charges that he had biased agency findings for political purposes.

These were controversial charges. Defenders of Congress launched a strong counterattack. They were quick to point out that the constitutional separation of powers guarantees Congress an independent role and makes it the equal of the executive. Allowing different electorates to select the president and Congress virtually ensures that the two branches will approach difficult policy questions with distinctive points of view. Congress, as the "people's branch," speaks for state and local constituencies; the president, chosen nationally, articulates broader, less parochial perspectives. The voters, more frequently in recent years, have used their franchise to entrust the presidency to one political party and the legislature to the other, thus creating a divided government; the result has been an exacerbation of interbranch policy partisanship that has made effective governance more difficult. The Constitution permits Congress to assert its preferences and those of the voters who have elected it, regardless of which party controls the legislature and which controls the executive.

Even so, members of Congress can claim significant policy accomplishments: energy and environmental protection legislation in the Carter years, a major overhaul of the tax code during the Reagan presidency, the Americans with Disabilities Act and the Clean Air Act revision in the Bush term, and, in the first months of the Clinton administration, legislation requiring employers to grant their workers unpaid leave of absence to deal with family emergencies (the Family and Medical Leave Act of 1993) and a "motor-voter" bill (passed in May 1993) to facilitate voter registration. Congress, according to its proponents, can and regularly does face up to and resolve pressing policy matters. Moreover, it effectively exercises oversight of the executive branch; congressional hearings and investigations have ferreted out malfeasance and inefficiency at the Environmental Protection Agency, in the Defense Department (procurement of weapons), and in the Department of Housing and Urban Development (housing subsidy programs). In short, much criticism of Congress is misplaced and unfair.[10]

Although not condoning illegality or immorality, supporters of Congress have stressed the positive side of lawmakers' perquisites. Decent pay has encouraged talented individuals to embark on legislative careers. Travel, contacts with the public, and expert staff support have enabled lawmakers to represent their constituents more effectively— to discern popular sentiments and to formulate and enact legislation establishing workable programs in keeping with them.

The defenders of Congress make a powerful case, but regardless of the merits of their arguments, the critics seem to have carried the day. The public approval rating of Congress declined sharply in the late 1980s. Poll after poll found voters wary of their lawmakers. For instance, in an April 1992 ABC News/Washington Post survey, 82 percent of the respondents agreed that "those we elect to Congress . . . lose touch with the people pretty quickly"; in March 1992, 72 percent had thought writing bad checks was business as usual for Congress. In the CBS News/New York Times poll conducted in July 1992, only one-fifth (20 percent) of the respondents said they "approved of the way Congress is handling its job." Proposals to limit congressional service to twelve years or less passed overwhelmingly in all fourteen states where they were included on the November 1992 ballot.[11]

Paradoxically, majorities of voters in these polls believed that the lawmakers from their states and districts were performing adequately. In the 1992 elections, 88 percent of the incumbents seeking reelection were returned to office (though often with reduced vote margins). Yet 43 House incumbents and 4 Senate incumbents lost their seats. Coupled with high levels of voluntary retirement, these losses brought 110 newcomers to the House and 14 to the Senate. These men and women took their places at a time when public confidence in the institution was at an all-time low. Many had campaigned on a reform agenda and they seemed ready to examine critically the way Congress does its job.

When the 103d Congress convened in January 1993, the public was still skeptical about the lawmakers' performance and ethics. The media focused on these issues, and reform proposals filled the air. Congress itself established a Joint Committee on the Organization of Congress to review these suggestions and to recommend changes that would improve policy-making performance and restore the goodwill of the citizenry. Congress endured a similar assault in the 1970s and responded with a series of major reforms. Their failure to achieve all that their proponents had hoped and expected contributed to the reform impulse of the 1990s. How and why Congress has periodically come under assault, what it has done in response to such attacks, the effects of the changes it has adopted to defend itself, and the prospects for additional reform are the subjects of this book.

NOTES

1. See George B. Galloway, *The History of the House of Representatives*, 2d ed., revised by Sidney Wise (New York: Crowell, 1976). See also Alvin M. Josephy, Jr., *On the Hill: A History of the American Congress from 1789 to the Present* (New York: Touchstone Books, 1979).
2. Arthur M. Schlesinger, Jr., popularized this phrase and the notion of an excessively powerful president. See *The Imperial Presidency* (Boston: Houghton Mifflin, 1976).
3. This view, of course, is an overstatement. Many legislators continued to be energetic and effective workers for social change. The critics claimed, however, that Congress as an institution had not distinguished itself as a source or proponent of innovative solutions to major policy problems. Except for the programs of the early New Deal (1933-1937) and Lyndon B. Johnson's Great Society initiatives of 1964 and 1965, Congress was more often cautious than creative. On this issue, see Bruce I. Oppenheinmer, "How Legislatures Shape Public Policy and Budgets," *Legislative Studies Quarterly* 8 (1983): 551-597; and Gerald C. Wright, Jr., Leroy N. Rieselbach, and Lawrence C. Dodd, eds., *Policy Change in Congress* (New York: Agathon Press, 1986).
4. The "perks" included, in addition to high salaries, mail franking privileges (the sending of mail at government expense to all "postal patrons" in a state or district), travel and telephone allowances, extensive staff assistance, inexpensive medical care, cheap haircuts, free flowers, subsidized parking, and a variety of other frills that critics deemed unnecessary and extravagant at a time of budgetary stringency.
5. For a sampling of critical and reformist views of congressional performance, see Hedrick Smith, *The Power Game: How Washington Works* (New York: Random House, 1988); George F. Will, *Restoration: Congress, Term Limits, and the Recovery of Deliberative Democracy* (New York: Free Press, 1992); Philip M. Stern, *'Still' the Best Congress Money Can Buy*, rev. ed. (Washington, D.C.: Regnery Gateway, 1992); and Jeffrey H. Birnbaum, *The Lobbyists: How Influence Peddlers Get Their Way in Washington* (New York: Times Books/Random House, 1993).
6. On the Iran-contra affair, see House Select Committee to Investigate Covert Arms Transactions with Iran and Senate Select Committee on Secret Military Assistance to Iran and the Nicaraguan Opposition, *Report of the Congressional Committees Investigating the Iran-Contra Affair* (Washington, D.C.: Government Printing Office, 1987); and *Report of the President's Special Review Board* (Tower Commission) (Washington, D.C.: Government Printing Office, 1987). Two other convictions were reversed on technical and legal rather than substantive grounds. In the last days of his presidency, seeking, he said, to lay the controversy to rest for the good of the nation (and, said numerous critics, to conceal

his own involvement in the matter as vice-president), George Bush announced pardons for six participants in the affair.

7. For recent analyses of executive-legislative relations concerning foreign policy, see Thomas E. Mann, ed., *A Question of Balance: The President, the Congress, and Foreign Policy* (Washington, D.C.: Brookings Institution, 1990); Cecil V. Crabb, Jr., and Pat M. Holt, *Invitation to Struggle: Congress, the President, and Foreign Policy*, 4th ed. (Washington, D.C.: CQ Press, 1992); and Randall B. Ripley and James M. Lindsay, eds., *Congress Resurgent: Foreign and Defense Policy on Capitol Hill* (Ann Arbor: University of Michigan Press, 1993).

8. The need to control crime was widely recognized; the means to do so, however, was the subject of considerable controversy, and the president could not accept the bill Congress enacted.

9. Several recent works treat the subject of presidential-congressional competition: Michael L. Mezey, *Congress, the President, and Public Policy* (Boulder, Colo.: Westview Press, 1989); James A. Thurber, ed., *Divided Democracy: Cooperation and Conflict between the President and Congress* (Washington, D.C.: CQ Press, 1991); Lance T. LeLoup and Steven A. Shull, *Congress and the President: The Policy Connection* (Belmont, Calif.: Wadsworth, 1993); and Robert J. Spitzer, *President and Congress: Executive Hegemony at the Crossroads of American Government* (New York: McGraw-Hill, 1993).

10. For the argument that not even divided government prevents Congress from enacting legislation establishing policy and conducting oversight, see David R. Mayhew, *Divided We Govern: Party Control, Lawmaking, and Investigations, 1946-1990* (New Haven, Conn.: Yale University Press, 1991).

11. "A Public Hearing on Congress," *Public Perspective* 4 (November-December 1992): 82-92, presents the results of numerous polls on the public's perceptions of Congress.

1. Congress and American Politics

No other legislature is quite like the U.S. Congress. Its ability to compete with the executive branch, and its considerable ability to impose its will on the direction and substance of national politics when and if it chooses to do so, distinguish it from most other twentieth-century assemblies. Even its critics acknowledge that Congress continues to pose serious policy-making challenges for the president; what the nation does in foreign affairs and domestic matters often, but not always, bears the stamp of the national legislature. Much of American political history, in fact, has been characterized by a power struggle between the president and Congress for policy-making primacy. Yet Congress has not always asserted its authority to the fullest extent. The alleged failure of Congress to leave its mark on public policy gave rise to the reform movement that began in the mid-1960s.

Congress and the Constitution

Reform was both attractive and possible because the decline of the legislature was neither inevitable nor irreversible. Congress retained the constitutional and statutory means to exert a major impact on the form and content of public policy. The Constitution clearly assigns to Congress, as one of the "separate institutions sharing power," important policy-making responsibilities. It has the power to declare war and appropriate money to sustain the military, as well as to authorize and fund major domestic programs. The way Congress employs its constitutional power to meet its obligations at any moment in history goes far to determine what the nation does or does not accomplish. Congress can, when a majority of its members wish to act, impose its collective preferences on the body politic. It does not only act affirmatively, however; it also is able (and more likely) to block initiatives that others—the public, interest organizations, and the courts, as well as the president—propose. If Congress has not used its powers, it is because most lawmakers have chosen to defer to executive expertise or to permit others to make decisions that they, as elected legislators, have decided not to make for themselves.

Congress has other obligations beyond policy making. The Legislative Reorganization Act of 1946 authorizes it to maintain "continuous watchfulness" over the departments, agencies, and bureaus that constitute the administrative branch of government. In general, the aim of this process of congressional oversight of the executive is to keep bureaucrats, from cabinet secretaries on down, honest and efficient.[1] The Senate, exercising its "advice and consent" prerogative, must approve the president's nominations for the top political posts in the administration. For example, the Senate subjected Ronald Reagan's choice for attorney general, Edwin Meese, to close scrutiny because of a series of charges that Meese had used his position as a White House adviser to the president to reward friends for loans and for other favors they had done for him and his family. The Senate directed the appointment of a special counsel to investigate the accusations, which delayed confirmation for many months, and exacted from the nominee pledges to avoid even the appearance of ethical impropriety in the future. Congress also writes the civil service statutes that specify the conditions and qualifications of employment in the federal bureaucracy below the level of the president's political appointees. As a result, individuals who oppose presidential initiatives may be entrenched in the executive branch as career civil servants. Policing the personnel of the executive may, of course, bring Congress in conflict with the president.

Oversight also entails congressional examination of bureaucratic performance. Legislative committees regularly seek to determine whether administrators get a dollar's worth of value for a dollar spent. Members of Congress are predictably outraged when they discover that the government has paid defense contractors $7,622 for a coffee machine, $748 for a pair of pliers, or $640 for a custom-made toilet cover.[2] In the long run, the fact or threat of legislative investigation may deter bureaucrats from pushing forcefully for adoption of presidential initiatives. Oversight goals may be couched in terms of efficiency, but they have clear programmatic implications. Revelations of defense industry abuses prompted Congress to sharply cut back procurement of the MX missile to levels well below those the president favored. Here, too, oversight may exacerbate differences of opinion between the legislature and the executive.

Congress is the "people's branch": it should speak for and to the citizenry. Members should both listen to and act on behalf of their constituents, informing and educating them about the activities in the nation's capital. Representation takes several forms.[3] Senators and representatives are expected to translate public preferences into policies that result in practical programs. They are also expected to "deliver the goods"—in the form of public projects and contracts for local industries—to their constituents and to perform for them a variety of "casework" services, such as tracing lost Social Security or income tax refund checks and providing information about how the federal bureaucracy operates. Representation also has a symbolic dimension. If for no other reason than to promote their reelection, members feel an obligation to present a favorable image of themselves to the folks back home. Thus, they develop a "home style," a way of relating to residents through regular contacts with their states and districts.[4] By making appropriate gestures to constituents—listening to them, showing empathy for them, and explaining legislative activities to them—members of Congress hope to earn their trust and confidence and to gain at least some freedom to pursue their own policy preferences.

Constituency relations, then, assume great importance in members' lives, for policy making as well as in oversight and representation. The opinions and complaints that members hear from constituents may alert them to policy needs or deficiencies and compel them to respond. Representation may also generate differences with the executive. To the extent that the public favors one set of programs and the president favors another, legislators have to choose. Politically, the most prudent course may be to defer to constituents and to oppose the chief executive. When unpopular positions—raising taxes, committing troops, defending abortion—are avoided, difficult problems may remain unresolved.

In short, whatever Congress does when it legislates (or fails to act), oversees, and represents is likely to bring it into conflict with the executive. The Constitution virtually guarantees that the legislature will view its work differently than will the president. The latter is chosen by all the people and is the focus of national attention, the central actor in the political drama. By contrast, members of Congress are elected by states and local constituencies that vary widely in population characteristics and social and economic conditions. Senators represent the interests of large, populous states (California, New York, Texas) as well as sparsely settled states (Alaska, Utah, Idaho); energy-producing states (in the Southwest) and energy-consuming states (in New England); Farm Belt states and states where urban, inner-city areas dominate; industrial "smokestack" states (the Frost Belt) and service-industry states (the Sun Belt).

Districts represented in the House of Representatives are often more homogeneous—composed almost totally of working-class, farm, suburban, or black constituencies. On controversial issues, these citizens frequently send their legislators loud and clear messages. In such circumstances, members may well speak for interests requiring responses that bring Congress in conflict with the president.

Moreover, the federal system, which undercuts the possibility of centralized, disciplined, national political parties, contributes to members' independence of the president. The parties' national organizations (even that of the president's party) have little leverage with members, who are essentially local candidates. Senators and representatives, who run in single-member districts that select winners by plurality vote, largely control their own electoral fates. Increasingly in recent years, they have gotten support from party organizations, but they continue to run their own races in response to local conditions. They recruit their own campaign workers, solicit their own campaign funds, plan their own schedules, and select their own campaign issues. They regularly win reelection, they believe, as a result of their own efforts, with little debt owed to the national party, which has few sanctions by which to discipline members who defect from nationally established party positions.[5] Electorally entrenched by their constituencies, members are free to oppose the president when that seems to be a wise strategy; whether for policy reasons or political purposes, they can pursue their own interests without fear of real reprisals from the chief executive.

In sum, the Constitution, with its checks and balances, separation of powers, and principle of federalism, makes Congress independent of the executive. Congress has the constitutional authority to impose its policy preferences; its members have the political freedom to do so. For better or worse, sooner or later Congress and the president will clash over the content of public policy. The Constitution ensures such conflict.

Politics, Values, and the Assessment of Congress

Whether this conflict is good or bad is, of course, a matter of philosophy, of political preference. Some observers profess satisfaction with the status quo, preferring minimal policy change most of the time to an overly powerful, imperial president. Congress, they believe, should serve to restrain the executive. Others, however, want action; they see major problems that need solution, and they deplore the immobilism that, in their view, inevitably results from the executive-legislative balance. The problem is particularly acute in periods of divided government, when one party controls the presidency while the other has a majority in one or both houses of Congress. Either position may spawn proposals for reform. The former group, believing that, after the New

Deal of the 1930s, Congress gradually relinquished its ability to resist the president, proposes changes to strengthen the legislature's capacity to countervail the executive. The latter group, assessing the same circumstances, ironically sees something quite different: an overly powerful Congress. It suggests reforms intended to reduce the legislature's opportunities to obstruct presidential leadership, to block innovative policy initiatives that the president is most likely to produce.

As time passes and political circumstances change, however, these groups are likely to alter their views, depending on the particular policy at issue. For example, liberals, those predisposed to social activism and government intervention in the economy, have decried Congress's reluctance to embark on major new programs since the reforms of the New Deal and the Great Society. Yet when a president proposed to eliminate desirable programs already on the statute books, the same liberals applauded Congress's refusal to repeal these policies. They were more than happy to see the legislature block many conservative proposals that Richard Nixon advanced between 1968 and 1974.[6] Presumably, they were equally content with its resistance to many Reagan and Bush administration initiatives (1981 to 1992), especially cutbacks in the size and scope of numerous federal programs. Conversely, conservatives, those who favor a free market and minimal government intervention, cheer when Congress blocks new federal initiatives and hiss when it fails to heed the bidding of presidents, such as Ronald Reagan and George Bush, who share their philosophy. Today's reforms influence tomorrow's congressional performance; change may have consequences the reformers never considered or intended.

Broad Visions

Both liberals and conservatives evaluate Congress in terms of current political (particularly policy) values; they seldom step back to assess the big picture: what Congress might be like in the best of all possible worlds. A few, however, have set forth comprehensive and presumably timeless theories concerning the legislature's proper political role that, in a sense, transcend the politics of the moment and current policy preferences. Four such visions warrant brief discussion here: the executive force theory, the responsible parties theory, the "literary" theory, and the congressional supremacy theory.[7]

The Executive Force Theory. Proponents of the executive force theory are pessimistic about Congress's capacity to govern.[8] They stress the need to solve pressing political, economic, and social problems and deny that the legislature can contribute meaningfully to policy formulation. In their view, the executive is the likely catalyst for progress;

Congress, given its basic structures and processes, can only impede innovation. Because it is a decentralized, fragmented institution representing multiple interests—especially the rural, small-town, conservative constituencies of middle America—the legislature is incapable of acting decisively. It is better suited to oppose than to create, to react than to invent.

In consequence, if policy making is to meet the nation's needs, the president must be permitted to lead, unobstructed by a recalcitrant Congress. Executive proposals and initiatives should move smoothly through Congress so they can be adopted and implemented. Reform should reduce legislative ability to frustrate presidential policy making. Independent sources of power—committees and subcommittees, for instance—should be curbed. Rules of procedure that permit legislative minorities to block action require modification. This executive supremacy view, in sum, stresses presidential leadership and reduces Congress's role to reviewing after the fact, legitimizing, and perhaps modifying, decisions the president makes.[9] The president proposes, and the legislature disposes according to his wishes.

The Responsible Parties Theory. An alternative way for the executive to deal with congressional obstructionism is to encourage disciplined, cohesive, responsible political parties.[10] If the members of the majority party, given their command of the legislative terrain as the assembly's chief organizational agents, always marched smartly and decisively in rank, their policy proposals would be accepted at each stage of the lawmaking process. Moreover, if the president commanded the party troops, they would advance his programs without risk of rearguard delay or defeat.

Proponents of responsible parties promote reforms to enlist rank-and-file members of Congress in the partisan armies. In general, they would empower the national committees of the parties to manage the electoral process by giving them a legal monopoly over campaign finances. By controlling the representatives' nomination, the committees could dictate their actions. To break ranks would, in effect, end their political career; the nomination would be given to a new, more loyal recruit. The rules of Congress would be rewritten to ensure that disciplined majorities could more easily carry the legislative day. According to the responsible parties theory, the president proposes, and his partisan army loyally obeys his marching orders. Here, too, Congress would eschew policy making; the emphasis is rather on legitimizing and nonpolicy representation (for example, constituent service).

The "Literary" Theory. What proponents of the executive force and responsible parties theories consider vices are virtues to proponents of the "literary" theory.[11] The latter pay homage to the written tradition of checks and balances and separation of powers in the Constitution. In their view, Congress should restrain the power-seeking executive during both policy formulation and policy implementation. New policies, departures from the status quo, should evolve slowly, only after careful deliberation of all alternatives, and only after a genuine national consensus emerges. Thus a decentralized legislature, which is influenced by multiple interests and can act only cautiously, is highly desirable.

These virtues have been lost in the twentieth century, the so-called age of executives, and reform is required to restore the status quo ante, say the literary theorists. To that end, they resist all centralizing mechanisms. They prefer an election system that protects legislators' independence; they fear disciplined political parties that might ignore or misrepresent citizens' sentiments; they distrust executive leadership in any form; and most important, they favor congressional procedures that protect the power of individual legislators to speak, delay action, promote deliberation, and oversee the administration. Overall, they want Congress to propose *and* dispose—make policy, represent citizens, police the bureaucracy—in order to countervail the chief executive. They seek to restore Congress to what they view as its rightful place at the center of the political process.

The Congressional Supremacy ("Whig") Theory. Legislative supremacists stress the centrality of Congress to an even greater extent than do the literary theorists.[12] They consider Congress the first branch of government, the prime mover in national affairs, and they favor all the reforms that the literary theorists advocate as well as other changes intended, in effect, to strip the chief executive of the ability to dominate national policy making. The "Whig" theorists envisage a Congress that proposes and an administration (president and bureaucracy) that disposes in strict accordance with legislative desires. A supreme Congress will make policy—explicitly and on its own terms—as well as oversee the implementation of that policy.

Conclusion. Each of these broad visions of Congress includes a particular set of organizational and procedural reforms that could provide a model against which to evaluate specific reform proposals. Central to any assessment of reform are a general question about the obligation of government and a more specific question about the role of Congress in policy making. Proponents of the executive force and responsible parties theories stress action; the government must find prompt and effective solutions to national problems. In stark contrast, the literary and congressional supremacy theorists focus on caution and consensus; policy initiatives should evolve slowly, after due deliberation has produced wide agreement that new programs are needed.

All four visions have concomitant organizational requisites. Those who desire to foster active policy making (the executive force and responsible parties theorists) favor a centralized Congress. Dominant executives, sustained by an accommodating legislature, formulate and implement public policies. Those who prefer inaction look favorably on a decentralized legislature—with numerous autonomous decision-making centers—that can act only after considering many points of view as the basis for widely acceptable programs. In other words, the pro-executive theorists seek to minimize independent congressional policy influence, whereas the pro-legislative theorists seek to maximize it.[13]

Narrower Standards: Responsibility, Responsiveness, and Accountability

These broad visions of the "good" legislature have inspired more talk than action. They are hard to implement; each would in all likelihood require amending the Constitution, a difficult task under any circumstances, and especially so when it involves altering basic features of the political process such as the electoral system. Needless to say, given the sharp contrasts between the pro-executive and legislative supremacy positions, there is little basis for agreement. Furthermore, in the "real world" of practical politics, few with the opportunity and authority to change the way Congress operates—the members themselves—have taken a genuine interest in stepping back from day-to-day political pressures to examine Congress and its policy-making role in philosophical terms. Rather, they have tended to react pragmatically and to call for reform only if it seemed absolutely necessary. The strong criticisms of 1990 and 1991 prompted Congress to establish a Joint Committee on the Organization of Congress to assess the proposals and possibilities for reform. Members have tended to evaluate their institution's performance using three criteria: responsibility, responsiveness, and accountability.[14] These three standards relate to the broader visions but do not require the same levels of agreement or pose insuperable obstacles to taking specific steps toward reform.

Any assessment of the need for congressional reform raises fundamental questions about the place of Congress in the national government, a subject that the executive-legislative conflicts over "hot" issues such as Vietnam and Watergate brought to the top of the political agenda. What should Congress's role be? Should it relinquish its claim to participate meaningfully in policy making? Should it focus its attention and resources on overseeing the executive branch, sounding the alarm when presidents move in the wrong direction or when bureaucrats perform unsatisfactorily? Should the legislature be content simply to represent the public—transmitting expressions of popular opinion to those who actually make decisions, informing citizens about government programs, and performing nonpolicy casework services for constituents? Or should Congress revitalize its mode of operation and attempt to exercise policy initiative and leadership? The three criteria yield quite different answers to these questions, but each provides a starting point for analysis of the legislative branch.[15]

Responsibility. Responsibility focuses on problem solving. A responsible institution makes policies that are reasonably successful in resolving the major issues confronting the nation. In addition to success, the responsibility criterion emphasizes speed and efficiency. Can Congress formulate policies that deal promptly and effectively with national and international problems? Can it control inflation or reduce unemployment? Can it pass laws that strengthen the nation's defense, promote international trade, or encourage Third World social and economic development? If, as many critics of Congress have argued, the answer to such queries is "no," then reform to improve the *product* of the legislative process is clearly in order.

A responsible Congress is compatible with both pro-executive and pro-legislative visions. To the extent that Congress simply ratifies the president's program without delay or major revision, it acts as the advocates of the executive force or responsible parties theories prefer; it concurs with the executive, approving policies that presumably address the major issues of the day. Policy independence, however, is minimal; the legislature merely defers to the initiatives of the president. To the degree that Congress imposes its own programmatic priorities, however, it behaves consistently with the literary and congressional supremacy (Whig) theories; that is, it does what it thinks best, regardless of what is favored by the executive, interest groups, or public opinion. This may entail blocking what seem to be unwise executive initiatives or, a more problematic course, insisting on its own priorities. Here, Congress exercises genuine policy autonomy and influence, but it will most certainly encounter difficulty, especially when it seeks to impose its own preferences. Other political participants will mobilize to block congressional action. The president may veto legislation, a veto that can be overruled only if Congress musters a two-thirds majority in each chamber. Needless to say, asserting supremacy in the face of determined opposition will prove more challenging than joining a government wide policy consensus. A policy-oriented legislature may spend more time studying and debating legislation and will probably devote less effort to oversight and representational activities. In any case, the responsibility standard assesses Congress in terms of its ability to formulate workable public policies with dispatch.

Responsiveness. Responsiveness emphasizes *process* more than product, the content of policy. This is not to suggest an indifference to policy but merely to indicate that substance is secondary to the ways that the legislature operates. To be responsive, Congress must listen to and take account of the ideas and sentiments of those who will be affected by its actions: individual citizens, organized groups, local and state governments, and federal government executives. The lawmakers must provide an open channel of communication to those whom their decisions will influence; those with policy preferences or requests for services must have free and easy access to the legislators. On rare occasions, Congress responds almost immediately to an outpouring of public sentiment; in most instances, a responsive Congress will not act until all who have opinions have had the chance to voice them.

A responsive Congress tends to be a deliberate, slow-moving body. If it does not get unequivocal and forceful messages from the public (an infrequent occurrence), it is likely to delay innovative policy making, at least in the short run. Proponents of the executive force theory prefer prompt action and consider congressional caution and delay to have a debilitating effect on policy formulation. They grow impatient if the legislature takes time to listen to all points of view and to negotiate middle-of-the-road compromises that do not, in their opinion, resolve the nation's pressing problems. Congressional supremacists, by contrast, tend to appreciate responsiveness. Fearing an overly powerful president, they prefer a legislature that restrains the chief executive; they want Congress to listen, wait, and act only when a real national consensus emerges. They are not alarmed when Congress stresses oversight and casework activities at the expense of active policy making. Regardless of the theory invoked, however, the responsiveness standard emphasizes the benefits of openness and free communication between ruled and rulers and the requirement that the latter respond to the former. It plays down the costs of inaction and inefficiency.

Accountability. Congress should be held accountable for what it does or does not do; that is, its decisions should be evaluated regularly by the citizenry. If the electorate finds the decision makers wanting, they can "turn the rascals out." When voters disapprove of Congress's policy choices (including the failure to act) or perceive that members have unethically placed self-interest above the public good, they can use the ballot box to send new, presumably wiser and more honest individuals to Washington. The contrast between Congress and the federal judiciary is sharp in this respect. Justices of the Supreme Court, once appointed, serve for life and cannot realistically be removed (they can be impeached but never have been); members of Congress must face the voters every two or six years. Thus, the legislators must calculate the popular response, real or potential, to their actions. In short, accountability operates after the fact: decision-making failure may result in the loss of position and power, should the voters conclude that new office-holders would perform more successfully.

An accountable Congress is an institution on public display. Interested citizens can find out what the representatives they have elected are doing and saying in committee and on the floors of the House and Senate. Citizen scrutiny is likely to encourage caution. To avoid alienating blocs of voters, members will try not to make rash statements or take extreme stands on controversial issues. They may avoid tackling difficult problems by deferring to the president or delegating authority to the bureaucracy. If they do, they lose policy-making independence and leave program innovation to the president and the administration, to the satisfaction of executive force theory adherents. If, by contrast, they simply refuse to act without permitting others to decide critical questions, policy immobilism may ensue, to the pleasure, in principle, of the congressional supremacists. In short, accountability, whether real or potential, inclines members to avoid risks because their behavior and ethics are open to public examination.

Conclusion. These three narrower criterion of evaluation—responsibility, responsiveness, and accountability—are by no means mutually exclusive; they can be applied simultaneously. This is clear in the case of accountability. Regardless of whether voters judge congressional performance in terms of product or process, they can, in theory, find out what their representatives are doing and send into early retirement those whose performance they deem unacceptable. Similarly, in the abstract at least, Congress can act both responsibly and responsively; it can move rapidly, on the basis of full consultation, to adopt workable policies.[16] In practice, however, responsibility and responsiveness are likely to conflict. Therefore, it is unlikely that Congress or any other institution can be fully responsible and responsive. Responsibility requires rapid and efficient problem solving; responsiveness calls for careful attention to a wide variety of viewpoints. A problem may grow worse or effective solutions may become obsolete if time is spent waiting for numerous sentiments to be expressed. A Congress that acts quickly while the problem remains tractable may be prevented from receiving views that are hard to ascertain or imperfectly formulated.

Summary

The Constitution involves Congress deeply in the national policy-making process; the legislature shares with other political participants, particularly the president, the power to shape public policies. Armed with this power, it has and will continue to compete for policy-making primacy. If the chief executive sometimes seems "king of the Hill," it is because members of Congress, for their own reasons, have opted to defer to him. The issue underlying periodic efforts to reform Congress is not whether the legislature *can* make policy—it clearly can if it chooses to act—but whether the legislature *should* be central to policy formulation. If Congress assumes a serious policy-making role, questions immediately arise about the nature of that role, and the organization of the institution that plays it. If Congress eschews or minimizes policy activity, presumably it will devote itself to its other roles, oversight and nonpolicy representation.

Discussion of Congress's proper place in national politics, especially its relation to the president, has proceeded along two lines: pro-executive and pro-legislative. A few theoreticians have advanced broad visions of Congress. Proponents of the executive force and responsible parties theories would prefer to see the legislature support the president, who is the likely source of innovative solutions to fundamental problems. They envision a Congress that poses few obstacles to creative executive action. Adherents of the literary and Whig positions, by contrast, see Congress as the supreme policy-making force, free to block the excessive or unwise initiatives of a potentially tyrannical president. The pro-executive and pro-legislative positions have different reform agendas.

Most reformers, especially the members of Congress who enact into law whatever reforms are adopted, find such theories, and the multitude of particulars they entail, impractical. It is too difficult to amend the Constitution; broad visions engender too much controversy. They are inclined instead to propose specific steps to deal with specific problems. Some may focus on executive-legislative relations, others may stress internal congressional procedures. They ask whether particular reforms, or a series of reforms, will move Congress even a short distance toward some preferred vision of the "good" or "better" legislature. In this chapter, three evaluative criteria are emphasized. Reform may improve legislative policy making (responsibility), increase the opportunity for citizen communication with Congress (responsiveness), or make the activities of Congress open to public scrutiny (accountability). In the real world of practical politics, all three criteria are unlikely to be met simultaneously.

Assessment of Congress's place in the political process depends on which evaluative standard is assumed to be most important. Is Congress to be preeminently a responsible policy maker? Should it give up its decision-making functions and concentrate instead on overseeing the executive and serving as a conduit for popular opinion? Or is it more important that the citizens be able to hold their national legislature accountable? Alternatively, is it more realistic to look for an optimum mix of responsibility, responsiveness, and accountability that will permit Congress to survive and work effectively?[17]

The chapters of this book establish a framework for exploring these questions. As pointed out in the Introduction, the continuing criticism of Congress underscores the constancy of reform concerns. In this chapter we have examined Congress in the larger context of national politics and introduced broad criteria (the executive force and congressional supremacy theories) and narrower standards (responsibility, or policy-making efficiency; responsiveness, or representativeness; and accountability, or opportunity for citizen control) by which to assess its performance. The specific charges that planted the seeds of the 1970s reforms are discussed in Chapter 2. Chapter 3 traces the reform movement that flowered in the 1960s, reached its zenith in the 1970s, and declined thereafter; it also reviews the steps that have been taken to make Congress more effective. Chapter 4 assesses these reform initiatives as they have evolved since the 1980s in terms of the reformers' intentions and the results they attained. The reform agenda that Congress currently confronts is the subject of Chapter 5. Addressing the normative issues directly, Chapter 6 returns to the executive force and congressional supremacy theories of what the legislature can or should be, suggests additional steps that might be taken to achieve those ends, and proposes that majoritarian democracy in Congress might maximize both responsiveness and responsibility.

NOTES

1. On oversight, see Morris S. Ogul, *Congress Oversees the Bureaucracy: Studies in Legislative Supervision* (Pittsburgh, Pa.: University of Pittsburgh Press, 1976); Lawrence C. Dodd and Richard L. Schott, *Congress and the Administrative State* (New York: Wiley, 1979); Charles H. Foreman, Jr., *Signals from the Hill: Congressional Oversight and the Challenge of Social Regulation* (New Haven, Conn.: Yale University Press, 1988); Joel D. Aberbach, *Keeping a Watchful Eye: The Politics of Congressional Oversight* (Washington, D.C.: Brookings Institution, 1990); Randall B. Ripley and Grace A. Franklin, *Congress, the Bureaucracy, and Public Policy*, 5th ed. (Pacific Grove, Calif.: Brooks/Cole, 1991); Bert A. Rockman, "Legislative-Executive Relations and Executive Oversight," *Legislative Studies Quarterly* 9 (1984): 387-400; Mathew D. McCubbins and Thomas Schwartz, "Congressional Oversight Overlooked: Police Patrols versus Fire Alarms," *American Journal of Political Science* 28 (1984): 165-179; and Morris S. Ogul and Bert A. Rockman, "Overseeing Oversight: New Departures and Old Problems," *Legislative Studies Quarterly* 15 (1990): 5-24.
2. *Congressional Quarterly Weekly Report*, May 25, 1985, 986-987.
3. See Hanna F. Pitkin, *The Concept of Representation* (Berkeley: University of California Press, 1967); and Heinz Eulau and Paul D. Karps, "The Puzzle of Repre-

sentation: Specifying the Components of Responsiveness," *Legislative Studies Quarterly* 2 (1977): 233-254.

4. Richard F. Fenno, Jr., *Home Style: Representatives in Their Districts* (Boston: Little, Brown, 1978).

5. David R. Mayhew, *Congress: The Electoral Connection* (New Haven, Conn.: Yale University Press, 1974); Barbara Hinckley, *Congressional Elections* (Washington, D.C.: CQ Press, 1981); Gary C. Jacobson, *The Politics of Congressional Elections*, 3d ed. (New York: HarperCollins, 1992); Gary C. Jacobson and Samuel Kernell, *Strategy and Choice in Congressional Elections*, 2d ed. (New Haven, Conn.: Yale University Press, 1983); Edie N. Goldenberg and Michael W. Traugott, *Campaigning for Congress* (Washington, D.C.: CQ Press, 1984); and Marjorie Randon Hershey, *Running for Office* (Chatham, N.J.: Chatham House, 1984). For a broader perspective on elections and representation, consult Lyn Ragsdale, "Responsiveness and Legislative Elections: Toward a Comparative Analysis," *Legislative Studies Quarterly* 8 (1983): 339-378.

6. Gary Orfield, *Congressional Power: Congress and Social Change* (New York: Harcourt Brace Jovanovich, 1975).

7. For an extended treatment of these visions of Congress, see Roger H. Davidson, David M. Kovenock, and Michael K. O'Leary, *Congress in Crisis: Politics and Congressional Reform* (Belmont, Calif.: Wadsworth, 1966), 15-36; and John S. Saloma III, *Congress and the New Politics* (Boston: Little, Brown, 1969), chaps. 1-2. Admittedly, normative perspectives have been advocated largely by those outside Congress, mostly academics. For a long-term view by a House insider, see Richard Bolling, *Power in the House* (New York: Capricorn Books, 1974). Bolling recognizes, however, that "the role of the political leader is vastly different from that of the philosopher, political theorist, or anyone who tries to analyze social problems. . . . All of these can and should be purists. . . . The political leader's role is to achieve as promptly as possible an *effective* solution" to these problems (20-21). Reform is likely to reflect a short-run perspective that favors such practical solutions.

8. James M. Burns, *Congress on Trial* (New York: Harper, 1949); James M. Burns, *The Deadlock of Democracy* (Englewood Cliffs, N.J.: Prentice-Hall, 1963); and Joseph S. Clark, *Congress: The Sapless Branch* (New York: Harper and Row, 1964).

9. Concerning this possible change in Congress's role, see Samuel P. Huntington, "Congressional Response to the Twentieth Century," in *The Congress and America's Future*, 2d ed., ed. David B. Truman (Englewood Cliffs, N.J.: Prentice-Hall, 1973), 6-38.

10. American Political Science Association, Committee on Political Parties, *Toward a More Responsible Two-Party System* (New York: Rinehart, 1950); Richard Bolling, *House Out of Order* (New York: Dutton, 1965).

11. James Burnham, *Congress and the American Tradition* (Chicago: Regnery, 1959).

12. Alfred de Grazia, *Republic in Crisis* (New York: Federal Legal Publications, 1964); and Alfred de Grazia, coord., *Congress: The First Branch of Government* (Washington, D.C.: American Enterprise Institute, 1966).

13. In "Congressional Responses," Huntington accurately describes the legislators' dilemma: "If Congress legislates, it subordinates itself to the executive; if it refuses to legislate, it alienates itself from public opinion. Congress can assert its power or it can pass laws, but it cannot do both" (7). Reform, at least that

guided by a broad view of Congress's place in national politics, forces an explicit choice between subordination to the executive and exercise of responsive legislative authority.

14. Observers inside and outside Congress do not always, or even regularly, use these narrower standards to assess criticisms of the legislature. In *Power in the House*, former representative Bolling (D-Mo.) cites the need for a "responsible budgetary process" (259). In *Both Your Houses: The Truth about Congress* (New York: Praeger, 1972), Warren Weaver, a Capitol Hill correspondent, describes the legislature as "clumsy" and "unresponsive" (3). Most critics voice specific complaints about excessively powerful personalities. These legislative shortcomings fall easily into categories that relate to alleged inefficiency, lack of sensitivity to public opinion, and inaccessibility to citizens' scrutiny. Responsibility, responsiveness, and accountability are thus convenient rubrics for assessing the common criticisms of Congress.

15. These are not the only criteria available for evaluating the legislature's performance. For others, see Roger H. Davidson and Walter J. Oleszek, "Adaptation and Consolidation: Structural Innovation in the House of Representatives," *Legislative Studies Quarterly* 1 (1976): 37-65; Charles O. Jones, "How Reform Changes Congress," in *Legislative Reform and Public Policy*, ed. Susan Welch and John G. Peters (New York: Praeger, 1977), 11-29; Walter J. Oleszek, "A Perspective on Congressional Reform," in Welch and Peters, *Legislative Reform and Public Policy*, 3-10; Samuel C. Patterson, "Conclusions: On the Study of Legislative Reform," in Welch and Peters, *Legislative Reform and Public Policy*, 214-222; Leroy N. Rieselbach, "Congressional Reform: Some Policy Implications," *Policy Studies Journal* 4 (1975): 180-188; Burton D. Sheppard, *Rethinking Congressional Reform: The Reform Roots of the Special Interest Congress* (Cambridge, Mass.: Schenkman Books, 1985); and Center for Responsive Politics, *"Not for the Short Winded": Congressional Reform, 1961-1986* (Washington, D.C.: Center for Responsive Politics, 1986).

16. Presidents also claim to act both responsibly and responsively, and they seek congressional support on that basis. Richard Nixon believed his Vietnam policy was both successful (responsible) and approved by most citizens (responsive). Ronald Reagan argued that his administration, with congressional support, handled major economic and defense issues during his first term both responsibly (solved problems) and responsively (represented large popular majorities). George Bush made a similar claim that his record, especially in foreign policy, was responsible and responsive. (The electorate, however, seemingly rejected the claim, for it gave Bush only 38 percent of the vote and put Bill Clinton in the White House.)

17. The last contingency is the most likely result of reform, to the extent that it is even possible to anticipate what reform will produce. Members will inevitably be reluctant to give up what they consider their legitimate prerogatives. The issue, in realistic rather than utopian terms, is how to combine legislative functions most effectively and organize Congress most efficiently to approximate any observer-critic's particular vision.

2. The Prereform Congress: A Critical Assessment

Observers of Congress in the 1950s and 1960s—those who preferred a responsible legislature that could compete on even terms with the president for policy influence as well as those who preferred a responsive legislature attentive to constituent concerns—found Congress wanting. They leveled three charges, which can be expressed boldly in the following terms: (1) *Congress was, at best, only imperfectly responsible;* it had yielded much of its decision-making authority to the executive branch, especially in foreign relations. (2) *Congress was only modestly responsive;* it often listened, but it did not act and did little to elicit opinions from less frequently heard societal groups. (3) *Congress was being held accountable far more in theory than in practice,* an unsatisfactory situation that was not entirely the fault of the legislature itself. Critics of Congress marshaled persuasive evidence to substantiate each of these charges and recommended an extensive reform agenda.[1] The legislature's performance, they asserted, could be improved on all fronts. What they may have failed to appreciate sufficiently, however, is that reforms designed to improve performance in one area may have unintended and unanticipated repercussions in other areas of legislative activity.

To the reformers of the 1950s and 1960s, Congress's troubles did not seem momentary aberrations. Its fundamental organization had undergone only modest alterations in the past half-century. The 1910-1911 "palace revolution" in the House of Representatives, which constrained the powers of Speaker Joseph Cannon, marked the beginning of the modern legislative era. From then through the 1960s, with the single and notable exception of the Legislative Reorganization Act of 1946, the main principles of congressional organization and procedure evolved slowly but continuously. Change tended to be adaptive and incremental. For example, in 1961 the membership of the House Rules Committee was increased to strengthen party leaders' control over the flow of legislation to the floor, but the panel continued to thwart the Speaker and his lieutenants periodically. The Senate adopted the "Johnson Rule" (named after former majority leader Lyndon B. Johnson), that allowed junior members to select a committee on which to serve before the senior senators got a second assignment; the change permitted newcomers to win places on more important committees more easily. (The majority party member with the longest continuous service on a committee automatically assumed the committee chair.) Despite the rule, senior senators retained what many perceived as excessive influence. (The rule did not affect seniority; it pertained to committee assignments, not to the chair.) Senators who served during the Harding or Coolidge administrations, returning to the Capitol fifty years later, would have recognized clearly the basic strategies of congressional politics in the Kennedy-Johnson era.[2]

A Decentralized Institution

In general, by the mid-1960s Congress had become "institutionalized"; that is, it followed standard operating procedures and practices.[3] Year after year, legislators sat on the same committees, confronted the same issues, and dealt with those issues in the same manner as before. The congressional modus operandi was fragmentation and decentralization, with authority and influence widely although not equally dispersed among the 535 senators and representatives. Many legislators had a direct and immediate impact on congressional decisions, mainly concerning matters within the jurisdictions of the committees on which they served. In such circumstances, congressional politics was coalition politics; proponents of particular proposals used such tactics as bargaining, compromise, negotiating, logrolling, and mutual back scratching to assemble fragments of political power and form winning coalitions. Seeking support in committee, on the floor, and in conference, they tried to push bills through the multiple stages of the legislative process until they finally landed on the president's desk.

Several explanations can be given for the dispersal of power in Congress, which, by the mid-1960s, had resulted in decision making by bargain and compromise. The electoral process stimulates member independence of central authority—both presidential and partisan. Electoral triumph, especially in the smaller House districts, is almost always the product of the candidates' own efforts in their constituencies.[4] Given this fundamental fact, most legislators devote prime attention, particularly early in their careers, to serving their districts, "where the votes are" and where the ultimate decisions about their continuation in office are made. Incumbents, having learned the ropes, begin their reelection efforts with substantial advantages over their challengers. Therefore, few incumbent representatives were turned out of office during the prereform period, but a sufficient number lost every two years to reinforce the inclination of those who survived to court their constituents and to resist national, centralizing forces that might jeopardize their electoral security.

The internal organization (formal and informal) of Congress also sustained the individual legislator's independence. The specialized standing committees, the chief agents of congressional decision making, constituted the major decentralizing force in Congress. They operated relatively free of restraint; what they decided was often what the chamber enacted. These committees, especially in the House, were the repositories of congressional expertise; members tended to be legislative specialists on the topics within the panel's substantive jurisdiction. Members of other committees were often prepared to defer to such expertise, to accept standing committee recommendations. Of course, they expected and generally received reciprocal deference in their own areas of specialization.

The standing committee, then, was a relatively independent body with substantial influence over legislative activity. Its chair, as the single most important member of the panel, wielded the greatest influence. The chairs varied considerably in the degree to which they exercised their powers, but, protected by the seniority rule, many had the independence to shape what their committees did. Their ability to make their own views (or views close to their own) prevail within their committees, and the reciprocal deference among committees, contributed to the fragmentation of legislative authority.[5]

The political parties, which might have centralized legislative authority, were weak in this period. The party leadership—the Speaker of the House, floor leaders, and the whips—had few genuine sanctions enabling them to enforce discipline among party members holding disparate views. As noted, legislators tend to vote their districts' preferences rather than following the party line if a difference between the two occurs. Moreover, application of the seniority rule in selection of committee leaders and the protection afforded by committee expertise and power often militate against party support. Party leaders in the 1960s were not without some influence, but it was based on persuasion rather than compulsion. Therefore, parties sometimes acted cohesively, but on balance they lacked the power to countervail, regularly and effectively, the centrifugal forces generated by these aspects of the electoral and committee systems.[6]

In the 1960s, numerous congressional rules and procedures sustained a system of multiple centers of influence and promoted bargaining as a way to resolve conflict in Congress, thus contributing directly to the legislature's fragmentation and decentralization.[7] They required a bill to move past many "veto points," at each of which the measure either succeeded or died. They also defined and defended committee jurisdictions, thereby serving to insulate the panels, to minimize the possibility that such rules and procedures would be circumvented, and to guarantee that the major decisions would be made in committee. The position of legislative minorities was buttressed in the House by the Rules Committee and the rule of unlimited debate, and in the Senate by the well-known if not notorious filibuster.[8]

Finally, like any other organization, Congress operated in a context of mores and practices, nowhere codified but demonstrably observable. In the 1960s, these informal traditions, or norms, fostered dispersion of power. Senators and representatives alike were enjoined to specialize in a few policy areas, to defer to one another's expertise, to treat each other courteously, and, in general, to behave in ways that minimized hostility and friction. This "legislative culture" permitted the lawmakers to try to carve out for themselves a niche where each could eventually exert some influence over congressional decision making. Many succeeded, content to possess a fragment of power even at the cost of having authority beyond their narrow focus of concern.[9]

Thus, Congress during the 1960s appeared to its critics to be a highly decentralized, fragmented institution. Electoral considerations, the committee structure, formal rules and procedures, and informal norms and expectations diffused authority widely among the lawmakers. Decision making was accomplished chiefly by negotiation and compromise; bargaining was the only viable means to assemble the fragments of power into workable coalitions. Political parties, the potential centralizing force, proved unable to overcome the divisive forces.[10]

In consequence, the critics found Congress incapable or unwilling to act decisively. They pointed to its failure to provide comprehensive national health insurance for all citizens; partial coverage—Medicare for the elderly, Medicaid for the poor—they deemed inadequate. They also faulted Congress for delay in redressing the civil rights grievances of black Americans. Only after extraordinary developments in the mid-1960s—the assassination of President John F. Kennedy in 1963, the unprecedented and televised civil rights movement, and a landslide Democratic electoral victory in 1964—was the legislature goaded into enacting major civil rights legislation. Critics cited similar failures with respect to aid to education and environmental protection. Decentralization, they argued, made creative policy making difficult if not impossible. To win reelection, members often deferred to the president or delegated to the bureaucracy rather than confront politically controversial policy choices.

Responsibility: Policy Making in Congress

Policy making in a decentralized legislature is a complicated, pains-taking process. To enact policy legislation, those in favor must move their bill through subcommittee, full committee, the Rules Committee (in the House), and out onto the floor where a majority must vote for passage. If the process can be repeated in the other house and a confer-ence committee can resolve all differences in the two chambers' ver-sions, then and only then will some new policy, or a modification of an old policy, be *authorized*. Money must be *appropriated* to implement most programs. The entire process is then repeated; appropriations bills are sent through the subcommittees and full Committees on Appropriations in the House and Senate.[11] It is the need to move across, around, or over these imposing hurdles that makes congres-sional politics a coalition-building process. To assemble a winning co-alition at each of these stages requires bargaining skill and patience that must be sustained over many weeks and months.

Given this picture of congressional practice, it is not surprising that critics judged the national legislature to be deficient on responsibility grounds. In the early New Deal period and during the Great Society era of the mid-1960s, an exceptional coincidence of events gave the Democratic party both control of the presidency and an overwhelming majority in both houses of Congress.[12] Solid legislative majorities make the weakness of party discipline tolerable and provide the dominant party with incentives to advance a major legislative program.[13] Ordi-narily, however, conditions are far less favorable.

When partisan control of government is divided, with one party controlling the presidency and the other holding a majority in at least one house of Congress (as was the case in ten of the years between 1950 and 1972), the prospects for cooperative and inventive lawmaking are substantially reduced. The government's failure to reduce domestic petroleum consumption when faced with the severe supply shortages created by the 1973 Arab oil embargo is typical of conflictual policy making under conditions of divided control.[14] Even when the presi-dent and the congressional majority share a party label, responsible lawmaking seldom follows, for nominal majorities show a decided ten-dency to evaporate when the roll is called. Thus, policy making in Congress is a series of slow, arduous negotiations that often cross rather than follow party lines.

Policy making by negotiation is especially apparent in domestic af-fairs, where Congress retains much authority and is less likely to defer to executive initiatives; the result usually reflects the impact of legisla-tive deliberation and decision. Congress seems to prefer to respond to presidential proposals, to expect the chief executive to set the national agenda. Congressional criticism, particularly when the Democrats command a majority, is commonplace when, in the lawmakers' judgment, the president is lax in proposing a legislative program. Once that program is announced, however, the legislators are more than willing to alter the president's proposals drastically or to reject them entirely. Throughout the prereform period, numerous conflicts over executive proposals to cut farm price subsidies or to reduce federal support for rivers and harbors projects (which Congress regularly rejected) or to change national health insurance or for civil rights legislation (which Congress was frequently unwilling or unable to pass) testified to the legislature's ability to resist and defeat undesired presidential initiatives.[15]

When Congress is prepared to substitute its own priorities for those of the executive, it provides ammunition to those who criticize it for irresponsibility. As has been suggested, the congressional process is less than efficient. To assemble a winning majority takes time; many independent interests must be accommodated. Critics of Congress during the 1950s and 1960s pointed to extended hearings, lengthy markup sessions,[16] and filibusters and other dilatory tactics as evidence of the legislature's inability to act decisively. These critics did not always recognize that time may be the essential ingredient in legislative decision making, for although delay may cripple or defeat legislation, on some occasions it may be the essential ingredient in legislative decision making, permitting action by allowing a specific compromise to be reached. Nevertheless, their basic argument was sound: Congress moved slowly. Furthermore, the negotiated agreements that did command a majority were often modest in scope because proposals for major change were sacrificed to secure the support of critical power holders.[17]

In 1965, for example, President Lyndon Johnson proposed a bold and expensive initiative to deal with poverty and crime in inner-city slums. As originally drafted, the "demonstration cities" legislation would have given a dozen or so cities large sums, to be spent under the watchful eye of federal bureaucrats, to promote racial integration and the renovation of blighted areas. Passage of the program, however, required compromise: proponents had to drop integration as a goal, relax the national government's administrative control over the program, and, more important, make many more cities (eventually 150) eligible to participate. Each compromise added congressional votes to the coalition supporting the model cities legislation—those of southern conservatives who objected to federal control of local political activities and representatives of cities that were added to the list of recipients. The "demonstration project" that was intended to show that massive federal intervention could renew decaying urban centers had become simply another "pork barrel project" that distributed funds widely and ineffectively among the constituencies of many members of Congress.[18] Such policy transformations are common congressional practice.

In sum, Congress seemed in no hurry to respond to interest groups or executives, but preferred to develop its own domestic programs in its own way and at its own pace. Those who saw responsibility as requiring more efficient development of more imaginative and innovative programs found congressional performance unsatisfactory.

Judged by the criterion of responsibility, congressional performance in foreign relations seemed even more unsatisfactory. From the end of World War II to the early 1970s, presidents had capitalized on several advantages, allowing them to dominate foreign policy making. The power as commander in chief, one of the Constitution's most explicit grants of authority, enables the chief executive to commit military forces on his own initiative, as Harry Truman did in Korea. A near monopoly on access to the sources of expertise (the State Department, Foreign Service, Pentagon, and intelligence community all report directly to the White House) permits the president to cast foreign policy issues in terms favorable to his proposals. The Supreme Court, in *United States v. Curtiss-Wright Export Corp.* (299 U.S. 304 [1936]), determined that the president is "the sole organ of the nation" in international relations, thus giving the chief executive a forceful claim to manage the nation's diplomatic contacts. Finally, and perhaps most important, the lessons of history had taught Congress that its decentralized organization and slow-paced decision making were frequently inappropriate, especially when speed or secrecy was required, as in foreign policy making.

For all these reasons, Congress had come to defer to presidential expertise in military matters. The Armed Services committees were merely "real estate" panels, concerned with the management of military installations and content to leave the more critical issues of military strategy and procurement to Pentagon generals and White House officials.[19] Several diplomatic initiatives, such as President Richard Nixon's rapprochements with China and the Soviet Union, originated in and were conducted by the executive branch. Tariff agreements were negotiated under broad congressional delegations of power, which were renewed and extended at regular intervals. Wars were under total presidential control; in Korea and Vietnam, Congress supported military efforts initiated by presidents without invoking its constitutional right to declare war.

Congress could have influenced American foreign policy at any time. Control over the purse strings, which the Constitution grants to Congress, enables it to deny funds for executive policy initiatives. The increasing unpopularity of the Vietnam conflict prompted numerous proposals to cut off money for military involvement in Southeast Asia.

But only during the last days of U.S. involvement did Congress succeed in forcing the president's hand. In June 1973 the legislature tacked onto a $3.3 billion supplemental appropriations bill, intended to keep the government operating in the new fiscal year beginning July 1, a provision to cut off funds for bombing in Cambodia. President Nixon vetoed the bill and the House sustained his action, but so that the government would not go out of business for lack of money, he accepted a compromise and signed a second supplemental bill prohibiting spending for military purposes in Indochina after August 15, some six weeks hence, without prior legislative approval. On the whole, however, the substance of the nation's Indochina policy—from its inception in the Eisenhower and Kennedy administrations to the end of direct American involvement during Nixon's presidency—reflected the policy choices of the chief executive rather than Congress.

Congress could also have reclaimed for itself the power to set tariffs, which it had delegated legislatively to the president, or the power to designate some independent agency to negotiate trade agreements, but it did not. The legislature tried with only modest success to keep closer tabs on military matters by insisting that funds for weaponry be authorized on an annual, not a long-term, basis.[20] The lawmakers did make changes in the foreign aid program: they made major cuts in the president's fund requests, reallocated money from military to economic purposes, and denied money to countries (Vietnam, Cambodia, Angola, and—temporarily—Turkey). But the president remained at the center of foreign policy making; Congress was only peripheral. As Sen. Adlai E. Stevenson III (D-Ill.) put it, "Congress is . . . unfit to formulate foreign policy or to effectively oversee its implementation in all parts of a fast moving world." [21] In the eyes of the legislators and the public, responsibility for America's international relations rested with the White House, not Capitol Hill.

Placing responsibility for domestic and foreign policy on the president rather than on Congress seemed, then, to have some justice to it. The legislature was not preeminent in policy making much of the time, and it achieved such influence only after extended deliberation and debate. Congress was not the responsible initiator of public policy; rather it slowly molded, and gave legitimacy to, policies that usually originated in the executive branch.

Responsiveness: Representation in Congress

When the spotlight shifted from responsibility to responsiveness, Congress was found to have performed more successfully. Its vices, which some critics felt inhibited responsible policy choice, now became its virtues because they were perceived as fostering responsiveness. Congress's openness, decentralization, and bargaining style of decision making seemed admirable. Its slow pace allowed time for those with a stake in policy outcomes to communicate their sentiments to members. The multistage lawmaking process identified points of access where nonlegislators could exert pressure on the legislators. Congress was usually more than willing to listen to what outsiders had to say. During the 1950s and 1960s, it had ample opportunity to consider messages from interested parties, including the president, pressure groups, and ordinary citizens. As noted, Congress chose to react to executive initiatives rather than to set its own agenda. Moreover, the president possessed a full arsenal of weapons that constituted what Richard Neustadt has called his "power to persuade." [22] Specifically, the president used his public popularity and professional reputation (his standing with other Washington decision makers) to try to influence lawmakers; it was difficult for them to resist a popular and determined leader. He could argue on the merits of an issue, using speeches, press conferences, special messages, and his personal ability (and numerous opportunities) to command attention. He could draw on party loyalty by wording his messages to appeal to partisan interests. He could deal with congressional committees by sending his chief aides and experts to testify at hearings; by courting the important committee members, especially the chair and ranking minority member; and by accepting committee amendments to bills to win votes. He could attempt to win over crucial supporters—committee chairs, party leaders, influential senators and representatives—through personal contacts. If he secured their support, they in turn could use their authority to persuade their followers to back him.[23]

In congressional politics, the president's persuasive power depends on his ability to do lawmakers favors and to provide goods and services—such as endorsing particular bills, offering patronage positions, and helping political campaigns financially or by making personal appearances. If the president is highly regarded, such electoral assistance may benefit the local legislative nominee. Although it is never entirely clear precisely to what extent any president uses these forms of persuasion—bargains struck are not always explicit and seldom widely publicized—they enable the president to work from a position of strength to influence congressional decision making.[24]

President Johnson, for instance, broke a decade-old logjam in 1964 by persuading Congress to declare a "war on poverty." The bold legislation that resulted, the Economic Opportunity Act, contained provisions to provide jobs, education, student aid, and an assistance package for the rural poor; and to establish the Job Corps, a training program for urban youths. The president made the legislation the central focus of his 1964 reelection campaign and put the numerous experts within the executive branch to work designing a broad package with widespread political appeal. When the bill was before Congress, Johnson gave it his personal attention. Northern Democrats, mostly liberals, could be counted on to back him. Southern support was courted: Phil M. Landrum (D-Ga.), a conservative with impeccable credentials (he had cosponsored a restrictive labor reform bill hated by liberals), was persuaded to sponsor the act.

Johnson also took his case to the public; the war on poverty theme was a winner. How could the opposition, mostly Republicans, favor poverty or oppose equal opportunity? White House lobbyists swarmed all over Capitol Hill, and they played rough: "Republicans protested the threats and pressures they claimed were being used upon individual congressmen." [25] When necessary, the president made substantive concessions; for example, he mollified conservative foes by accepting an amendment permitting governors, as protectors of states' rights, to veto most projects proposed for their states. In the end, the president captured enough southern conservatives and Republicans to win comfortable majorities in both chambers of Congress.

Because President Johnson's constituency differed from those of individual lawmakers—and the differences between the president's national orientation and the members' more parochial perspective were widely noted[26]—points of view were introduced into legislative deliberations that otherwise might not have been heard or at least might have been less forcefully expressed. Congress, in short, was responsive to the president.

The legislature was also responsive to the views of organized interests. Lawmakers often worked closely with pressure group representatives (lobbyists) to promote mutually desired legislation. This is not to argue, as some observers did, that pressure group activity was decisive in lawmaking outcomes. Indeed, the most persuasive evidence from the 1950s and 1960s suggests that special interests did not call the legislative tune (and did not really pay the piper either); rather their representatives worked in collaboration with, and sometimes at the request of, sympathetic members of Congress.[27]

Lobbyists sought to establish and maintain free and open lines of communication with members of Congress who were in a position to help them promote their specific causes. They often ran service operations that supplied information, assistance, and contacts to lawmakers working to advance the views they wished to promote. In return for such support, the lobbyists hoped to be able to "make a pitch" to legislators to further their clients' interests. The pressure group belied its name; it was more often a coalition partner than an irresistible force in the legislative process.[28]

Even this reliance on low-key tactics, on friendship and trust rather than on bribes or threats, provided interest groups with ample opportunity to present their opinions. Their representatives regularly appeared as witnesses at committee and subcommittee hearings. They supplied research findings and documentary evidence directly to relevant legislators and members of their staffs. Group positions thus became visible to the lawmakers whose own positions often had not yet crystallized. (In some cases, however, groups provided only data that supported the legislators' existing judgments; they introduced no new perspectives.) If responsiveness is defined as maintaining open and operative channels of communication, Congress in these years was responsive, at least to organized group interests.

And here was the rub. The national legislature heard and had the chance to respond to the views of well-organized, well-financed interests—such as business, labor, agriculture, veterans, and the professions—but the views of other, less affluent interests were unheard and consequently unheeded. Access to Congress, its critics were quick to charge, was unequal. Because of congressional decentralization some groups had ties to important leaders whereas others had connections only with the rank and file. Important interests—the poor, blacks, women, and consumers—were often inadequately organized. Lacking money, experience, and lobbying know-how, such groups were unable to present their positions persuasively. What legislators heard, in short, was far from the full story; their intake of information depended on what messages were being sent as well as which communications they chose to hear.[29]

One other audience, the unorganized public, was a focus of legislative attention. Members of Congress were not prepared to accept the executive branch or interest groups as the legitimate and incontrovertible voice of the people. To get a general sense of popular sentiment, they examined opinion polls and, perhaps more closely, their constituents' views expressed in conversations, letters, and local newspaper columns and editorials. A few members, recognizing the imperfect nature of these information sources,[30] commissioned their own surveys; others relied more on intuition, their own sense of what their constituents believed. Most lawmakers did not really know how the folks back home felt about any but the most dramatic issues of the day.

On the whole, Congress at mid-century was moderately responsive to a variety of interests. It could not avoid getting messages (which were loud and clear in many instances) from the chief executive; indeed, Congress demanded such communications. The many interest groups transmitted their views to legislators, who found them helpful and often solicited them. Lawmakers also felt the need to gauge local sentiment; to avert possible electoral consequences, they were careful to consider citizen opinion before they acted. Moreover, the decision-making process in Congress contributed to responsiveness. The legislature's decentralization and fragmentation, as well as the slow pace of its bargaining, guaranteed numerous points of access and the time to transmit messages. Congress not only listened, but when conditions were right—when the messages were clear and decisive—it acted. During the Great Society era of the mid-1960s, it passed significant new legislation on employment, education, equal rights, health care, and environmental protection.[31] A long time in coming, these initiatives suggested that Congress would respond if the pressures were great enough. On all fronts, however—chief executive, interest group, individual—critics found room for improvement. These defects became the targets of reformers seeking to increase the legislature's responsiveness.

The Accountability of Congress

These defects explain why the public was indifferent and did not attempt to hold Congress more accountable for its actions. Accountability, or citizen control by means of the ballot box, requires that three conditions be met. First, the voters, those making the judgment, must be aware of the behavior of the legislators whom they are to hold to account. Second, the voting citizens must have some views of their own, some desirable policy goals that they expect the legislators to attain. Third, if legislators' behavior is not consistent with citizen preferences, voters must be able to express their dissatisfaction by choosing candidates, in the party primary and general election, whose views coincide with their own. Congressional observers in the 1950s and 1960s found that these three conditions were not being adequately met. The public was hard pressed to hold Congress to account.

Because the prerequisites for accountability were seldom present, members of Congress in this period were free to act without citizen control on all but the most dramatic, emotionally charged issues.[32] With regard to the first condition, citizens were generally unaware of the major details of legislative behavior. Polls regularly revealed that approximately half of those in the same population were unable to name their elected representatives. Few understood the complexity of the congressional decision-making process; many were not even familiar with the most visible act, the roll call vote.

To add to the confusion, legislators exploited the possibilities of a decentralized organization. They acted inconsistently, working against a bill in committee but voting in support later when a roll call vote was taken. In the House, they could take one position in teller votes, when they filed past tellers and were counted for or against a measure but were not listed individually, and another in recorded votes, when each individual's stand was clearly entered in the public record. Congressional procedures enabled members to be all things (both friend and foe) to all bills and immeasurably complicated a citizen's effort to understand congressional politics. The media of communication did not help. Understandably, the actions of a single chief executive were more newsworthy and easily reported than those of the multimember legislature. Dramatic events in Congress were the exception not the rule, and coverage of the legislature was modest, even in the most comprehensive media. Thus, the few citizens who tried to be attentive to legislative politics had a hard time fully comprehending what their representatives were up to in Washington.

Citizens who had their own views and policy goals—the second condition required for accountability—were scarcer still. Voting studies from the 1950s amply demonstrate that voters cast their ballots more on the basis of party identification—their continuing loyalty to one of the major political parties—than on the basis of their views about the issues of the day.[33] Although there is reason to believe that the 1950s marked the nadir of citizens' issue orientation—a case of the "bland leading the bland"—it is doubtful that the increase in their concern about issues and congressional performance in the following decade created a sufficiently well informed electorate.[34] The voters' rejection of presidential candidates who sought to offer a choice— Barry Goldwater in 1964 and George McGovern in 1972—seems to reflect a general perception of the losers' "unsuitability" more than an awareness of their specific views on substantive issues (although admittedly, the former may have followed from the latter). If this was true for presidential contests, it certainly was true for less well publicized legislative races. Voters' choices in congressional elections in the 1950s and 1960s seldom reflected an awareness of the details of candidates' issue positions.

The third condition for accountability, the opportunity for meaningful choice, was not satisfied either in this period. In theory, electoral contests provide voters with the chance to substitute candidates with whom they agree for incumbents whom they oppose, but in practice, the effects of elections were limited for two reasons: the voters were relatively uninformed, and their preferred candidates often had only a slight chance of winning. If citizens knew neither what the incumbent did in Washington nor what the major issues were in any campaign, they were unlikely to render an unequivocal, issue-related verdict at the polls, even when a clear, substantive choice existed between incumbent and challenger (and it did not in numerous districts). Most constituencies were "safe" for the incumbent or for the incumbent's political party. In fact, there was little turnover in Congress throughout the prereform period; more than two-thirds of the House seats remained Republican or Democratic. The shifts that did occur in Congress reflected what happened in about 100 highly competitive House districts.[35]

Moreover, change was not uniform. Variations in the voting patterns of district electorates tended to cancel out the possibility that one set of views would gain ascendancy in Congress. Voters in some districts chose liberal challengers over conservative incumbents, but the reverse occurred in other districts. When the balance in the competitive districts tipped in one direction, as it did for the Democrats in 1964, a strong legislative majority was created, resulting in substantial policy change in Congress. Most commonly, however, the competitive districts did not swing uniformly in favor of one party, and the overall composition of Congress varied little from year to year. These modest changes in composition did not appreciably affect the ideological outlook of the entire legislature.[36]

In the elections held every second year, citizens on occasion did vote "no," at least in a few states and districts. But studies have shown that these ballots were cast on the basis of little information about the incumbents' legislative performance, with scant concern about the issues that separated sitting lawmakers from their challengers; in many districts there was only a slight chance that a new member of Congress would be sent to Washington. Stability was the chief characteristic of the national legislature during the 1950s and 1960s. Electoral reversals occurred in a few states and districts, but they were rarely sufficient to alter Congress's substantive outlook more than marginally.

Summary

The Congress of the 1950s and 1960s was a stable, institutionalized assembly with fixed routines for conducting its business. Its dominant characteristic was decentralization; power was dispersed among 535 members who relied on bargaining and coalition building in their decision making. The legislature's formal rules and informal norms sustained fragmentation, and the political parties—a potential force for centralizing congressional operations—were too weak to overcome the divisive tendencies that were a product of congressional organization and procedure. These circumstances engendered substantial criticism of Congress and set the stage for the reform drama that unfolded during the 1970s.

These critics seldom invoked broad philosophic visions of the legislature—either the pro-executive or pro-legislative views—to guide their assessments; such theories remained the preserve of a few academics and interested observers. Most critics, particularly the members of Congress themselves, focused instead on practical, day-to-day matters that revealed congressional defects. Commentary came from both the political left and the political right. Liberals wanted more policy action, conservatives preferred less; both felt frustrated in their inability to find out and control what Congress, as an institution, and its members were doing. Each group had its own reform agenda, and in the 1960s each came to the conclusion that reform was imperative.

The sum of the critics' arguments was that Congress was less than ideal in terms of responsibility, responsiveness, and accountability. It simply was not equipped to be responsible on a regular basis; its organization and procedures were not designed to allow efficient and speedy formulation of policy. Congress had delegated much of its policy-making power to the president, especially in international relations. Only the war in Indochina had, by the late 1960s, provided much incentive for Congress to flex its muscles and try to recapture some of its atrophied authority. The legislature's performance with respect to the responsiveness criterion was more successful. The organizational shortcomings that inhibited responsibility encouraged representativeness. Many interest groups (but not all, and particularly not those lacking money and skill) could find the time and the locus in the legislature to present their views prior to the enactment of policy legislation. Congress was better suited to listen than to act, and was also more inclined to do so. Finally, Congress was held accountable, in the sense that dissatisfied citizens could, and occasionally did, retire some of its members. For the most part, however, citizens lacked the knowledge, the incentive, or the opportunity to exercise meaningful control over public policy by holding lawmakers to account. In short, whichever evaluative criterion was employed, critics of various persuasions found Congress wanting and were determined to reform it. When the 1960s came to an end, conditions were favorable for launching a major effort to change Congress, and the reformers quickly undertook to do so.

NOTES

1. See Chapter 1 and notes 8-16 thereto.
2. On the evolution of congressional organization and the legislative process in the period after 1910, see George B. Galloway, *The History of the House of Representatives*, 2d ed., revised by Sidney Wise (New York: Crowell, 1976); John R. Hibbing, *Congressional Careers: Life in the U.S. House of Representatives* (Chapel Hill: University of North Carolina Press, 1991); Nelson W. Polsby, "The Institu-

tionalization of the U.S. House of Representatives," *American Political Science Review* 62 (1968): 144-168; Nelson W. Polsby, Miriam Gallaher, and Barry S. Rundquist, "Growth of the Seniority System in the U.S. House of Representatives," *American Political Science Review* 63 (1969): 787-807; Charles S. Bullock III, "House Careerists: Changing Patterns of Longevity and Attrition," *American Political Science Review* 66 (1972): 1295-1300; Joseph Cooper and David W. Brady, "Institutional Context and Leadership Style: The House from Cannon to Rayburn," *American Political Science Review* 75 (1981): 411-425; Steven S. Smith and Christopher J. Deering, *Committees in Congress*, 2d ed. (Washington, D.C.: CQ Press, 1990), chap. 2; and Randall B. Ripley, *Congress: Process and Policy*, 4th ed. (New York: Norton, 1988), chap. 2.

3. Polsby, "Institutionalization."

4. John W. Kingdon, *Candidates for Office* (New York: Random House, 1968); David A. Leuthold, *Electioneering in a Democracy: Campaigns for Congress* (New York: Wiley, 1968); Jeff Fishel, *Party and Opposition: Congressional Challengers in American Politics* (New York: McKay, 1973); Marjorie Randon Hershey, *The Making of Campaign Strategy* (Lexington, Mass.: Lexington Books, 1974); David R. Mayhew, *Congress: The Electoral Connection* (New Haven, Conn.: Yale University Press, 1974); and Gary C. Jacobson, *The Politics of Congressional Elections*, 3d ed. (New York: HarperCollins, 1992).

5. On committees in the 1960s, see William L. Morrow, *Congressional Committees* (New York: Scribner's, 1969); and George Goodwin, Jr., *The Little Legislatures: Committees of Congress* (Amherst: University of Massachusetts Press, 1970).

6. On parties and party leadership during the 1960s, see Randall B. Ripley, *Majority Party Leadership in Congress* (Boston: Little, Brown, 1969); Lewis A. Froman, Jr., and Randall B. Ripley, "Conditions for Party Leadership: The Case of the House Democrats," *American Political Science Review* 59 (1965): 52-63; Charles O. Jones, *The Minority Party in Congress* (Boston: Little, Brown, 1970); Louis P. Westefield, "Majority Party Leadership and the Committee System in the House of Representatives," *American Political Science Review* 68 (1974): 1593-1604; and Randall B. Ripley, *Power in the Senate* (New York: St. Martin's Press, 1969).

7. For a full discussion of the rules and their strategic implications in the 1960s, see Lewis A. Froman, Jr., *The Congressional Process: Strategies, Rules, and Procedures* (Boston: Little, Brown, 1967).

8. Subject to the approval of the full House, the Committee on Rules defines the terms (such as the length of time for debate and the permissibility of amendments) governing the chamber's consideration of a bill. On some occasions in the 1950s and 1960s, the committee refused to permit legislation that had been approved by other standing committees to reach the floor. See James A. Robinson, *The House Rules Committee* (Indianapolis, Ind.: Bobbs-Merrill, 1963); and Spark M. Matsunaga and Ping Chen, *Rulemakers of the House* (Urbana: University of Illinois Press, 1976). The filibuster rule in the Senate (technically, the cloture rule) specifies the conditions under which debate can be terminated and a vote forced. Legislative minorities, especially those opposed to civil rights, used unlimited debate in the prereform era to force the majority, which was eager to pass other legislation, to make concessions or to abandon bills entirely. See Raymond E. Wolfinger, "Filibusters, Majority Rule, Presidential

Leadership, and Senate Norms," in *Readings on Congress*, ed. Raymond E. Wolfinger (Englewood Cliffs, N.J.: Prentice-Hall, 1971), 296-305. On the rules in general, see Walter J. Oleszek, *Congressional Procedures and the Policy Process*, 3d ed. (Washington, D.C.: CQ Press, 1989).

9. On norms, see Donald R. Matthews, "The Folkways of the U.S. Senate: Conformity to Group Norms and Legislative Effectiveness," *American Political Science Review* 53 (1959): 1064-1089; Ralph K. Huitt, "The Outsider in the Senate: An Alternate Role," *American Political Science Review* 55 (1961): 566-575; William S. White, *Citadel: The Story of the U.S. Senate* (New York: Harper, 1956); Herbert B. Asher, "The Learning of Legislative Norms," *American Political Science Review* 67 (1973): 499-513; and Richard F. Fenno, Jr., "The Internal Distribution of Influence: The House," in *The Congress and America's Future*, 2d ed., ed. David B. Truman (Englewood Cliffs, N.J.: Prentice-Hall, 1973), 63-90.

10. This description of what Kenneth A. Shepsle calls the "textbook Congress" dominated discussion of the legislature from the mid-1940s to the mid-1960s and was the prevailing conventional wisdom about how the assembly worked. See Shepsle, "The Changing Textbook Congress," in *Can the Government Govern?*, ed. John E. Chubb and Paul E. Peterson (Washington, D.C.: Brookings Institution, 1989), 238-266.

11. On appropriations politics in the 1960s, see Richard F. Fenno, Jr., *The Power of the Purse: Appropriations Politics in Congress* (Boston: Little, Brown, 1966); Stephen Horn, *Unused Power: The Work of the Senate Committee on Appropriations* (Washington, D.C.: Brookings Institution, 1970); and Aaron Wildavsky, *The New Politics of the Budgetary Process* 2d ed. (New York: HarperCollins, 1992), chaps. 2-3.

12. The Hoover administration's inability to cope with the Great Depression led voters in large numbers to choose Franklin Roosevelt and the Democrats in the elections of 1932, 1934, and 1936. The singular combination of the assassination of President Kennedy and the 1964 Republican debacle, with Barry Goldwater at the top of the ticket, gave Democrats a genuine working majority for a brief period in the mid-1960s.

13. For an assessment of the possibilities for genuine policy change in Congress, see Gerald C. Wright, Jr., Leroy N. Rieselbach, and Lawrence C. Dodd, eds., *Policy Change in Congress* (New York: Agathon Press, 1986).

14. See Walter A. Rosenbaum, *Energy, Politics, and Public Policy* (Washington, D.C.: CQ Press, 1981).

15. Most commonly, conflict revolved around the efforts of Congress to impose its preferences—for public works, emergency housing, and milk price support legislation—on an unwilling president. For capsule summaries of these policy struggles, see Randall B. Ripley and Grace A. Franklin, *Congress, the Bureaucracy, and Public Policy*, 5th ed. (Pacific Grove, Calif.: Brooks/Cole, 1991). The president's response was to veto objectionable bills: Richard Nixon vetoed 40 public bills; Congress overrode (by a two-thirds vote in each house) only 5 of those vetoes. The legislature was more successful in imposing its preferences on Gerald Ford, overriding 12 of his 66 vetoes.

16. In these sessions the committee goes over the bill line by line, often substantially amending it. The full committee or the entire chamber then acts on the final version of the proposed legislation.

17. Sometimes a powerful individual can single-handedly block legislation. Wil-

bur D. Mills (D-Ark.), chairman of the House Ways and Means Committee, personally blocked enactment of national health insurance for the elderly. Only when he had become convinced of the need for such a program and steered an acceptable bill through his committee did Medicare become law. See Theodore R. Marmor, *The Politics of Medicare*, rev. ed. (Chicago: Aldine, 1973); John R. Manley, *The Politics of Finance* (Boston: Little, Brown, 1970); and Randall Strahan, *New Ways and Means: Reform and Change in a Congressional Committee* (Chapel Hill: University of North Carolina Press, 1990).

18. See Randall B. Ripley, *The Politics of Economic and Human Resource Development* (Indianapolis, Ind.: Bobbs-Merrill, 1972), chap. 5; and R. Douglas Arnold, *Congress and the Bureaucracy: A Theory of Influence* (New Haven, Conn.: Yale University Press, 1979).

19. Lewis A. Dexter, "Congressmen and the Making of Military Policy," in *New Perspectives on the House of Representatives*, 3d ed., ed. Robert L. Peabody and Nelson W. Polsby (Chicago: Rand McNally, 1976), 3-25.

20. Raymond H. Dawson, "Congressional Innovation and Intervention in Defense Policy: Authorization of Weapons Systems," *American Political Science Review* 56 (1962): 42-57.

21. Quoted in Judy Gardner, "Congress More Cautious in Post-Vietnam Era," *Congressional Quarterly Weekly Report*, June 28, 1975, 1349.

22. Richard E. Neustadt, *Presidential Power and the Modern Presidents: The Politics of Leadership from Roosevelt to Reagan* (New York: Free Press, 1990).

23. Of course, contemporary, postreform presidents continue to use many of these techniques to persuade Congress.

24. Presidents did not in the 1950s and 1960s, nor does the president now, make all these contacts personally. A large liaison staff is at the president's disposal to assist in persuading members of Congress to go along with his policy proposals. On liaison in the prereform period, see Abraham Holtzman, *Legislative Liaison: Executive Leadership in Congress* (Chicago: Rand McNally, 1970). Executive branch lobbying efforts in this period were not always supportive of the chief executive's programs, although they often seemed to be. The agencies sometimes asked Congress to depart from official executive requests because they were not satisfied with the authority or the amount of funds requested for them. Some bureaus (the Army Corps of Engineers, for instance) developed cozy relationships—often referred to as *iron triangles* or *subgovernments*—with congressional committees and concerned interest groups and became virtually immune to executive control. The Army Corps, as the chief construction agency for rivers and harbors projects, sought to enlarge its mission; congressional subcommittees (the House Appropriations Committee's Public Works Subcommittee, for example) were eager to increase their influence and their ability to serve their constituents; citizens and the interest groups that represented them were happy to have the benefits that public projects provided. Each component of the iron triangle had an incentive to push for bigger construction programs, and presidents were regularly frustrated in their efforts to hold the fiscal line. See John A. Ferejohn, *Pork Barrel Politics: Rivers and Harbors Legislation, 1947-1968* (Stanford, Calif.: Stanford University Press, 1974); Arthur A. Maass, "Congress and Water Resources," *American Political Science Review* 44 (1950): 576-593; Douglass Cater, *Power in Washington* (New York: Random House, 1964); and

J. Leiper Freeman, *The Political Process*, rev. ed. (New York: Random House, 1965).

25. James L. Sundquist, *Politics and Policy: The Eisenhower, Kennedy, and Johnson Years* (Washington, D.C.: Brookings Institution, 1968), 146. This paragraph draws largely on Sundquist's account (chap. 4) of the war on poverty.

26. Samuel P. Huntington, "Congressional Responses to the Twentieth Century," in *The Congress and America's Future*, 2d ed., ed. David B. Truman (Englewood Cliffs, N.J.: Prentice-Hall, 1973), 6-38.

27. For instance, Raymond A. Bauer, Ithiel de Sola Pool, and Lewis A. Dexter, in *American Business and Public Policy*, 2d ed. (Chicago: Aldine-Atherton, 1972), pt. 4, suggest that lobby groups had less clout than was generally believed, that they were often understaffed and inadequately financed, and that they sought to avoid pressure tactics and "hard sell." See also Lester W. Milbrath, *The Washington Lobbyists* (Chicago: Rand McNally, 1963); and Lewis A. Dexter, *How Organizations Are Represented in Washington* (Indianapolis, Ind.: Bobbs-Merrill, 1969). For the classic view of interest groups as more powerful policy-making participants, see David B. Truman, *The Governmental Process*, 2d ed. (New York: Knopf, 1971); and Grant McConnell, *Private Power and American Democracy* (New York: Knopf, 1966).

28. This stress on the supportive role rather than the aggressive posture of interest groups does not mean that more traditional techniques of influence were not used. Such groups did hire intermediaries, who were influential constituents of the legislators, to express interest group sentiments. Public relations campaigns and even bribery were also used. Some lobbyists, seeking to reward their friends and punish their enemies, did get involved in the electoral process. But on balance, such tactics were relatively costly and inefficient. Direct communication was more effective and was the preferred method of group involvement.

29. For the classic exposition of the "mobilization of bias," the unrepresentativeness of the most active and powerful associations, in the interest group system, see E. E. Schattschneider, *The Semi-Sovereign People* (New York: Holt, Rinehart and Winston, 1960).

30. Citizens with more education, higher incomes, and more leisure time communicate more often than do low-income constituents and are quite atypical of the electorate as a whole. Thus, members are unlikely to get a fair sampling of constituent opinion. See Angus Campbell, Philip E. Converse, Warren E. Miller, and Donald E. Stokes, *The American Voter* (New York: Wiley, 1960); and Campbell et al., *Elections and the Political Order* (New York: Wiley, 1966).

31. Sundquist, *Politics and Policy*.

32. This point should not be overemphasized. As noted, electoral uncertainties did compel members of Congress to worry about constituents' reactions and thus there was some link between governor and governed. But the legislators' sensitivity to constituent opinion was probably stronger than was empirically necessary, given the reality of voters' attention to Congress. In fact, legislators had few worries about most single actions or votes. See John W. Kingdon, *Congressmen's Voting Decisions*, 3d ed. (Ann Arbor: University of Michigan Press, 1989). Rather, members needed to cultivate the impression among their constituents that they were alive, well, and, most important, working hard for the state or district.

33. See Campbell et al., *The American Voter* and *Elections and the Political Order;* and Donald E. Stokes and Warren E. Miller, "Party Government and the Saliency of Congress," *Public Opinion Quarterly* 26 (1962): 532-546. Stokes and Miller found that in the off-year congressional election of 1958, only 7 percent of those polled gave issue-related reasons for their votes. For confirmatory evidence from 1970, see Stanley R. Freedman, "The Salience of Party and Candidate in Congressional Elections: A Comparison of 1958 and 1970," in *Public Opinion and Public Policy*, 3d ed., ed. Norman R. Luttbeg (Itasca, Ill.: Peacock, 1981), 118-122.

34. See, for example, David RePass, "Issue Salience and Party Choice," *American Political Science Review* 65 (1971): 389-400; Richard W. Boyd, "Popular Control of Public Policy: A Normal Vote Analysis of the 1968 Elections," *American Political Science Review* 66 (1972): 429-449; and Gerald M. Pomper,"From Confusion to Clarity: Issues and American Voters, 1956-1968," *American Political Science Review* 66 (1972): 415-428.

35. Charles O. Jones, "Inter-party Competition for Congressional Seats," *Western Political Quarterly* 17 (1964): 461-476. In 1968, when Richard Nixon barely edged out Hubert Humphrey for the presidency, only 8 (of 404) House incumbents seeking reelection were defeated (3 in the primary, 5 in the general election). At the other extreme was the Democratic landslide in 1964, when Lyndon Johnson buried Barry Goldwater: 50 incumbents (of 394 whose names were on the lists) lost their seats (5 in the primaries, 45 in the fall contest). Thus even major swings brought only modest-sized new contingents to Congress; because there was no new blood, the ideological composition of Congress changed only slightly.

36. One study found that in the 1966 off-year House elections (the 90th Congress, 1967-1968), the losing candidates, as a group, bore a striking ideological similarity to the winners. Had the defeated nominees won, the resulting House would have been slightly more liberal in foreign policy but slightly more conservative in domestic matters. If the national electorate had strongly endorsed one party or shown a distinct ideological (liberal or conservative) preference, the 90th Congress would have been strikingly different. But such unidimensional swings in partisan or ideological preferences, encompassing virtually all electoral districts, are unknown in American political history. See John L. Sullivan and Robert E. O'Connor, "Electoral Choice and Popular Control of Public Policy," *American Political Science Review* 6 (1972): 1256-1258. For a discussion of the occasional elections that do produce genuine policy change, see Gary C. Jacobson and Samuel Kernell, *Strategy and Choice in Congressional Elections*, 2d ed. (New Haven, Conn.: Yale University Press, 1983); and David W. Brady, *Critical Elections and Congressional Policy Making* (Stanford, Calif.: Stanford University Press, 1988).

3. Reform and Change Since 1970

U
nder the lash of numerous critics, Congress in 1970 began to enact a series of wide-ranging reforms designed to improve its performance. The reformers shared one ambition: making Congress "better." But what constitutes a better Congress? There was and is little agreement. A few reformers have proposed changes intended to make Congress more consistent with a broad vision of what it should be, but these proponents of executive force or congressional supremacy theories have found that few are interested in their theoretical insights. Other reformers have focused on smaller but more manageable matters, suggesting specific steps designed to make Congress more responsible, more responsive, more accountable, or some combination of these desirable yet often incompatible qualities. This pragmatic perspective, which was influenced by the events of the 1960s in particular, dominated the reform movement that gained strength in the 1970s; Congress moved in several directions rather than seeking consistency with any one reform vision. Ironically, even though the reforms sought improvements in the responsibility, responsiveness, and accountability of Congress, their net impact, at least until the mid-1980s, may have been to preserve, or even increase, the decentralization of the legislature.

The major contemporary reforms were adopted during the 1970s; by the end of the decade, reform had largely ceased to be a serious concern. The 1980s, by contrast, were a period of evolution—of gradual change, not dramatic reform; the reforms previously adopted were implemented by those affected by them—in particular, the parties and committees. At that decade's conclusion, some observers professed to detect the emergence of a "postreform" Congress—less fragmented, more centralized, and, in consequence, more capable of responsible policy making.[1] As noted in the Introduction, however, twenty years of reform and change had failed to create a Congress that its critics found satisfactory. In the early 1990s, prompted by perceived policy-making failure and numerous ethical lapses, calls for wholesale reform again resounded in Washington and throughout the nation.

To determine the causes, course, and consequences of congressional change is no easy task. *Reform*—defined as the intentional effort to reshape institutional organizations and processes—is only one, and perhaps not even the most important, type of organizational change. *Change,* a broader concept, can affect basic institutional patterns or procedures; be intended or inadvertent, evolutionary or revolutionary; and occur randomly and unobtrusively. In addition, the content of public policy, and the advantages—money, power, symbolic preferment—that statutes or other legislative activities confer, may reflect either reform (as defined) or change, or both. Thus change is basic; it can have a variety of causes, and it can result in new forms of organization and action and new institutional outcomes. Accordingly, reform is best seen as a type of change, an *explicit* effort to bring about preferable results through specific organizational or procedural alterations. The aim of this chapter and the next is to sort out the causes and types of change, including reform, and to assess its impact, if any, on Congress's performance.

As David Rohde and Kenneth Shepsle make clear, change may result from a multiplicity of forces.[2] *Events* occurring outside the legislature may directly affect it. Domestic recession or international crisis may pose problems that highlight congressional deficiencies; lawmakers' failure to cope with old or new issues is likely to encourage reformers to come forward with proposals to make Congress work better. Such external developments may raise new issues, may produce *agenda change*, with which Congress may feel compelled to deal, and which requires new institutional organizations and processes.[3] Finally, *membership turnover* may bring to the legislature new personnel with different backgrounds, experiences, and perspectives; these newcomers may operate the existing congressional machinery in ways quite at variance with old routines, or they may seek to rebuild the legislative engine to achieve more efficient performance.[4] Alternatively, events may induce or compel incumbent members of Congress to reassess their views, leading to either policy change or reform, or both.[5] In short, events and new members, which are neither planned nor predictable, may contribute to legislative change as much as or more than any planned movement.

Members of Congress are the chief agents of reform; unless and until they choose to act, there will be none.[6] Lawmakers deal with reform, as they do more "substantive" issues, incrementally. They are seldom if ever moved by broad visions of the ideal Congress; rather they respond, in the short run, to the circumstances of the moment.

Reforms tend to be political, pragmatic, and more or less spontaneous reactions to seemingly irresistible forces. They have been piecemeal, not wholesale; individually modest, not radical; ad hoc, not the products of comprehensive planning.

In addition, the reformers' motives are mixed, not pure, making it difficult to determine precisely the purposes of the changes they propose. Some ostensible goals are far easier to defend than others; the rationale for institutional engineering may belie its true intent, however. Few would fault Congress for wanting to regain the public prestige lost during the late 1960s.[7] And the desire to make the legislature more effective and efficient in producing public policy is hardly controversial. It is somewhat riskier, however, to propose reforms that increase legislative influence relative to that of the executive; there are those who prefer presidential power to congressional power. Likewise, to suggest reforms to bring about desired policies, or to attempt to reverse unfavorable outcomes, is likely to elicit opposition from those satisfied with the legislature's current output (or lack thereof). Finally, the personal considerations of members—the desire to increase their electoral success or legislative power—may underlie their reform sentiments, although these concerns are seldom advertised.

Overall, then, it is hard to know with certainty what reformers have wanted to accomplish. The reforms they adopted, then implemented incrementally and sequentially, have been compromises that were not always consistent with one another. Moreover, the reforms are hard to distinguish from the consequences of other, unplanned changes that occurred in the same period. Any efforts to specify what the reforms have actually produced are treacherous. This disclaimer notwithstanding (valor being the lesser part of discretion), it is possible to identify three categories of reforms—those promoting responsibility, responsiveness, and accountability—that Congress adopted and that contribute to improved congressional performance today.[8]

Two broad aims seem to have motivated these efforts. The first was to make Congress more responsive and accountable: to "democratize" it, that is, to give more members and citizens more influence and increase their opportunity to participate meaningfully in congressional deliberation and policy making. The second was to make Congress more responsible, to reassert congressional power and influence unwisely lost to the executive branch, to make Congress a more effective policy maker. These efforts occupied the better part of a decade, and the reforms they produced were implemented without reference to broad theories or even to other reforms of that period.

The Road to Reform

The events of the late 1960s, along with new issues (or old issues in new guises) and personnel turnover in Congress, set the stage for the reformers of the 1970s to win approval of much of their agenda. Vietnam was surely the catalyst. When President Lyndon Johnson asked Congress for a free hand to escalate the fighting in Indochina, the legislators were more than happy to comply: no representatives and only two senators voted against the Gulf of Tonkin resolution that gave the president carte blanche to conduct an armed conflict as he saw fit. But as the war dragged on toward an ultimately unsatisfactory conclusion and as the American public became increasingly impatient with the nation's inability to "win" the fight, lawmakers became increasingly frustrated. They sought, without success until the very end, to influence the course of the war once it had become obvious that presidential policy was not working. Their failure to move either Johnson or Richard Nixon to alter the course made clear their impotence vis-à-vis the "imperial presidency" and led to calls for a reassertion of legislative authority.[9]

Controversy over the federal budget taught a similar lesson: Congress was at a serious disadvantage in any policy competition with the executive branch. The costs of the Vietnam conflict unbalanced the federal budget; the effort to pay for both "guns and butter"—the war and a multitude of Great Society social programs—had led to soaring inflation and budgetary deficits. Spending seemed out of control, and Congress's budgetary mechanisms appeared incapable of checking expenditures. Nixon confronted Congress directly: he insisted that it adopt a cap on federal spending and began to impound duly appropriated funds that he thought were excessive.[10] Members of the legislature concluded, grudgingly although correctly, that they were poorly prepared to push their own fiscal priorities in the face of such presidential power and persuasion.

During the mid-1960s, the nation confronted a set of difficult and emotional policy concerns. Civil rights issues aroused racial antagonisms. The Supreme Court's 1954 decision in *Brown v. Board of Education* had declared segregated schools unconstitutional. The civil rights movement, consisting of peaceful marches and protests that often turned violent, brought black Americans' claims forcefully to public attention. The Civil Rights Act of 1964 and the Voting Rights Act of 1965 increased the salience of their cause. The civil rights issue was no longer simply a residue of slavery, restricted to the southern states; problems of housing, access to public accommodations, busing to achieve school desegregation, equal employment opportunity, and voting rights affected all sections of the nation and the lawmakers who represented them.[11] Other issues, such as environmental protection, energy, school prayer, and abortion—previously ignored or treated gingerly—rose to the top of the policy agenda, and lawmakers found that they were ill-prepared to deal with them. Congress, suffering from a collective, institutional inferiority complex, called for reform.[12]

Throughout the United States there was a new spirit of democracy, of expanded political participation in this period. Johnson's War on Poverty program stressed community action and sought to involve ordinary citizens, the beneficiaries of social programs, in the planning and implementation of federal welfare activities. Previously unrepresented or underrepresented groups—not only the poor and the minorities but consumers and women—began to organize and to press their claims on the government: the public interest movement (or citizen lobby) flourished.[13] The Democratic party, fearing that rank-and-file partisans played too small a part in the presidential selection process, totally revised its nominating procedures. New party rules, adopted after 1968, drastically reduced the role of party professionals—the alleged "bosses"—and created a system in which the nominee was chosen, for all practical purposes, by citizens in state caucuses and primary elections.[14] In short, more involved citizens made louder and more numerous demands on their elected representatives, who, burdened by a growing work load, found themselves increasingly hard pressed to respond.

The electoral process further transformed Congress in the 1970s; there was a great infusion of new blood. Membership turnover, low during the 1960s, rose sharply. In the 91st Congress (1969-1971), there were 36 freshman representatives (23 members of the 90th Congress retired; 13 lost their reelection bids); that is, 8 percent were serving their first term while 18 percent were in their tenth term or more. A decade later, in the 96th Congress (1979-1981), there were 77 freshman representatives (18 percent of the House), replacing 49 retirees, 24 defeated members, and 4 who either resigned or died; members with 10 or more terms of service constituted 13 percent of the House.

In the Senate, the story was the same: turnover increased dramatically. In the 91st Congress there were 14 freshman senators (replacing 6 retirees and 8 losers); in the 96th Congress there were 20 (succeeding 10 retirees and 10 election victims). In the 91st Congress, 31 percent of the senators had less than a full term of service; ten years later, the figure was 48 percent.[15]

The newcomers recognized Congress's failings, inheriting from their predecessors a long-standing dissatisfaction with the legislature's performance. In the 1946 House elections, Republican challengers won 55 previously Democratic seats, mostly from northern liberals, and took control of the House. The Democrats regained the House majority in 1948, but the surviving conservative southerners dominated the party and, by virtue of the seniority tradition, gained a disproportionate share of powerful committee chairmanships. They allied in a conservative coalition with the Republicans in Congress to block liberal policy initiatives. Consequently, throughout the 1950s there was constant but unavailing agitation by liberals to modify the seniority system, gain power in congressional policy making, and enact progressive legislation.

The newcomers of the 1960s and early 1970s were younger, more policy oriented, and more independent; as a result, they were less predisposed to follow the modus operandi than was the earlier generation of lawmakers. They balked at the traditions of the institution, refusing to accept norms like apprenticeship that required them to refrain from active participation in congressional deliberations until they had supposedly "learned the ropes," or to defer to the wise counsel of committee leaders—chairs and ranking minority members—until they had acquired the requisite specialization. They were, in short, unwilling to take the advice of Speaker Sam Rayburn (D-Texas): "To get along, go along."[16] Moreover, many of these new members found it electorally advantageous to run for Congress by running "against" Congress,[17] to criticize the legislative establishment and, on arriving in Washington, to adopt a reformist view of congressional organization and procedure. The changed circumstances that helped to protect most incumbents from November surprises at the polls—more attention to creating effective personal campaign organizations and the ready availability of funds from the proliferating PACs[18]—gave new members the independence they needed to pursue their own political agendas, agendas that included reform.

Thus the reform spirit grew, spurred by Congress's inability to influence American foreign policy in Vietnam. Watergate, the extraordinary congeries of scandals that was more far-reaching than the bungled burglary at the apartment complex that gave it its name, provided the final impetus. President Nixon, preoccupied with defending himself and his subordinates, had little time to devote to the legislature. As the Watergate revelations unfolded, his popularity plummeted, as did his persuasive power. Nixon's political weakness gave Congress the courage and the opportunity to act to redress its grievances against the executive branch. Nixon's resignation (and his successor's controversial pardon of the "disgraced" ex-president) handed the Democrats a major triumph in the 1974 midterm elections: 75 freshman Democrats, many of them liberals, were elected to the 94th Congress (1975-1976) and they sustained the reform spirit.[19]

This extraordinary concatenation of circumstances stirred up a wave of congressional self-evaluation and analysis; without these external pressures, it is doubtful that members of Congress would have felt the need to undertake reform. In 1965, Congress established the Joint Committee on the Organization of Congress. The committee's wide-ranging examination of the legislature's organization and procedures led to passage of the Legislative Reorganization Act of 1970. In 1972 Congress established a second committee, the Joint Study Committee on Budget Control, which laid the groundwork for the Congressional Budget and Impoundment Control Act of 1974.

Each chamber pursued its own course as congressional introspection grew. The House established three separate reform panels: the (Bolling) Select Committee on Committees in 1973-1974; the (Obey) Commission on Administrative Review in 1977; and the (Patterson) Select Committee on Committees in 1980.[20] Not to be outdone, the Senate launched the (Hughes) Commission on the Operation of the Senate in 1975, the (Stevenson) Temporary Select Committee to Study the Senate Committee System in 1976, and the (Culver) Commission on the Operation of the Senate in 1975.[21] An impressive welter of ideas emerged from these committees; many were adopted (most were not).

The liberal Democratic Study Group (DSG)[22] nurtured the seeds of reform, which first bore fruit when Congress enacted the Legislative Reorganization Act of 1970. Policy problems that appeared intractable extended the growing season, new members tilled the fields, and the reformers brought in a bumper crop of changes during the ensuing years. But they did not inevitably reap what they had intended to sow (in fact, they did not always know precisely what they had planted), and their harvest was often bitter.

A Democratizing Trend: Responsiveness and Accountability

Nevertheless, these conditions produced significant reform; they created for members of Congress both incentives and opportunity to alter the ways in which the legislature conducted its business. The first major thrust of the reform movement was to make Congress more democratic by offering more senators and representatives a greater opportunity to influence congressional policy making, oversight, and representation. This effort was motivated by two aims: responsiveness and accountability. The reforms engendered by the first sought to permit more voices from inside and outside the legislature to be heard, and perhaps heeded, prior to congressional deliberations and decisions. Those produced by the second sought to ensure that those debates and choices took place in the open, presumably subject to citizen scrutiny. In this more democratic Congress, more members, responding to more interests, would contribute to its activities, and they would do so in plain sight of the public. Most of these reforms were in place by the end of the 1970s; minor adjustments have been made periodically since then.

Redistributing Committee Power to Increase Responsiveness

As a first step in redistributing committee powers, the House and later the Senate loosened the hold of committee leaders on their panels. Many members, especially liberal and junior legislators, chafed under the restrictions on their participation and policy influence that the old committee-dominated regime imposed. The committee chair, often in collaboration with the ranking minority member, dominated the panel. Formal leaders were chosen by seniority; the majority party member with the longest continuous service on a committee automatically became its chair. In the eyes of the critics, this meant that longevity, both physical and political, rather than expertise or political skill, determined who would manage committee deliberations. Specifically, because so many "safe" Democratic seats were in the South, conservatives from states below the Mason-Dixon line acceded with inordinate frequency to the top committee posts and used the power of those positions to block northern liberals' policy initiatives.[23]

In 1971, both parties in the House decided they could employ criteria other than seniority to choose chairs; each empowered its party caucus, the meeting of all party members, to vote on whether to accept the recommendations of the party committee on committees for the position of chair or ranking minority member. The Republican procedure called for a conference vote on its committee on committees' nomination, a recommendation not necessarily based on seniority. The Democrats adopted a plan, sometimes described as a "kamikaze system," whereby ten committee members could force a vote on their chair in the Democratic caucus. The requirement to stand up publicly to oppose powerful chairs served to deter challengers, but liberals on the District of Columbia committee did seek to oust chairman John L. McMillan (D-S.C.) because they objected to his long-standing opposition to home rule for Washington, D.C., McMillan survived by a 196-96 caucus vote. This challenge may have contributed to his defeat in his district's 1972 primary.

In 1973, the House Democrats went one step further: they determined that the full caucus should vote on the nominee for each committee chair and, if one-fifth of the members so desired, by secret ballot. In practice, all decisions followed seniority; the number of negative votes against the senior committee member ranged from 2 to 49 and in no instance constituted one-third of the total votes cast. The

Republican conference raised two challenges, but in both cases the seniors retained their chairs by three-to-one margins. There was a hint of change in the Senate in 1973 when Republicans adopted a proposal by which committee members would elect the ranking minority member from among their own number without regard to seniority; no ranking minority members were unseated under the new process. Two years later, the Senate Democrats accepted a plan (not used until the beginning of the 95th Congress in 1977) for a secret ballot vote for chair in full caucus on request of the caucus; in such voting, members need not consider seniority.

It was the House Democrats, however, who first used new procedures to mount a successful challenge to a sitting committee chair. In 1975, they permitted rank-and-file members of the caucus to nominate candidates for that position if the caucus had rejected the committee on committees' original choice. The caucus—its ranks enlarged by the addition of 75 freshmen, mostly liberals—actually did depose three elderly southern committee chairmen: W.R. Poage (Texas), age 75, of the Agriculture Committee; F. Edward Hebert (La.), 74, of the Armed Services Committee; and Wright Patman (Texas), 81, of the Banking, Currency, and Housing Committee. These aged oligarchs were succeeded by younger northerners: Thomas Foley (Wash.), age 45; Melvin Price (Ill.), 70; and Henry Reuss (Wis.), 62. Foley and Price had been the second-ranking Democrats on the Agriculture and Armed Services Committees, respectively; Reuss stood fourth on the seniority ladder in the Banking Committee.[24] Wayne Hays (Ohio), rejected by the committee on committees for renomination for another term as chairman of the House Administration Committee, averted defeat in the caucus; freshmen whose campaigns he had supported with funds at his disposal as chairman of the House Democratic Congressional Campaign Committee helped reverse the initial decision.[25] Later in 1975, the Democratic caucus used the procedures that had been followed for selecting committee chairs in selecting subcommittee chairs of the Appropriations Committee, positions that have important budgetary responsibilities.

A decade later, at the start of the 99th Congress (1985-1986), the House Democratic caucus replaced octogenarian Melvin Price with Les Aspin (Wis.), a younger liberal, as chairman of the Armed Services Committee.[26] In 1991, the Democrats struck again, removing two chairmen—Frank Annunzio (Ill.) of the House Administration Committee, and Glenn M. Anderson (Calif.) of Public Works; each was widely viewed as ineffective and unresponsive. Two years later, the caucus eased its most senior member, the ailing 83-year-old Jamie Whitten (Miss.), from the Appropriations Committee chairmanship.[27] Overall, the seniority tradition has been followed more often than not, but it is now clear that it is not sacrosanct; chairs are on notice that they may be unseated if their peers deem their behavior unacceptable.

If committee leaders had been less powerful—had emphasized their duties as presiding officers rather than being independent actors—the conflict over seniority would have been less heated. In the prereform period, committee chairs commanded substantial influence. In consequence, the democratizing trend produced a number of reforms that limit the ability of chairs to dominate their panels. The Legislative Reorganization Act of 1970, for example, allows the ranking majority member to preside over committee business if the committee leader is absent. If a committee chair in the House fails to move for floor consideration of a bill within seven days after the Rules Committee proposes a rule defining the conditions for floor debate, a committee majority can so move. The 1970 act also guarantees all members the opportunity to participate fully in committee hearings (for instance, it empowers minority members to call their own witnesses), limits the ability of chairs to use proxy votes (it mandates that they be in writing and used only for specific legislative business), and grants extra staff assistance to minority party members.

In addition, the 1970 reorganization act allows senators to serve on only three committees (two major, one minor) and to chair only one committee and one subcommittee of a major panel; these provisions were effective beginning with the 92d Congress (1971-1972).[28] During the 1970s, the House also acted to reduce the concentration of power. The Democrats took numerous steps. No member could chair more than one legislative subcommittee, serve on more than two full committees, or be a member of more than one exclusive committee.[29] Each Democrat was entitled to serve on one exclusive or one major committee. Members who chaired exclusive or major committees could not chair any other committee or a subcommittee of a committee other than the one they led. No member could serve on more than a total of five subcommittees.[30] Thus both the Senate and the House effectively guaranteed members "a piece of the action" earlier in their careers and ensured that committee chairs could no longer monopolize leadership positions on their panels.

Most important, perhaps, in the House, the reforms transferred much full committee power to the subcommittees. As noted, new rules made it easier for junior members of a full committee to attain positions of authority on that panel's subcommittees. In 1973, the Democratic caucus designated all party members on each standing committee as constituting the committee caucus and empowered them to choose subcommittee chairs, establish subcommittee party ratios, and set subcommittee budgets. The boldest step taken by the caucus in 1973, however, was to adopt a "subcommittee bill of rights."[31] This manifesto declared that full committees should respect the jurisdiction of each of their subcommittees. All legislation referred to a full committee was to be parceled out to the appropriate subcommittee within two weeks of referral. Subcommittees were empowered to elect their own leaders; write their own rules; employ their own staffs; and meet, hold hearings, and act on legislation. Each subcommittee was entitled to its own budget. This bill of rights was a declaration of subcommittee independence from the full committee and its chair. In 1974 the Democratic caucus required all full committees with more than twenty members to create a minimum of four subcommittees.

In the 1970s House Democrats also established procedures to facilitate members' accession to positions of subcommittee power. They instituted bidding procedures that permitted all members, even the most junior, to secure desirable subcommittee assignments and leadership posts. Bidding was in order of seniority. Each full committee Democrat was guaranteed a choice of one subcommittee membership before any could claim a second subcommittee slot; each member thus could seek an advantageous subcommittee assignment, and each could secure a reasonably senior slot on some subcommittee. A similar process governed the selection of subcommittee chairs: members requested (bid for) the top spot on their preferred subcommittees; the full committee caucus ratified their choices, by secret ballot when there was competition for a particular subcommittee chair. In sum, these reforms not only restricted the number of positions any member could hold but virtually guaranteed that the available assignments would be shared by all the committee members, thus facilitating broad participation in subcommittee activity.

Control over the staff was dispersed as well. Under the 1971 House reforms, the chair of the full committee could no longer hire all panel staff members. Each subcommittee leader (chair and ranking minority member) was granted authority to employ a professional staff member for the committee. In 1975 the Senate went further, allowing all senators to have some committee staff members of their own. Previously, the chair of the full committees and subcommittees had controlled staff recruitment, but the new procedure permitted all senators not already authorized to hire staff personnel to recruit an aide to assist them with each of their three full committee assignments.[32] These changes effectively reallocated committee power from senior leaders to rank-and-file members.

The democratizing impulse also led to direct attacks on two powerful House committees: Rules, and Ways and Means. The Rules Committee determines the conditions under which legislation is considered on the House floor. A "closed" rule (which its critics call the "gag" rule) allows the Rules Committee to limit or eliminate the opportunity to propose amendments to pending bills; thus the committee can, and sometimes did in the 1950s and 1960s, prevent a majority from voting its will. To reduce this possibility, the Democrats in 1973 adopted a complicated procedure requiring the party delegation on rules to allow a floor vote on any amendment if fifty party members called for a vote and the full party caucus agreed.[33]

The Ways and Means Committee also felt the lash of the democratizers. Under the chairmanship of Wilbur Mills (D-Ark.), the committee did not use subcommittees; all business was conducted in full committee with Mills presiding. The 1974 resolution requiring all committees with more than 20 members to establish at least four subcommittees was aimed directly at Ways and Means; permanent, expert, independent subcommittees were intended to undercut Mills's power. Subsequently, the Democratic caucus enlarged that committee by half, from 25 to 37 members, thus enabling more, and more liberal, representatives to secure seats on the panel. In 1990, the caucus assumed the authority to elect Ways and Means subcommittee chairs. Like the changes aimed at the Rules Committee, these reforms were designed to make Ways and Means more responsive to the will of rank-and-file Democrats.

Taken together, the committee reforms of the 1970s, which have since been modified only slightly,[34] sought to decentralize Congress and to make it more democratic. Change was particularly marked in the more hierarchical House. The reformers believed that committee chairs would be less able to direct and dominate their panels, for they would have to share their authority with subcommittee leaders and full committee majorities. In other words, more members, operating from power bases within committees and subcommittees, would have a share of congressional authority. More lawmakers, voicing differing sentiments and articulating a broader range of constituent opinions, would participate in reaching solutions to pressing problems and influence the bargaining that eventually would produce new policies. Democratizing reforms, in sum, were expected to increase congressional responsiveness.

These democratizing reforms could serve additional purposes. For the individual member, ensconced in a subcommittee seat with concomitant budgetary, staff, and other resources, the ability to influence policy meant increased participation in policy subsystems, the "iron triangles" or "issue networks" that often permit congressional personnel, interest group representatives, and executive branch bureaucrats to shape basic policy choices.[35] Since the subcommittee has jurisdiction over certain policy topics, its members could contribute to the decisions on matters that the subsystem manages. Of course, policy influence was readily convertible into reelection currency if members advertised their activities and claimed credit for their accomplishments.[36] A newly won subcommittee slot permitted more members to "deliver the goods" (such as a rivers and harbors project or a defense contract) to their states and districts. Democratization was readily defensible. (Who could quarrel with the values of equality and participation?) But it also may have concealed other less defensible, more mundane and personal political considerations.

The growing term limits movement, which originated outside the Beltway, has sought, in one sense at least, to make the legislature more responsive. Though term limits are constitutionally questionable—they may impermissibly add to the qualifications the Constitution (Article I, sections 2 and 3) specifies for service in Congress—fifteen states voted in referenda to limit congressional service to six to twelve years in the House and two terms (twelve years) in the Senate. Proponents of limits hoped to eliminate member dependence on special interests and PAC campaign contributions and to encourage the lawmakers to pay attention to the concerns of ordinary citizens.[37]

"Sunshine" Reforms: Less Secrecy, More Accountability

Democratization of Congress had a second aim: to make the legislators more accountable and thus to improve Congress's public image. The reforms were a direct response to the demands of an increasingly hostile public. The prestige of Congress had been weakened not only by policy failure but by a series of widely publicized scandals (ranging from ordinary, old-fashioned corruption and conflicts of interest to Adam Clayton Powell and Abscam, nontyping typists and Tidal Basin exhibitionism).[38] Paradoxically, constituents retained considerable confidence in their own individual representatives but concluded that Congress collectively was performing poorly.[39] To change this perception, the legislature adopted a series of reforms designed in large part to expose its operations to citizen scrutiny. To the extent that the voters could ascertain what their representatives were doing, and satisfy themselves that these activities were ethical, they would be able to hold Congress accountable and accept it as legitimate and untainted.

Congress adopted several reforms to make its activities more accessible to interested citizens.[40] The Legislative Reorganization Act of 1970 allowed televising, broadcasting, and photographing of committee hearings within limits left to the discretion of the individual panels. In 1978, the House began broadcasting its formal floor sessions, and with the advent of cable television systems, the programs reached a wider segment of the population over the C-SPAN network. The Senate initially balked at televising its proceedings, however, fearing that such coverage would encourage its members to "grandstand" rather than to focus on legislative business and would show the institution at its worst.[41] In 1986, the Senate relented and, after a six-week trial run, let the television cameras in on a permanent basis.

In 1973, the House mandated that all committee sessions should be open to the public unless a majority of the panel voted in an open meeting to close them; this included the markup sessions, in which committees prepared final drafts of bills (previously conducted by most committees behind closed doors), and conference committee meetings, in which differences between House and Senate bills on the same subject were resolved. The Senate adopted similar sunshine rules in 1975. House committee members were required to vote by recorded roll call each day to close a committee meeting, and only the full chamber, also in a recorded roll call vote, could close a conference committee session. In both chambers executive sessions can still be held on secret or controversial matters, but those who would exclude outside observers must persuade their committee colleagues that there is good reason to keep the public out.

The 1970 act also required that committees record and make publicly available each lawmaker's committee votes. Under the old rules only vote totals, not the positions of individual members, were recorded in committee. Also prior to the 1970 act, under certain circumstances no votes were recorded; in the voice, standing, or unrecorded teller votes, the positions of individual legislators remained unknown.[42] Only formal roll call votes were recorded. The 1970 act provided that, on demand of twenty House members, the names of those participating in teller votes would be listed as the members walked up the aisle. Eventually, the House switched to voting by machine—using an "electronic device"—to speed up the roll call process as well as to record individual positions more visibly. In 1993, the rules were altered to eliminate teller votes entirely. These reforms were intended to enable attentive citizens to identify the supporters and opponents of particular legislative measures when they voted in committee and on the floor.[43]

In the same vein, reforms were passed that forced disclosure of members' campaign finances. In 1971, Congress enacted a modest piece of legislation, the Federal Election Campaign Act (FECA). In 1974, following Watergate disclosures of manifold campaign finance abuses—satchels containing illegal cash contributions, money laundering, funding of criminal activities—the legislature adopted sweeping amendments to the FECA. Donations to primary, runoff, and general election campaigns were strictly limited to $1,000 by individuals and $5,000 by organizations. Spending ceilings were also imposed on candidates. Both donors and recipients were obligated to report, fully and promptly, even modest campaign contributions. The law created a Federal Election Commission (FEC) to oversee the statute; the FEC receives and makes available to the public candidate spending reports. A variety of interest organizations (particularly Common Cause, a public interest lobby) analyze campaign finance information and publicize the sources of funds received by members of particular congressional committees and lawmakers promoting particular policies.

The constitutionality of the FECA was challenged, and in *Buckley v. Valeo* (1976) the Supreme Court struck down the provision imposing spending ceilings on candidates on the grounds that it violated First Amendment guarantees of freedom of expression. The decision did sustain both the contribution limits and the reporting requirements of the act. Thus, although candidates were free to spend unlimited funds, they had to raise the money by combining relatively small contributions and to report in some detail the purposes for which they spent it. The PACs soon became, and have remained, prominent sources of funds for congressional candidates. The act limits each PAC's contribution to $5,000 per candidate per election, but groups of related PACs representing single sectors of industry—such as oil or defense—have emerged as major suppliers of campaign money. Although each can give no more than $5,000, together they can provide candidates with large sums. Still, they must report what they give. The intent of these reporting requirements, enforced by the FEC, was to make known the sources and uses of campaign funds and thus lessen popular suspicions about legislators' finances.[44]

In 1977 and 1978, the Senate and House, respectively, adopted stricter codes of ethics to replace the ethics legislation enacted in 1958 and 1968. The new regulations were designed to eliminate conflicts of interest by requiring members to disclose their general financial history to interested citizens and the media. In particular, senators and representatives were required to report their earned income, income from dividends and interest, honoraria received for lectures and other activities, the value and donor of gifts tendered, holdings in property or securities, and their outstanding financial obligations. Such disclosures would enable concerned citizens to ascertain to whom, if anyone, legislators were financially beholden and to assess whether their personal interests impinged on matters about which they were to vote or otherwise act.

In addition, the new ethics codes imposed limits on lawmakers' acquisition and use of funds. Members were allowed to earn less in the form of honoraria for giving speeches or offering advice to interest groups; income from such activities could not exceed 15 percent of their congressional salaries.[45] Members were also barred from taking, in any single year, gifts from interest groups or their lobbyists worth more than $100.[46] They were forbidden to collect "slush funds" (designated "office accounts") to supplement their official allowances and prohibited from spending campaign funds to defray their personal expenses. Candidates for reelection were also prohibited from sending franked mail within sixty days of a primary or general election. Annual franked mailings for all members were restricted to not more than six times the number of addresses in the state or district represented. Representatives running for reelection were prohibited from sending franked mail to residents outside the districts they currently represented. Although members believed franked mail was essential to the representative function—which was to inform and educate constituents—reformers, including some in Congress, felt the perquisite conferred an unfair electoral advantage on incumbent legislators, and they moved successfully to restrict the practice. The intent here, as with the financial disclosure provisions, was to restore public confidence in Congress.

Because these steps did not allay public hostility, Congress made additional changes to enforce more rigorous ethical standards. The main vehicle was the Ethics in Government Act of 1989, which imposed limits on gifts that members could accept: representatives could take no more than $200 in gifts valued at $75 or more each; senators were limited to a total of $300 worth of gifts and no more than $100 worth from anyone with an interest in pending legislation. Two years later, both chambers eased the restrictions: members now cannot accept gifts worth more than $250 a year (those valued at less than $100 did not count), and they need not report allowable gifts on their disclosure forms. Travel and "personal hospitality" are exempt from the restrictions, but travel reimbursement is limited to seven days for trips out of the country and to four days (House) or three days (Senate) for trips within the country; no legislator can accept hospitality from any individual lasting more than four consecutive days or thirty days total.

The 1989 act also tightened conflict of interest regulations. House members voted themselves a salary increase, from $96,600 for 1990 to $125,000 for 1991, and indexed their pay to inflation, providing for automatic annual cost-of-living increments (thus eliminating the necessity of a public floor vote). In return, they gave up honoraria for speeches and articles, though they retained the opportunity to direct that payments of up to $2,000 be given to charities of their choice. Representatives must disclose the source and amount of the latter funds as well as meet more rigorous reporting requirements for travel reimbursement and the listing of their assets, liabilities, and financial transactions. Senators had initially declined to bar honoraria, but took only a cost-of-living wage adjustment for 1990; in 1991, however, the Senate fell into line with the House, accepted the higher salary, and adopted the same rules on honoraria. In addition, in 1989 the House but not the Senate imposed a limit (15 percent of salary) on the amount of outside earned income—from law practices or service on corporate boards of directors, for instance—that members could accept. The House eliminated the opportunity for retiring or defeated members to convert leftover campaign funds (which often totaled several hundred thousand dollars) to personal use; after 1992, legislators were to be unable to amass huge war chests for self-serving purposes. Both chambers also barred retiring or defeated members from lobbying the legislative branch for one year after leaving Congress.[47]

Following the Keating Five scandal—which led the Senate Ethics Committee in 1991 to rebuke five senators for improper contacts with regulatory agencies on behalf of a financially troubled savings and loan association—the Senate struggled to distinguish between legitimate efforts on behalf of constituents and undue interference in the bureaucratic process. In 1992, it rewrote its Rule 17 to define acceptable contact with regulators as including inquiries about the status of administrative decision making, expressions of opinion, or requests for reconsideration of agency rules. In addition, the rewritten rule prohibits conduct that reflects badly on the Senate's reputation.[48]

Unflattering publicity about excessive perquisites of office induced Congress to clamp down on them as well. The notorious House bank, which had condoned members' writing of overdrafts on their checking accounts, went out of business. Legislators gave up subsidized medical care, cut-rate gymnasium privileges, bargain prices on items purchased from the congressional gift shop, inexpensive car washes, and free flowers. They did retain free parking and the right to ignore District of Columbia parking regulations, their exemptions from certain federal laws (such as the Occupational Health and Safety Act and the Freedom of Information Act), and a generous interpretation by the FEC of the purposes for which they can spend their campaign funds. To put its affairs in order, the House appointed a director of non-legislative and financial services to take charge of such matters as postal services and the management of computer facilities. Thus members continued to worry about their standing with the public and redefined acceptable practices in an effort to restore Congress's popularity.[49]

On their face, these sunshine reforms of the 1970s—open procedures, campaign finance regulations, and ethics codes—and their periodic fine-tuning since then, were designed to make it possible, although not necessarily easy, for the public to assess the degree to which members of Congress pursue their own interests at the expense of the public's. But in adopting even such praiseworthy reforms as increasing congressional visibility, and thus accountability, the lawmakers may have had less readily defensible intentions. Although little noted in the press or by the public, there were clear implications for the political parties in the requirement that Congress perform in public. The more visible any action, the more that competing pressures—from the president, interest groups, and the public generally—come into play; the greater the extent and intensity of such pressures, the less likely members will be to defer to party leaders and support the party line.[50] Financial disclosure requirements might also be expected to influence, at least indirectly, the substance of policy. Forced to acknowledge the sources of their funds and obligations, members might be less likely to support their bankrollers' programs for fear of accusations of conflict of interest. Moreover, controls on campaign spending have an obvious impact on election results. Limits on challengers' ability to fill their campaign coffers strengthen the well-documented advantage of incumbents (especially in the House).[51]

To increase member participation in legislative decision making, Congress also expanded the rights of the minority party.[52] The Legislative Reorganization Act of 1970 guaranteed the minority at least ten minutes of debate on any amendment printed in the *Congressional Record* one day before debate on the legislation. It also gave the minority the opportunity to call its own witnesses, at least on one day of committee hearings, and allowed it three days in which to file its concurring or dissenting views on committee reports. In 1975, the minority gained the right to hire a minimum of one-third of the committee staff. Floor debate on conference committee reports was to be divided equally between majority and minority party members. These changes were intended to increase the minority's opportunities to make its voice heard in legislative deliberations.

During the 1970s reform period, House Democrats also moved to increase rank-and-file participation in the affairs of the party caucus. They required the Democratic caucus to meet more frequently, at least once a month; they authorized all members, not merely the party leaders, to place items for discussion on the caucus's agenda. Furthermore, they permitted a majority of any state delegation to nominate a Democrat for a particular committee assignment; previously, the Committee on Committees had the exclusive power to nominate candidates for committee slots. The Democratic caucus also required the chair of the Democratic Congressional Campaign Committee, which provides assistance to party candidates for Congress, to be elected by the full caucus membership. In addition, the party required the Speaker to name as House conferees members who were directly involved with a bill and preferably those who supported its major provisions. This requirement was aimed at preventing the conferees from subverting the intent of the full House by yielding too easily to the Senate position on the bill. Finally, all members won the right to attend any full committee or subcommittee meeting (except that of the Ethics Committee), even if the session was closed to the public.

Overall, reforms redistributing committee power and increasing the visibility of congressional operations were designed to enlarge participation, by members and by citizens, in legislative decision making. Democratization, the reformers argued, should foster responsiveness and accountability, and thus increase public support for the embattled Congress.

A Trend toward Responsibility

The second basic thrust of the reform movement was a concerted effort to revive and revitalize Congress as an effective—that is, responsible—policy maker. The critics charged that Congress had abdicated its programmatic responsibilities, ceding much of its authority to the executive branch. Attempts during the 1970s to reclaim the legislature's proper policy primacy moved along several tracks. The reformers mounted a direct challenge to the president, enacting laws that strengthened Congress's ability to make its preferences prevail over his. They also sought to improve efficiency by increasing the ability of the majority party in Congress to move its legislative program forward; a cohesive majority could act decisively, either to support a chief executive or to impose congressional priorities on a recalcitrant one. Finally, the legislature adopted new rules and procedures intended to reduce the opportunity for minority party members to impede the legislative process. All of these measures attempted to centralize legislative operations; more centralized authority, the reform proponents believed, would make Congress more efficient.

Taming the Executive: Reclaiming Power

During the prereform period, presidential assertiveness and congressional acquiescence had combined to create an imbalance between the two branches. That there was an "imperial presidency," symbolized by Vietnam and Watergate, suggested that the legislature had lost or ceded its traditional powers to declare war, to control the federal budget, and to oversee the bureaucracy. Reform would enable Congress to regain its rightful role in the policy process, imposing its preferences on the president when it seemed sensible to do so.

To buttress its position relative to the executive, Congress reasserted its prerogatives in foreign policy, an area where executive dominance had long been a congressional concern. As far back as 1954, Senate reformers had tried to limit presidential discretion in foreign affairs by passing the proposed Bricker amendment to the Constitution. This amendment, which was defeated by a single vote, would have curbed the practice of conducting diplomacy unilaterally through executive agreements rather than bilaterally through treaties, which require the advice and consent of the Senate.[53]

Other congressional efforts to restrict executive domination of foreign relations reached fruition in 1973 with the passage, over President Nixon's veto, of the war powers resolution. Frustrated by its inability to influence more than marginally the conduct of the war in Indochina and emboldened by the administration's Watergate embarrassments, Congress circumscribed the authority of the commander in chief to commit U.S. military forces to combat without explicit congressional approval. The act enabled Congress to compel the executive to withdraw any such troops sent into the field within sixty days (ninety days if required by the logistics involved in removing the military units).[54] In theory, the president would seek congressional approval before sending U.S. troops into battle; without consultation, there would be a real risk of legislative reversal of the chief executive's decision.

The War Powers Act requires the president, in the event of a crisis, to consult the legislature "in every possible instance" before committing the nation's armed forces to hostile or potentially hostile territory. If he does deploy the troops, he must report that action in writing to Congress within forty-eight hours. This report triggers the sixty-day congressional review period, and unless the lawmakers declare war or in some other way approve the use of force (by appropriating funds, for example), the president must bring the troops home. In addition, the legislature can end American involvement in the conflict by passing at any time a concurrent resolution to that effect. (A concurrent resolution, passed in identical form by both House and Senate, does not require the president's signature.)[55] Interestingly, the War Powers Act reflects congressional concern about its collective, institutional ability to oppose the president; Congress framed the statute so that legislative *inaction* would trigger U.S. troop withdrawal. The chief executive can send the armed forces into hostilities on his own initiative, but he is obligated to withdraw them unless Congress acts to approve the commitment.

Congress also reasserted its policy-making authority in the area of budgetary reform. Impartial observers as well as critics had long agreed that Congress was failing to exercise its power of the purse effectively. Indeed, President Nixon justified his impoundment of appropriated funds on the grounds that Congress had been fiscally irresponsible.

In the prereform budget process, the chief executive submitted to

Congress a single, unified budget, which congressional appropriations committees then split into a dozen or more bills that were given separate but unrelated treatments. At no point did the interested lawmaker have occasion to review the total budget and to compare proposed expenditures with available revenue.[56] Rather, the full picture was not visible until all appropriations measures had been passed; thus the last bills in the series became major targets for reduction as the sums committed in the earlier bills began to mount. Funds cut at one point could be restored later in supplemental appropriations bills, a fact that probably encouraged legislators to make cuts for partisan purposes in the full knowledge that such reductions need not be permanent. What seemed necessary to remedy these defects—as well as to reduce Congress's competitive disadvantage in respect to executive expertise and to give the legislature the opportunity to establish its own spending priorities—was to coordinate and centralize congressional consideration of the budget.

Congress made the effort in 1974. Building on the recommendations of the 1972 Joint Study Committee on Budget Control, the legislature passed the Congressional Budget and Impoundment Control Act. This comprehensive bill created special budget committees in the House and Senate that can draw on the resources of the Congressional Budget Office (CBO), a unified joint staff of skilled budgetary experts. The CBO is the legislature's equivalent of the executive branch's Office of Management and Budget (OMB); it provides Congress with independent information and analysis, thus reducing its need to rely on data generated by the executive. Each year the budget committees are required to produce (by April 15), and Congress is required to pass (by May 15), a *first budget resolution* that clearly specifies "targets" for federal spending,[57] recommended levels of revenue, the size of the deficit (or surplus), and the total public debt. Spending targets, allocated among nineteen separate categories, are not binding; they merely indicate the budget committees' recommendations.

After passage of the first budget resolution, the appropriations committees of the House and Senate and the revenue committees (House Ways and Means, Senate Finance) take over. They may accept the budget committees' figures or they may reject them. Even in the former case, they have substantial freedom to maneuver because the resolution specifies only grand totals and does not set spending ceilings for particular programs or agencies (although the budget committees may suggest them). The tax and spending panels conduct business as usual, as do the other standing committees, which continue to authorize spending for programs within their jurisdictions much as they did before passage of the 1974 budget act. These committees and the full chambers must complete action on the authorization and appropria-

tions bills not later than a week after Labor Day. The budget committees and Congress must then produce a *second budget resolution* that
"reaffirms or revises" the first resolution. The second resolution,
which must be adopted by September 15, is binding and sets forth the
government's economic policies for the new fiscal year, which begins
October 1.[58] Any proposed legislation that requires spending in excess
of the ceilings or that fails to meet the revenue requirements of the
second resolution is subject to a point of order—an objection that may
block passage—raised on the floor of either chamber.

The budget committees have an additional weapon to control the
spending of the legislative panels: *reconciliation.* The 1974 act empowers them to propose, in a bill, that the legislative committees reduce or
increase spending or revenue within their respective jurisdictions to
conform to the budget resolution. Again, these directives are in aggre-
gates and do not refer to line items; the reconciliation instructions,
which the full chamber must pass, may order a committee to save a
certain amount, but the committee retains the right to determine
which programs within its jurisdiction will be cut. Severe restrictions
on available funds may force committees to change entitlement programs, such as Social Security and food stamps, that usually escaped
scrutiny under the prereform budget procedures. The committee decisions made in response to reconciliation instructions are merged in a
reconciliation bill that Congress must pass by September 25, just prior
to the beginning of the new fiscal year.

The Congressional Budget and Impoundment Control Act of 1974
also includes curbs on the executive practice of impounding funds
authorized and appropriated by Congress. If the president wishes to
defer spending, either house can compel expenditure of the funds by
passing a resolution to that effect. If the chief executive seeks to terminate programs, he must persuade both houses to rescind, or cancel, the
appropriation within forty-five days; if the chambers do not act, he
must spend the funds. Here, too, Congress wrote the law so that the
legislature could have its own way with a minimum of effort. To rescind appropriations, the president must secure a resolution from both
houses; inaction by either obligates him to spend the money. A request
to defer expenditures requires that one house act positively; if neither
house votes a resolution of disapproval, the request to defer is automatically approved. These anti-impoundment procedures enable Congress
to insist on its own spending priorities and to curb the chief executive's
power to spend selectively.[59]

Overall, the 1974 budget act provides the legislature with new budgeting resources in the form of the budget committees and the CBO, a
new means of looking at the broad contours of the federal budget so
that it can determine its own spending and revenue priorities in a

timely manner, and a method to control impoundment of funds and force presidential compliance with its spending decisions. Passage of the bills, however, required a political compromise that merged innovative mechanisms with older, established procedures that served the needs of individual lawmakers. In fact, the bill became law because it served the members' mixed motives.

Virtually all observers agreed at the time that the old budgetary process was in shambles and that something had to be done. Congress as an institution was under fire for its failings, and the act was, symbolically at least, a counterattack. Reformers argued that the revised procedures would help Congress recapture lost power, improve its performance, and adopt new and better policies. Most important, it would achieve these goals without undue disruption of the existing budgetary process. The vested interests of appropriations and tax committee members would survive. The new methods did not replace old ways of doing business but were grafted onto them. They defined and to some extent circumscribed the power and influence of the old centers of authority, but they were not expected to reallocate that power and influence substantially. Reformers saw many potential benefits and few costs in the refined process.

Initially, the new process had modest success (see Chapter 4), but it did not achieve the purposes its proponents had envisioned. Resolutions were passed, reconciliation procedures were employed, but no budget discipline was imposed and the deficit soared. By the end of 1985, it was clear to Congress and to the public that the process was not working. The result was the Balanced Budget and Emergency Deficit Control Act of 1985, popularly known as the Gramm-Rudman-Hollings Act (GRH) after its sponsors, Senators Phil Gramm (R-Texas), Warren B. Rudman (R-N.H.), and Ernest F. Hollings (D-S.C.).[60]

Recognizing that political considerations prevented deficit reduction, that there was no political will to make hard budgetary choices, the sponsoring senators proposed an automatic device to force a reduction in the deficit. GRH set maximum deficit limits: $171.9 billion (the amount the budget resolution specified) for fiscal 1986; $144 billion for 1987; and, subsequently, after annual decrements of $36 billion, zero in fiscal 1991. If these targets were not met, cuts were mandatory. The OMB and the CBO were to prepare a report for the Government Accounting Office (GAO) estimating the size of the deficit and comparing that figure with the total permitted by GRH. The comptroller general, head of the GAO, was to determine whether there was an "excess deficit." A report that the deficit was greater than permitted by GRH would automatically trigger budget cuts, known as a "sequester," that the president would impose.[61] The report would go to the president on September 1; Congress would have forty-five days to cut spending or raise revenues to reduce the deficit to the prescribed limit; if it did not succeed, the sequester would take effect.

In principle, the automatic cuts were to be divided equally between the defense and nonmilitary portions of the budget. In reality, such Draconian, across-the-board spending reductions were politically untenable. The law, in consequence, exempted from the cuts such politically untouchable entitlement programs as Social Security and food stamps. Other programs could be reduced only to a limited extent. After all the exemptions were written into law, only about one-third to 40 percent of the budget was subject to the automatic reductions. These items would take a heavy blow if the sequester was imposed. Indeed, the sponsors of the law hoped that it never would be; the prospect of "meat-ax" cuts, they believed, would force Congress to use the regular process, which was to be in operation before October 15, to produce a budget that met the GRH targets and thus avoided the automatic cuts. GRH was a mechanism of last resort; it would operate only if the ordinary routines—the budget resolution and the reconciliation bill— failed to keep the deficit within the legally required limits.[62]

To decrease the likelihood of a sequester, GRH codified some of the changes in the budget process that had been made over the years to give some teeth to the enforcement of budgetary discipline. The act made the totals in the budget resolution binding, obviating the need for a second resolution. No new legislation could go to the floor until a budget resolution had passed, and no resolution that exceeded the allowable deficit target would be in order on the floor. The budget resolution allocated funds among the committees, and GRH permitted points of order to be raised on the floor against any legislation that committees reported if those bills exceeded a panel's allocation. Moreover, the points of order could be waived only by a three-fifths majority (rather than by a simple majority) vote. Under these rules, the 1974 budget act procedures might produce a budget that complied with the deficit targets, and the automatic sequester could be avoided. If not, the automatic cuts would kick in and the deficit would be set on a downward course.

To complicate matters of implementation, the courts found the trigger mechanism, the comptroller general's report, to be an unconstitutional violation of the separation of powers doctrine, because although the comptroller's role in the GRH process was an executive function, the officeholder was removable by Congress. In anticipation of such a possible adverse court ruling, the drafters of the law had included a fallback procedure. Congress was to enact and send to the White House legislation specifying the cuts required to meet the GRH deficit targets. The decision was the legislature's; this alternative did not include the automatic trigger of the original scheme. In 1987, Congress responded to the courts' ruling by giving an executive agency, the OMB, authority to trigger the sequestration process. The OMB was hedged about with sufficient restrictions that its ability to favor presidential positions was minimal, however. At the same time, recognizing that the Gramm-Rudman-Hollings process was not working well (the deficits were not declining as scheduled), Congress revised the timetable for eliminating the annual deficit and extended the deadline from 1991 to 1993.

Under GRH, the deficit did not decrease, and in 1990 Congress could not craft a budget for fiscal 1991 that complied with the law, even formally. In the aftermath of a 1990 budget "summit" between administration officials and congressional leaders, at which President George Bush abandoned his famous "read my lips, no new taxes" pledge, a budget, technically in compliance with GRH only because the allowable deficit limit was set at $327 billion, was passed by Congress. Recognizing the clear failure of budgeting for fiscal 1991, Congress included in the 1990 reconciliation bill, which contained the budget agreement, the provisions of a proposed Budget Enforcement Act (BEA) that substantially revised the budget process.[63]

The act put in place a new budget calendar, giving the president more time to submit the administration's budget, now due on the first Monday in February. If Congress cannot adopt a budget resolution by April 15, the budget committees must adopt the president's proposals for spending as guidelines for the appropriations committees. The new process eliminates the binding limits set by GRH on the deficit. Instead, firm spending limits for 1991-1993 were set in three separate areas: discretionary (controllable) outlays for defense, foreign aid, and domestic programs. Legislation that exceeds these caps, which are adjusted annually for inflation, will be out of order on the House and Senate floors. In 1994 and 1995, these areas will be covered by a single cap, much like the pre-1991 GRH procedure. In addition, defense, foreign aid, and domestic programs are separated, "fenced off," from one another. Funds saved in one area cannot be transferred to another; there can be no "peace dividend" from the reduction of military spending below the mandated ceiling because such money cannot be used to offset new spending in either of the other areas.

For mandatory spending—entitlements such as veterans' benefits and food stamps—and for taxes, the new procedure imposes a "pay-as-you-go" scheme. The cost of any new program must be offset by a reduction in another, older one. In the same vein, any lowering of taxes requires a compensating rise in revenues from other sources or a cut in entitlement spending. Program changes, although permissible, must be "deficit-neutral," that is, they must not add to the total deficit. The new procedures use modified automatic sequesters to enforce the spending ceilings and pay-as-you-go provisions. If appropriations bills exceed the prescribed spending caps in any of the three designated areas of discretionary spending, a sequester may be triggered automatically at any one of three points in the budgetary calendar to bring outlays down to the mandatory limit in that area. If mandatory spending increases the deficit, a sequester makes up the difference by reducing all nonexempt outlays (GRH specified exemptions from, and limits to, the automatic cuts) enough to restore revenue neutrality.

Deficit targets remain (the deficit is to decline to $117 billion by 1995), but they are not binding. Social Security trust fund moneys do not figure in deficit calculations. For 1991-1993, permissible deficit levels will be adjusted along with spending caps to take inflation and other economic conditions into account. For 1994-1995, the president may choose to adjust deficit targets for economic or technical reasons. If he does not do so, and the limits are exceeded, a sequester follows. The BEA, in short, stresses spending limits rather than inflexible deficit totals.[64]

In addition to establishing the CBO as part of the 1974 budget reforms, Congress created the Office of Technology Assessment (OTA) to advise members on the implications of scientific developments. Furthermore, Congress increased the budgets and enlarged the staffs of two existing agencies: the Congressional Research Service of the Library of Congress and the GAO. It also greatly increased members' personal and committee staffs and expanded the use of computers to improve members' access to information.[65] In these ways Congress sought to compete more effectively with the executive; no longer would it readily defer to an administration presumed to have access to superior information and analysis.

During the 1970s Congress began to assert, more forcefully than in previous decades, already established powers. The Legislative Reorganization Act of 1946 had formalized the legislature's obligation to exert "continuous watchfulness" over the agencies and bureaus of the executive departments. This surveillance was facilitated by the increase in both information resources and vantage points, particularly in the form of independent subcommittees. Use of the legislative veto also increased. The legislative veto is a procedure permitting either the House or the Senate, or both chambers, to review proposed executive branch regulations or actions and to block or modify those with which they disagree. As noted, both the war powers resolution and the impoundment title of the 1974 budget act contain congressional veto provisions, as do more than 150 other statutes enacted during the decade. Before 1983, the veto took numerous forms, depending on the particular piece of legislation. It could be exercised by an individual subcommittee or a full committee (or even informally by a panel's chair), by either the House or the Senate, or by both passing a concurrent resolution. Some forms required congressional approval of executive activities in advance; others allowed the legislature to reverse, after the fact, administrative rules and regulations. Whatever the form, however, Congress could, within a specified period, block bureaucratic behavior it found objectionable. Some scholars and lawyers have asserted that the veto was unconstitutional, that it encroached on the president's prerogatives, for Congress exercised the veto independently, without the chief executive's approval.[66]

But the legislature has found the veto device attractive. It enables Congress to delegate authority to executive departments without permanently ceding control over what the bureaucrats actually do. Lawmakers can duck hot issues but correct administrative "errors" if bureaucrats' proposals seem unwise or politically damaging; they can defer to experts but later countermand their decisions if they have made poor choices. The legislative veto and other forms of oversight have enabled Congress to exercise more thorough surveillance of the bureaucracy and greater influence over the executive branch.[67]

Here, too, the imbalance in institutional power between the two elected branches was used as a convenient justification for reform in the 1970s. To correct that imbalance, reformers argued, the legislature needed to reassert its authority over military, budget, and administrative matters. But other purposes may well have supplemented the avowed justification. Ideology figured prominently in both the war powers resolution and the 1974 budget bill. Those who opposed involvement in Southeast Asia, mainly liberals, led the fight to curb the powers of the commander in chief. Liberals and conservatives joined forces to support budgetary reform for quite different reasons: liberals expected the new process to provide more funds for social programs and less for defense; conservatives expected the reverse and were also eager for the budget committees to control spending—particularly of the "backdoor" variety—and balance the budget.

In addition to ideology, policy and personal power considerations prompted reform. On one hand, the centralizing effects of the 1974 budget act would certainly expedite the budget process, but they also would exact a major price from the traditionally powerful revenue and appropriations committees. Members of these panels were obviously reluctant to hand over policy responsibility to the budget committees. On the other hand, use of the legislative veto might help Congress centralize control over a sprawling bureaucracy, and if exercised by committees, it would increase the authority of congressional participants in those now ubiquitous "cozy triangles," or policy subgovernments. William Schaefer and James Thurber have argued that the veto is more likely to help members attain reelection goals and increase personal power than to promote coordinated congressional control of administration.[68] Again, what seemed to be a relatively acceptable motive—to redress legislative grievances against an overly powerful presidency—may have concealed almost as much as it revealed about the congressional reformers' real intent. But whatever the members' underlying motives during the reform decade of the 1970s, Congress did move forcefully to tame the executive.

Centralizing the Parties: Improving Efficiency

Perceived inefficiency in congressional performance was the motivation for a second group of reforms to improve legislative responsibility. The House Democratic Study Group, comprising liberals long dissatisfied with Congress's failure to adopt creative social programs, provided the impetus. A decentralized decision-making process impeded coherent policy formulation, and the reformers professed a desire to make it easier for Congress to act. They hoped to convert the Democratic caucus into a disciplined force for progressive legislation. To this end, they rallied majority Democrats to impose some party discipline.

Goaded by the DSG, the caucus liberals took three steps to strengthen the party apparatus. First, extending modest changes made in 1973, the Democratic caucus in 1975 established a new procedure for making committee assignments. In 1973, the party leaders—the Speaker, the floor leader, and the whip—were permitted to sit with the Ways and Means Committee Democrats, who had traditionally served as the party's committee on committees, to make committee assignments. In the same year, the Democrats also established a 24-member Steering and Policy Committee, composed of the party's elected leaders (the Speaker, floor leader, and caucus chair), 12 members elected by the Democratic caucus to represent geographic regions, and 9 others appointed by the Speaker (including the party whips and representatives of the Congressional Black Caucus, women members, and freshman Democrats).[69] In 1975, the Democratic caucus dramatically stripped the Ways and Means contingent of its committee on committees' powers, transferring them to the Steering and Policy Committee. The shift put the party's committee assignments in the hands of a more liberal body in which the party leaders had a strong voice.[70] The caucus retained the right to vote on each nominee for a committee chair and to approve Steering and Policy's slates for panel assignments.

In 1993, at the start of the 103d Congress, the Democratic caucus imposed additional controls on the committee chairs. It adopted a new procedure that permitted an open vote, after open nominations from the caucus, on a nominee for committee chair if 14 members of the

Steering and Policy Committee (now 35 in number) voted against the sitting chair. The new procedure replaced the old rule that allowed such an open vote only if the full caucus had rejected outright Steering and Policy's initial nomination for the chair. In addition, Steering and Policy was empowered to declare the chairmanship of a full or sub-committee vacant, or to remove a committee member, at any time (not merely at the beginning of a new Congress), subject to caucus approval. Such possibilities were expected to remind chairs that they served on sufferance of the party and its leaders.

During the initial reform period, the House Democrats also took steps to increase centralization—to strengthen the party leadership—at the expense of the committees. New House rules limited the number of subcommittees that the full panels could have: major committees could have no more than 6 subcommittees, minor committees could have no more than 5. Exclusive committees—Appropriations, Rules, and Ways and Means—were exempt from the rules. In all, 16 sub-committees were eliminated, reducing the total from 137 to 121. The reform was relatively painless because, given the high turnover produced by the 1992 elections, there were sufficient vacancies at the helm of subcommittees that no sitting chair was deprived of a top leadership post. The caucus also limited, to five (including service on select committees), the number of subcommittee assignments that an individual member could have. This change triggered the permanent abolition of the four select committees; the full House refused, in a 237-180 vote, to reauthorize the Select Committee on Narcotics Abuse and Control and subsequently permitted the remaining three committees to go out of existence.[71] These reforms reduced, at least marginally, the number of independent power centers in the decentralized legislature, and, so the reformers hoped, would make the party leaders' task of increasing party unity a bit easier.

The second action was taken beginning in 1973, when the caucus increased the personal power of the Speaker to move legislation forward. In addition to his powerful role in the Steering and Policy Committee, the Speaker now had the right to nominate the Democratic members of the Rules Committee, subject to caucus approval. By so doing, the reformers hoped to yoke that panel firmly to the leadership. The caucus also assumed the power to instruct the Rules Committee to act in specific ways, presumably to prevent favored programs from expiring while being considered by that sometimes defiant panel. The Speaker also gained new ability to regulate the flow of legislation to and from committee. He was authorized to refer bills to more than one committee, either simultaneously or sequentially, and to set time limits on committee consideration of measures. He could also create ad hoc committees to facilitate coherent treatment of complex policy issues.

(Speaker of the House Thomas P. O'Neill, Jr. [D-Mass.], used this device effectively to coordinate President Jimmy Carter's 1977 energy programs.)

The Democratic party leader also supplemented existing techniques of vote gathering. The whip system was enlarged to improve communications between leaders and the rank and file. In the 103d Congress, the whip apparatus includes the majority whip, 4 chief deputy whips, 11 deputy whips, a floor whip, an ex-officio whip, 2 whip task force chairs, 56 at-large whips, and 14 assistant whips representing different geographical regions. Thus, 90 of the 258 House Democrats (35 percent) held positions in the whip system. (House Republicans and members of both parties in the Senate have extensive if less influential whip organizations to aid their party leaders.) In addition, the Speaker was allowed to create informal task forces of members interested in particular bills to advise, plan strategy, and lobby for the legislation. Involving more members in the formulation of policy was intended to increase party cohesion. On the Senate side, the (Stevenson) Temporary Select Committee to Study the Senate Committee System proposed a modest reform, passed in 1977, that gave the leadership new controls over bill referrals and scheduling.[72]

The third action taken by the Democratic caucus was to strengthen party discipline by insisting that Democrats maintain working majorities on the exclusive Appropriations, Rules, and Ways and Means committees.[73] They set the membership ratios at roughly two to one (two Democrats for each Republican), regardless of the balance between the parties in the full chamber. This step increased the likelihood that party (liberal) legislation would receive favorable treatment in these panels. The caucus also retained the authority, if two-thirds of its members chose to exercise it, to instruct House committees to report legislation.[74]

In sum, reforms influencing committee assignments, the Speaker's authority, and party membership on committees centralized the power of the Democratic party in the House. A more responsible Congress was, ostensibly, the reformers' chief goal.

Both chambers also sought to realign and rationalize their committee jurisdictions. In the House the defenders of the status quo managed to remove all but the most routine aspects of the Bolling committee's 1974 reform proposals. The resulting reform was little more than cosmetic with respect to committee jurisdictions; the old order, which preserved existing vested interests, remained largely intact. The reform legislation proposed to abolish the Post Office and Civil Service committees; to divide Education and Labor into two separate committees; and to alter considerably the jurisdictions of Ways and Means, House Administration, and Merchant Marine and Fisheries. Although more sweeping recommendations were discussed (for example, to rotate committee members so that vested interests would not develop in particular assignments and to combine the authorization and appropriations phases of the budget process, which were then distinct, in a single committee), they were never taken seriously; it was evident from the outset that such "radical" notions could not command majority support. A more modest change proposed by the Bolling panel was to bar committee chairs from casting absent members' votes by proxy; such a step would reduce the leader's ability to shape committee decisions.

These proposals aroused howls of protest from lawmakers who saw them as threats to their own influence. Members of committees slated for abolition quickly took the lead in opposing the Bolling committee's legislation. Representatives serving on panels whose jurisdictions would be circumscribed sought to retain control of policy areas of concern to them. Committee chairs, fearful of losing some bases of authority, expressed skepticism about the wisdom of the reforms. Committee staff members, anxious about their jobs, joined the opposition, as did interest groups, eager to preserve their close and well-established relations with committees. The Bolling proposals cut too close to the bone for too many members; they created more losers than winners. The result was predictable: the legislation was referred to the Democratic caucus's (Hansen) Committee on Organization, Study, and Review, which in effect bowed to the opponents, gutted the Bolling committee's proposals, and produced a set of reforms, more symbolic than meaningful, that the House eventually enacted into law.[75]

Senate reformers fared better; they won approval of modest but meaningful committee changes. The number of full committees declined from 31 in the 94th Congress (1975-1976) to 24 in the 95th (1977-1978). Subcommittees decreased from 174 to 117 in the same period. In consequence, the senators' average number of full or subcommittee assignments decreased from 18 to 11. In the 103d Congress (1993-1994), there are 16 full committees and 4 special and select committees, with a total of 86 subcommittees; senators averaged 7 or 8 assignments to these panels. More important, jurisdictions were rationalized, although considerably less than the Stevenson committee initially proposed.[76] Sharper demarcation of committee jurisdictions was intended to increase congressional efficiency by reducing overlapping, redundant, and time-consuming treatment of legislation.

Curbing the Minority: Rules Changes

Reformers also attempted to improve congressional effectiveness by reducing the opportunities for partisan or bipartisan liberal or conservative minorities to thwart the majority and by speeding up consideration of legislation. To supplement the centralization of congressional fiscal policy making made possible by the new budget process, the Senate significantly weakened the opportunity for minority use of unlimited debate, the *filibuster*. In March 1975, after weeks of acrimonious discussion and complex parliamentary maneuvering, the Senate voted to modify its infamous cloture rule (Rule 22), making it a little easier to cut off debate. Previously, a two-thirds majority of those present and voting (67 senators if all were in attendance; 64 or 65 under ordinary circumstances) was required to invoke cloture; under the new rule three-fifths of the full membership (60 votes) could end debate.

The new procedure was, in fact, a compromise; liberals had wanted a simple majority of those present and voting to be able to force conclusion of a filibuster.[77] Senate rules permitted 100 hours of debate after cloture was invoked, and filibuster proponents soon found that they could prolong the agony: if they introduced amendments prior to cloture, these would be in order after the vote, and they regularly prepared for such a contingency by introducing hundreds of amendments. The possibilities for a postcloture "filibuster by amendment" were restricted by a 1979 change that required the vote on final passage to come within the 100-hour period.[78] In 1986, the Senate went further: the postcloture debate was limited to 30 hours.

The House also expedited consideration of legislation and reduced the opportunities for excessive delay. The Legislative Reorganization Act of 1970 allowed committees to meet while the House was in session, except under special circumstances. It permitted suspension of both quorum calls and the reading of the *Journal* (a printed record of the proceedings of the previous session), unless a majority insisted on either. Quorum calls summon a certain number of members (100 in the Committee of the Whole, 218 when the House sits formally) to the floor for a vote. By the end of the decade, the repeated use of quorum calls as a dilatory tactic had been restricted. One vote, at the beginning of the legislative day, was often sufficient to establish a quorum. In 1993, rules changes further relaxed the restriction on the holding of committee meetings while the House was in session and sanctioned the use of a "rolling quorum" in committee: if members constituting a quorum put in an appearance *at any time* during a committee session the panel can conduct its business; a quorum need not be present at any one time for the committee to continue to meet. The new 1993 rules also reduce the ability of the minority to use privileged motions—which require automatic and immediate attention—to force the majority to act. The Speaker is given two legislative days to schedule floor debate on such motions, presumably to enable the party leadership to mobilize its troops and to engage the opposition on the most favorable terrain.[79]

The roll call process was also simplified during the 1970s. As noted earlier, an electronic voting system was instituted, and the House rules allowed clustering of votes on rules, passage of bills, and delivery of conference reports at particular times so that members did not need to come to the floor so frequently. Subsequent votes in the series could be limited to five minutes. The number of members required to demand a recorded vote in the Committee of the Whole was increased from 20 to 25. These were modest steps, to be sure, but they made it easier for the 435-member institution to conduct its business.

Like courting popular approval or strengthening the separation of powers, improving congressional responsibility (effectiveness or efficiency) was used as a convenient justification for reform. Strengthening the parties and the role of the Speaker of the House, undercutting minority power, and reorganizing committee jurisdictions had implications beyond efficiency, however. Centralization would increase the influence of Congress in relation to the executive, reformers argued; a strong legislature would be better able to impose its preferences on the administration. Moreover, a disciplined and productive legislature would look good to the citizens, leading to an improvement in its popular standing. More significantly, of course, policy and personal goals could also be achieved. Those in command of an efficient policy-making process—the party leaders—would have a loud voice in the programs that were adopted, as well as considerable power to promote their own personal goals. Jurisdictional realignments, especially in the Senate, did move some programs from one committee to another, but many more sweeping changes in committee jurisdiction were rejected. Clearly, whatever the intrinsic attractiveness of arguments about responsibility, they may not stand up to practical pressures relating to influence and ideology. In both chambers, particularly the Senate, an increase in responsibility through centralization remains elusive.

The Road Not Taken: The Limits of Reform

Reform requires certain facilitating conditions. When critics and members of Congress concur that reform is needed, the latter, the actual reformers, will be inclined to act. They feel obliged to respond to the institution's needs, but the distance they are prepared to travel is limited. They will do what they must, but they are seldom eager, in any altruistic sense, to follow paths that may diminish their personal power and prerogative. The reforms of the 1970s failed to attain the goals that some observers, particularly those who stressed the desirability of making Congress a more responsible policy maker, felt were most critical. Many proposals were rejected largely because they would have disrupted important relationships within Congress and between members and outside interests.

One serious charge leveled at Congress was that its archaic committee arrangements, especially the confused jurisdictions of multiple panels, greatly inhibited responsible policy formulation. Too many committees, with divided and uncertain tasks, slowed down the legislative process, imposed unmanageable burdens on individual members, and deterred decisive policy choices. To remedy this defect, reformers attempted to realign and clarify committee jurisdictions. But as noted earlier, the Bolling committee's most sweeping proposals were never enacted into law. This reform failed because of members' fears that they would lose their "turf" if the committee system was significantly restructured. A half-dozen years later a far more modest proposal—to create a new Energy Committee with jurisdiction over matters previously in the hands of the Commerce, Interior, and Public Works panels—met a similar fate. Proposed by Rep. Jerry Patterson's Select Committee on Committees (1979-1980), the plan was sidetracked in favor of rechristening Interstate and Foreign Commerce the Committee on Energy and Commerce.

Indeed, by 1977 the reform movement had ground to a halt. Proposals for reform continued to be discussed, but favorable action never followed. The House in 1977 established a Commission on Administrative Review, which produced an agenda of forty-two suggestions, including the creation of a new Select Committee on Committees, to improve congressional performance. The House overwhelmingly declined to consider the proposals.[80] The 1980 report of the Patterson panel recommended several rules changes to improve efficiency: reforms to minimize scheduling conflicts between committees, to empower the Speaker to assign primary responsibility to one committee when a bill was referred to more than one panel, and to limit the number of subcommittees on which a member could serve as well as the number of subcommittee assignments available to each member. These proposals never reached the House floor.[81]

The Senate also continued to nod in the direction of reform, but to no avail. In 1983, it received a report from two former senators, Abraham Ribicoff (D-Conn.) and James B. Pearson (R-Kan.), proposing a series of "quite radical" reforms, including fundamental reshaping of the committee system, major reform of the budget process, limitations on debate to take up a bill, and elimination of an individual senator's ability to block consideration by placing a "hold" on legislation.[82] No action was taken. In 1985, the Senate also failed to act on recommendations from Sen. Dan Quayle's Temporary Select Committee to Study the Senate Committee System. The committee proposed, most notably, to enforce rules limiting senators to service on three committees, to limit subcommittee assignments, and to abolish some thirty existing subcommittees.[83]

In short, experience shows that when Congress reaches the fork in the road and must make a choice between reform (particularly to promote responsible policy making) and personal prerogative, the outcome is seldom in doubt. Unless there are compelling reasons to follow the reform path—and there have been few since the mid-1970s—reform will be the "road not taken."

The inaction of the 1980s, after the substantial reforms of the previous decade, clearly illustrates the ephemerality of the reform impulse. In the Reagan-Bush years, little attention was given to reform issues; this was a period of slow and barely visible change, of incremental adjustment to the day-to-day needs of the members of Congress. That is not to say that small alterations do not affect the way the legislature works—Congress in the 1990s is different from its predecessor. But wholesale reform is a rare event, and minor changes in the ways Congress organizes itself to perform its tasks may escape notice. When the times, the membership, and the legislative agenda change, so do the ways Congress goes about its work. The widespread public perception in the late 1980s and early 1990s that Congress is a flawed assembly, and changes in the congressional membership (110 House newcomers in the 103d Congress), have contributed to a revival of the reform spirit.

Summary

A new generation of younger, more independent minded legislators challenged executive policy-making dominance and tackled institutional reform in the 1970s. They had been roused to action by the impotence of Congress during most of the Vietnam War and the weakness of the executive branch after Watergate. They were not inspired by grand visions of the ideal Congress and did not talk in terms of executive force or congressional supremacy theories. Rather, they acted in a manner typical of legislators—pragmatically and incrementally, with mixed motives—to reshape the organization and processes of the legislature. The reform movement of the 1970s produced numerous alterations that were intended to (1) democratize Congress by giving more people, both inside and outside the institution, access to and influence over its deliberations and decisions; and (2) improve congressional efficiency by increasing the lawmakers' ability to formulate sound public policy.

To foster congressional responsiveness and accountability, the reformers reallocated committee power (in particular, increasing that of independent subcommittees) and obligated Congress to carry on its operations in public—in the "sunshine." There was a modest retreat from decentralization at the end of the 1980s; nevertheless, the revamped committee procedures offer more members, confident of secure committee positions, a chance to influence congressional decision making. Open committee meetings, revised campaign finance regulations, and financial disclosure requirements help interested citizens find out whether their representatives are guilty of unethical behavior so that they can act accordingly at the polls. These reforms, in sum, aimed to make member and public participation in legislative affairs more meaningful; the reformers were eager—for personal, political, and policy reasons—to create a more democratic Congress.

To increase congressional responsibility, the reformers expanded the legislature's policy-making potential by reasserting legislative power vis-à-vis the executive, strengthening the political parties as centralizing mechanisms, and revising the rules to promote efficiency. The War Powers Act and the Congressional Budget and Impoundment Control Act affirmed the authority of Congress to impose its preferences on the president and his administration. Congress has continued to search for ways to exercise such authority. The reformers believed that more powerful political parties, with more active caucuses and a strengthened Speaker of the House, could more readily advance creative programs in an attempt to remedy the nation's pressing problems. Revised rules would inhibit, if not prevent, partisan or ideological minorities from erecting roadblocks to passage of innovative policies. A responsible Congress thus would be able to exert its authority when its members believed they had effective programs to present.

These reforms—to achieve responsiveness, accountability, and responsibility—are in one sense complementary. Reforms that produce an efficient, responsible Congress that makes sound decisions with reasonable dispatch and whose operations are subjected to citizens' scrutiny will restore public confidence. Ideally, an open, responsive legislature, whose parties are powerful enough to organize action, should be able to translate the diversity of political viewpoints into effective programs without unconscionable delay or debilitating compromise.

In another sense, however, the reforms are incompatible. The ideal of prompt action resulting from broad participation might well be unattainable in a fragmented, decentralized institution. So many voices bombarding such a large body of policy makers might make policy formulation impossible or require so many compromises that the programs actually adopted will be unworkable or ineffective. Extended accountability, subjecting members to many more pressures from groups and individual citizens external to Congress, could have the same result.

The reformers, who were by definition optimists, opted for the ideal scenario, to the extent that they looked at the broad picture at all. They assumed that each of the steps they proposed and adopted would produce the desirable outcomes they projected. Even when reform zeal waned after 1977, they sought to fine-tune the system to improve congressional responsiveness, responsibility, and accountability. The extent to which they have realized their hopes—what their changes have actually produced—is the subject of the next chapter.

NOTES

1. See, for example, David W. Rohde, *Parties and Leaders in the Postreform House* (Chicago: University of Chicago Press, 1991); Barbara Sinclair, "The Emergence of Strong Leadership in the 1980s House of Representatives," *Journal of Politics* 54 (1992): 657-684; Lawrence C. Dodd and Bruce I. Oppenheimer, "Maintaining Order in the House: The Struggle for Institutional Equilibrium," in *Congress Reconsidered*, 5th ed., ed. Lawrence C. Dodd and Bruce I. Oppenheimer (Washington, D.C.: CQ Press, 1993), 41-66; and Roger H. Davidson, ed. *The Postreform Congress* (New York: St. Martin's Press, 1992).

2. David W. Rohde and Kenneth A. Shepsle, "Thinking about Legislative Reform," in *Legislative Reform: The Policy Impact*, ed. Leroy N. Rieselbach (Lexington, Mass.: Lexington Books, 1978), 9-21.

3. Barbara Sinclair, *Congressional Realignment, 1925-1978* (Austin: University of Texas Press, 1982).

4. On this "replacement" effect, which brings new members with different outlooks to Congress, see Herbert B. Asher and Herbert F. Weisberg, "Voting Change in Congress: Some Dynamic Perspectives on an Evolutionary Process," *American Journal of Political Science* 22 (1978): 391-425; Paul Burstein, "Party Balance, Replacement of Legislators, and Federal Government Expenditures," *Western Political Quarterly* 32 (1979): 203-208; David W. Brady and Barbara Sinclair, "Building Majorities for Policy Changes in the House of Representatives," *Journal of Politics* 46 (1984): 1033-1070; and David W. Brady, *Critical Elections and Congressional Policy Making* (Stanford, Calif.: Stanford University Press, 1988).

5. On member "conversion," that is, change in incumbents' voting stance, see Barbara Sinclair, *Congressional Realignment;* and Brady and Sinclair, "Building Majorities."

6. Charles O. Jones, "Will Reform Change Congress?" in *Congress Reconsidered*, ed. Lawrence C. Dodd and Bruce I. Oppenheimer (New York: Praeger, 1977), 247-260.

7. Glenn R. Parker, "Some Themes in Congressional Unpopularity," *American Journal of Political Science* 212 (1977): 93-109.

8. Some useful sources concerning the developments of the 1970s are: Lawrence C. Dodd and Bruce I. Oppenheimer, "The House in Transition," in *Congress Reconsidered*, 3d ed., ed. Dodd and Oppenheimer (Washington, D.C.: CQ Press, 1985), 34-64; Norman J. Ornstein, ed., *Congress in Change: Evolution and Reform* (New York: Praeger, 1975); Norman J. Ornstein and David W. Rohde, "Political Parties and Congressional Reform," in *Parties and Elections in an Anti-Party Age*, ed. Jeff Fishel (Bloomington: Indiana University Press, 1978), 280-294; Samuel C. Patterson, "The Semi-Sovereign Congress," in *The New American Political System*, ed. Anthony King (Washington, D.C.: American Enterprise Institute, 1978), 125-177; Susan Welch and John G. Peters, eds., *Legislative Reform and Public Policy* (New York: Praeger, 1977); Rieselbach, *Legislative Reform*; James L. Sundquist, *The Decline and Resurgence of Congress* (Washington, D.C.: Brookings Institution, 1981); Burton D. Sheppard, *Rethinking Congressional Reform: The Reform Roots of the Special Interest Congress* (Cambridge, Mass.: Schenkman Books, 1985); and Center for Responsive Politics, *"Not for the Short Winded": Congressional Reform, 1961-1986* (Washington, D.C.: Center for Responsive Politics, 1986).

9. See Sundquist, *The Decline and Resurgence;* Thomas M. Franck and Edward Weisband, *Foreign Policy by Congress* (New York: Oxford University Press, 1979); and Cecil V. Crabb, Jr., and Pat M. Holt, *Invitation to Struggle: Congress, the President, and Foreign Policy*, 2d ed. (Washington, D.C.: CQ Press, 1984).

10. For the details of this controversy, see Allen Schick, *Congress and Money: Budgeting, Spending, and Taxation* (Washington, D.C.: Urban Institute, 1980), chap. 3; Howard E. Shuman, *Politics and the Budget: The Struggle between the President and the Congress*, 2d ed. (Englewood Cliffs, N.J.: Prentice-Hall, 1988), chap. 7; Rudolph G. Penner and Alan J. Abramson, *Broken Purse Strings: Congressional Budgeting, 1974-1988* (Washington, D.C.: Urban Institute, 1988), chap. 2; and Aaron Wildavsky, *The New Politics of the Budgetary Process*, 2d ed. (New York: HarperCollins, 1992), chap. 4.

11. For a comprehensive treatment of the civil rights movement, see Robert Kluger, *Simple Justice* (New York: Knopf, 1976).

12. Steven S. Smith and Christopher J. Deering, *Committees in Congress* (Washington, D.C.: CQ Press, 1984), 36.

13. Jeffrey M. Berry, *Lobbying for the People* (Princeton, N.J.: Princeton University Press, 1977); and Andrew S. McFarland, *Public Interest Lobbies* (Washington, D.C.: American Enterprise Institute, 1975).

14. Austin Ranney, *Curing the Mischiefs of Faction: Party Reform in America* (Berkeley: University of California Press, 1975); William J. Crotty, *Decisions for Democrats: Reforming the Party Structure* (Baltimore: Johns Hopkins University Press, 1978); and Byron E. Shafer, *Quiet Revolution: The Struggle for the Democratic Party and the Shaping of Post-Reform Politics* (New York: Russell Sage Foundation, 1983).

15. Norman J. Ornstein, Thomas E. Mann, Michael J. Malbin, Allen Schick, and John F. Bibby, *Vital Statistics on Congress, 1984-1985 Edition* (Washington, D.C.: American Enterprise Institute, 1984), tables 2-7, 2-8, 1-6, and 1-7. Any two Congresses are, of course, not typical, but the evidence of high turnover is clear. The percentage of (relatively junior) representatives with three or fewer terms of service was 37 in the 91st Congress, 34 in the 92d, and 37 in the 93d; for the three subsequent Congresses, the percentages were 44, 49, and 50. The reasons

for this high turnover differed markedly in the two chambers, especially after 1976. Before that year, incumbents were almost certain to be reelected. From 1966 to 1974, for example, at least 88 percent of incumbent representatives and 71 percent of incumbent senators who sought another term were reelected. (The mean success rates for these five elections were 92 percent in the House and 79 percent in the Senate.) After 1976, however, the situation changed. House incumbents continued to retain their seats; even with the Reagan 1980 landslide, 90.3 percent of House incumbents were reelected. In the Senate, in sharp contrast, the incumbent advantage declined drastically. In the 1976, 1978, and 1980 elections, the incumbent victory rates were 64, 60, and 55.2 percent, respectively. (In the postreform period, 1980-1984, Senate incumbents regained their advantage, and most won handily.) In the 1970s, House turnover reflected voluntary retirement from Congress, whereas Senate membership change reflected voter preferences. See John R. Hibbing, *Choosing to Leave: Voluntary Retirement from the U.S. House of Representatives* (Washington, D.C.: University Press of America, 1982).

16. On "going along," see David W. Rohde, Norman J. Ornstein, and Robert L. Peabody, "Political Change and Legislative Norms in the U.S. Senate, 1957-1974," in *Studies of Congress*, ed. Glenn R. Parker (Washington, D.C.: CQ Press, 1985), 147-188; Barbara Sinclair, *The Transformation of the U.S. Senate* (Baltimore: Johns Hopkins University Press, 1989).

17. Richard F. Fenno, Jr., *Home Style: Representatives in Their Districts* (Boston: Little, Brown, 1978).

18. Herbert F. Alexander, *Financing Politics*, 3d ed. (Washington, D.C.: CQ Press, 1984); and Michael J. Malbin, ed. *Parties, Interest Groups, and Campaign Finance Laws* (Washington, D.C.: American Enterprise Institute, 1980). For a more general treatment of the "rise of the candidate-centered campaign," see Barbara G. Salmore and Stephen A. Salmore, *Candidates, Parties, and Campaigns: Electoral Politics in America*, 2d ed. (Washington, D.C.: CQ Press, 1989), chap. 3.

19 On this infusion of new blood in Congress, see Eric M. Uslaner, "Policy Entrepreneurs and Amateur Democrats in the House of Representatives: Toward a More Policy-Oriented Congress?" in *Legislative Reform*, ed. Rieselbach, 105-116; Thomas E. Cavanagh, "The Dispersion of Authority in the House of Representatives," *Political Science Quarterly* 97 (1982-1983): 623-637; and Burdett A. Loomis, "Congressional Careers and Party Leadership in the Contemporary House of Representatives," *American Journal of Political Science* 28 (1984): 180-202.

20. These committees and the commission were named after their chairmen: Richard Bolling (D-Mo.), David R. Obey (D-Wis.), and Jerry Patterson (D-Calif.). In addition, from 1970 to 1974 the House Democratic caucus instructed its eleven-member Committee on Organization, Study, and Review, chaired by Julia Butler Hansen (D-Wash.), to suggest reforms and review the proposals of the Bolling panel. The committee, which in the 103d Congress is chaired by Louise Slaughter (N.Y.), continues to review proposals and recommend reforms to the caucus.

21. The respective chairmen were Harold Hughes (D-Iowa), Adlai Stevenson III (D-Ill.), and John Culver (D-Iowa).

22. Arthur G. Stevens, Jr., Abraham H. Miller, and Thomas E. Mann, "Mobilization

of Liberal Strength in the House, 1955-1970: The Democratic Study Group," *American Political Science Review* 68 (1974): 667-681.

23. For a balanced view of the pros and cons of the prereform operation of the seniority system, see Barbara Hinckley, *The Seniority System in Congress* (Bloomington: Indiana University Press, 1970).

24. Barbara Hinckley argues that the three chairmen were vulnerable to removal because they were old *and* were southern conservatives *and* were autocratic in their dealings with committee members, and because a viable challenger was waiting in the wings. See "Seniority 1975: Old Theories Confront New Facts," *British Journal of Political Science* 6 (1976): 383-399.

25. An additional change in House committee leadership was made in 1975. After a series of widely publicized escapades with Fanny Foxe, an "exotic dancer," Wilbur Mills, age 63, long one of the most powerful men in the House and a thorn in the flesh of liberals eager to revise the tax structure, declined to seek reelection as chairman of the Ways and Means Committee. Presumably, he felt he could not retain his position. Al Ullman (Ore.), age 60, the second most senior Democrat on the committee, won the chairmanship. Subsequently, Mills publicly acknowledged that he suffered from alcoholism and began a lengthy period of treatment and convalescence. Mills eventually returned to work but retired at the conclusion of the 94th Congress. Incidentally, deposed chairmen Patman and Hebert also retired in January 1977.

26. Although Price was too promilitary for some representatives, many in the opposition held the view that at his age, and in failing health, he no longer had the strength to run the committee.

27. In the 1991 cases, the caucus turned to the second ranking Democrat, Robert A. Roe (N.J.), for Public Works and the number three Democrat, Charlie Rose (N.C.), for House Administration. These decisions, according to David R. Obey, sent a "message to all chairmen that they have to be more responsive." Joseph Moakley (D-Mass.) put it more graphically: "The days of snarling chairmen who look through junior members are long gone." For details of these events, see Janet Hook, "Younger Members Flex Muscle in Revolt against Chairmen," *Congressional Quarterly Weekly Report*, December 8, 1990, 4059-4061. In 1993, the second most senior Democrat, William H. Natcher (Ky.), age 83, replaced the 83-year-old Whitten, who had in the previous Congress yielded day-to-day management of the Appropriations Committee to Natcher. See Jill Zuckman, "Most House Chairmen Hold On; Freshmen Win Choice Posts," *Congressional Quarterly Weekly Report*, December 12, 1992, 3785-3788.

28. All standing Senate committees except Veterans' Affairs and Rules and Administration are considered major committees; thus the assignment limits apply to thirteen of the chamber's fifteen regular panels.

29. In 1973 the House classified its standing committees as *exclusive* ("power" committees, such as Appropriations, Rules, and Ways and Means), *major* (policy committees, such as Education, Banking, and Commerce), and *non-major* (committees to which assignment was less desirable, such as Post Office and House Administration).

30. At the beginning of the 103d Congress (1993), House Democrats reiterated the five-assignment limit, which had not been enforced rigorously, and extended it to count service on a select (temporary) committee as a subcommittee

assignment.

31. David W. Rohde, "Committee Reform in the House of Representatives and the Subcommittee Bill of Rights," *Annals* 411 (1974): 39-47; and Norman J. Ornstein, "Causes and Consequences of Congressional Change: Subcommittee Reforms in the House of Representatives, 1970-1973," in *Congress in Change*, ed. Ornstein, 88-114. See also Thomas R. Wolanin, "A View from the Trench: Reforming Congressional Procedures," in *The United States Congress: Proceedings of the Thomas P. O'Neill, Jr., Symposium*, ed. Dennis Hale (Chestnut Hill, Mass.: Boston College, 1982), 209-228; and Smith and Deering, *Committees in Congress*, chap. 2.

32. Susan Webb Hammond, "Congressional Change and Reform: Staffing the Congress," in *Legislative Reform*, ed. Rieselbach, 181-193; and Harrison W. Fox, Jr., and Susan Webb Hammond, *Congressional Staffs: The Invisible Force in American Lawmaking* (New York: Free Press, 1977).

33. In February 1975, this procedure was used to permit the first House vote on whether to retain the controversial oil depletion allowance. This tax benefit for oil producers, designed to stimulate exploration for new petroleum sources, had been denounced by its critics as a tax loophole. The Democratic caucus voted 153-98 to instruct the party's Rules Committee contingent to permit a vote on an amendment to a major tax reduction bill, which the Ways and Means Committee had rejected, to repeal the allowance. The members of Rules complied with the instruction, and the full House voted to eliminate the allowance.

34. At the beginning of the 103d Congress in 1993, the minority House Republicans sought to spread their influence among the rank and file. They imposed a three-year limit on service as ranking minority member on any committee, forbade the ranking full committee member from also serving as a ranking subcommittee member (starting in 1995), and gave freshman members "a spot" in the party leadership. See Phil Kuntz, "GOP Moderates Take a Hit in Caucus Elections," *Congressional Quarterly Weekly Report*, December 12, 1992, 3781-3784.

   In addition, the House has made some concessions to the full committees. In December 1990, just before the start of the 102d Congress, the Democratic caucus adopted a rule guaranteeing standing committees five days to review legislative proposals drafted by leadership task forces or noncommittee groups. See "House Democrats Kill Proposal for Contribution Loophole," *Congressional Quarterly Weekly Report*, December 8, 1990, 4068. In 1992, it permitted an authorizing committee to offer a preferential motion to insist on disagreement with Senate language added to appropriations bills; it required the Appropriations Committee to give authorizing committees 24 hours' notice before convening a conference committee and to provide the text of conference reports one day before House consideration. See Beth Donovan, "Busy Democrats Skirt Fights to Get House in Order," *Congressional Quarterly Weekly Report*, December 12, 1992, 3777-3780. These modest steps were aimed at protecting standing committee influence during the regular and conference stages of the legislative process. Increased committee involvement, of course, enhances congressional responsiveness.

35. The military-industrial complex is perhaps the classic example of an iron triangle. Allegedly, members of the Armed Services Committee and its subcommittees, defense contractors (Boeing Aircraft or the General Dynamics Corporation), and Pentagon generals and their subordinates combine to control

weapons procurement policy. The congressional participants gain influence (and their constituencies get defense contracts), the industry earns profits, and the military gets the hardware it desires for national protection. On subsystem politics, see J. Leiper Freeman, *The Political Process*, rev. ed. (New York: Random House, 1965); and Randall B. Ripley and Grace A. Franklin, *Congress, the Bureaucracy, and Public Policy*, 5th ed. (Pacific Grove, Calif.: Brooks/Cole, 1991), 6-8. See also Hugh Heclo, "Issue Networks and the Executive Establishment," in *The New American Political System*, ed. King, 87-124; and Jeffrey M. Berry, "Subgovernments, Issue Networks, and Political Conflict," in *Remaking American Politics*, ed. Richard A. Harris and Sidney M. Milkis (Boulder, Colo.: Westview Press, 1989), 239-260.

36. David R. Mayhew, *Congress: The Electoral Connection* (New Haven, Conn.: Yale University Press, 1974).

37. In another sense, however, term limits might make members of Congress less responsive and more responsible. Free of most if not all electoral concerns, legislators could eschew many parochial issues and focus instead on efficient policy making to promote the national interest. See Gerald Benjamin and Michael J. Malbin, eds., *Limiting Legislative Terms* (Washington, D.C.: CQ Press, 1992).

38. In 1967 Adam Clayton Powell (D-N.Y.) was excluded from the House, charged with a variety of offenses including "improperly spending public funds, falsely reporting his expenditures, contemptuous conduct, and reflecting discredit on the House," Robert S. Getz, *Congressional Ethics: The Conflict of Interest Issue* (New York: Van Nostrand, 1966), 188. Abscam (for Arab scam) was an FBI sting operation in which federal agents, posing as Arab sheiks, offered bribes to members of Congress, who accepted them. Wayne Hays kept his mistress on his staff payroll as a typist although she could not type. Wilbur Mills was present when his female companion, Fanny Foxe, took a plunge in the Tidal Basin. Ethical indiscretions continue to plague Congress in the 1990s, and the lawmakers are still struggling to regain public approval. For a discussion of legislative ethics, see Vera Vogelsang-Coombs and Larry A. Bakken, "The Conduct of Legislators," in *Ethics, Government, and Public Policy: A Research Guide*, ed. James S. Bowman and F.A. Elliston (Westport, Conn.: Greenwood Press, 1988), 79-102.

39. Richard F. Fenno, Jr., "If, as Ralph Nader Says, Congress Is 'The Broken Branch,' How Come We Love Our Congressmen So Much?" in *Congress in Change*, ed. Ornstein, 277-287; Glenn R. Parker and Roger H. Davidson, "Why Do Americans Love Their Congressmen So Much More Than Their Congress?" *Legislative Studies Quarterly* 4 (1979): 53-61; and Timothy E. Cook, "Legislature vs. Legislator: A Note on the Paradox of Congressional Support," *Legislative Studies Quarterly* 4 (1979): 43-52. This "schizophrenic" assessment of Congress persists and sensitizes senators and representatives to the need to increase popular support for the institution. For recent opinion poll results, see "A Public Hearing on Congress," *Public Perspective* 4 (November-December 1992): 82-92.

40. Charles S. Bullock III, "Congress in the Sunshine," in *Legislative Reform*, ed. Rieselbach, 209-221.

41. House leaders have retained careful control of the mechanics of television coverage. House employees operate the cameras, which focus only on the rostrum and avoid panning the (often empty) House chamber, so that the public is more

likely to receive a favorable image of the House and its deliberations.

42. Under House rules, a parliamentary framework known as the Committee of the Whole House on the State of the Union, which consists of all 435 members, is used to facilitate and expedite preliminary consideration of legislation. The Speaker need not preside, a quorum for conducting business is 100, not the 218 required when the House sits formally. Voting in the Committee of the Whole is by voice vote, standing vote (the presiding officer counts first the "yeas" and then the "nays" as each group in turn rises), or teller vote (each group, yeas and nays, comes forward in the chamber to be counted as the members pass between tellers). The 1970 reform required the recording of individual positions in the teller votes. See Norman J. Ornstein and David W. Rohde, "The Strategy of Reform: Recorded Teller Voting in the House of Representatives" (Paper presented to the 1974 annual meeting of the Midwest Political Science Association). When the Committee of the Whole concludes preliminary consideration, it "rises," the Speaker resumes the chair, and a quorum is again 218. The House then acts to review—ratify or reject—decisions made by the Committee of the Whole. On congressional rules, see Walter J. Oleszek, *Congressional Procedures and the Policy Process*, 3d ed. (Washington, D.C.: CQ Press, 1989).

43. In September 1993, House reformers, led by Rep. James Inhofe (R-Okla.) achieved a small but symbolically significant gain in the direction of improved accountability. They won a rules change that permits to be made public the names of members who sign a discharge petition (which brings to the floor legislation that committees decline to report); previously the signers were identified only after the required 218 signatures had been obtained. Proponents of the change charged that the old rule frustrated accountability by permitting lawmakers to claim they supported a bill when in fact they had avoided acting to move it toward enactment. Opponents worried that the new rule would subject members to undue pressure from outside groups and, in consequence, undermine legislative responsibility. Ironically, the change came when the reformers successfully discharged the Rules Committee, which sought to bottle up the proposal. See Phil Kuntz, "Anti-Secrecy Drive Putting Democrats on Defensive," *Congressional Quarterly Weekly Report*, September 11, 1993, 2369-2370; and Thomas Mann and Norman Ornstein, "No Smoke, No Barons," *Washington Post*, September 27, 1993, A19.

44. On the 1974 FECA amendments, see *Congressional Quarterly Weekly Report*, October 12, 1974, 2865-2870; on the *Buckley* decision, consult *Congressional Quarterly Weekly Report*, February 7, 1976, 267-274. More generally, see Gary C. Jacobson, *Money in Congressional Elections* (New Haven, Conn.: Yale University Press, 1980); Alexander, *Financing Politics*; and Frank J. Sorauf, *Inside Campaign Finance: Myths and Realities* (New Haven, Conn.: Yale University Press, 1992).

45. This limit was relaxed considerably by the 99th Congress (1985-1986): members were permitted to supplement their $75,100 salaries with honoraria of 30 percent, or $22,530. In 1991, however, the Senate banned acceptance of honoraria entirely.

46. *Congressional Quarterly Weekly Report*, March 5, 1977, and April 2, 1977; and Bullock, "Congress in the Sunshine." Both the House and Senate have ethics committees to investigate and resolve charges of improper behavior by members.

47. On the 1989 act and subsequent changes in ethics codes and financial disclosure requirements, see Congressional Quarterly, *Congressional Ethics: History, Facts, and Controversy* (Washington, D.C.: CQ Press, 1992); Kim Mattingly, "Tips on Staying Out of Trouble in 1990," *Roll Call*, Back to Congress Section, January 22, 1990, 39; and Phil Kuntz, "Pay Hike Tied to Looser Gift Rules in Deal on Hill Funding," *Congressional Quarterly Weekly Report*, August 3, 1991, 2128-2130.

48. Glenn R. Simpson, "Senate Quietly OKs Constituent Service Rule," *Roll Call*, July 13, 1992, 18; and John R. Cranford, "Leaders Propose Rules Changes," *Congressional Quarterly Weekly Report*, March 21, 1992, 711.

49. Timothy J. Berger, in "After the Perk Wars, What's Left?" *Roll Call*, November 14, 1992, 40-42, summarizes the changes in congressional perquisites.

50. Lewis A. Froman, Jr., and Randall B. Ripley, "Conditions for Party Leadership: The Case of the House Democrats," *American Political Science Review* 59 (1965): 52-63. See also Lawrence C. Dodd, "Coalition-Building by Party Leaders: A Case Study of House Democrats," *Congress & the Presidency* 10 (1983): 147-168.

51. Gary C. Jacobson, "Practical Consequences of Campaign Finance Reform: An Incumbent Protection Act?" *Public Policy* 21 (1976): 1-32. The political alignments on the issue of extending campaign finance reform—whether to reduce PAC contribution levels or to establish a system of public finance for congressional elections—nicely illustrate the problem of incompatible intentions. Republicans, the legislative minority throughout the reform period, vigorously opposed many features of the scheme that was adopted, as well as proposals for additions to it. They feared that the restrictions on fund raising would entrench the majority Democrats permanently. They continue to oppose any federal financing of congressional elections, especially limits on legislative campaign spending.

52. See Wolanin, "A View from the Trench," on reforms increasing minority party participation.

53. Reformers also had reservations about broad delegations of authority for executive control of foreign trade policy; they held that Congress should determine tariff levels on its own initiative.

54. There are those who argue that by giving the executive virtual carte blanche during the 60-day period, Congress actually *enlarged* presidential power, granting authority that the Constitution does not afford. On the war powers resolution, see the sources cited in note 9 to this chapter; also Pat Holt, *The War Powers Resolution* (Washington, D.C.: American Enterprise Institute, 1978); Robert A. Katzman, "War Powers: Toward a New Accommodation," in *A Question of Balance: The President, the Congress, and Foreign Policy*, ed. Thomas E. Mann (Washington, D.C.: Brookings Institution, 1990), 35-69; Louis Fisher, *The Politics of Shared Power: Congress and the Executive*, 3d ed. (Washington, D.C.: CQ Press, 1993), chap. 6; and Robert J. Spitzer, *President and Congress: Executive Hegemony at the Crossroads of American Government* (New York: McGraw-Hill, 1993), chap. 3

55. This procedure is one form of the *legislative veto*, by which Congress has sought to retain the ability to block specific administrative actions; it reserves the option, within a given period, to stop bureaucrats from implementing specific regulations even though it has empowered them to do so. The Supreme Court, in *Immigration and Naturalization Service v. Chadha* (1983), declared unconstitutional legislative vetoes that were not presented to the president for signature

or veto, but it remains unclear how, if at all, the decision will affect procedures under the War Powers Act.

56. Such calculations about the relationship between revenues and expenditures are extraordinarily difficult and complex. For example, agencies, especially those of the Defense Department, can "reprogram" funds; that is, with the approval of the appropriate committee or subcommittee, or ranking member thereof, they can spend them on activities other than those for which they were originally appropriated. Furthermore, money is often "in the pipeline"—appropriated but unspent—and a cut in subsequent appropriations will not affect programs until unspent funds are exhausted. Finally, agencies may spend using "backdoor" procedures—by borrowing, using permanent appropriations, or making mandatory expenditures thus exceeding the legislature's annual appropriations. Such abstruse provisions have made accurate calculations about deficits (or surpluses) and the costs of government extremely problematic. For a summary of conventional budgetary practices, see *Congressional Quarterly Weekly Report*, April 28, 1973, 1013-1018. See also Schick, *Congress and Money*; and Wildavsky, *The New Politics of the Budgetary Process*.

57. Actually, the spending figures that the act requires include budget authority (funds that can be obligated over a period of years) and budget outlays (sums that can be spent in the ensuing fiscal year). The two may differ because the latter may include budget authority granted in previous fiscal years.

58. Passage of the first and second resolutions is by concurrent resolution, which does not have the force of law. Both House and Senate must adopt the concurrent resolution, but it does not require the president's signature. The terms of the resolutions are implemented, however, by means of regular legislation.

59. On the budget process and the politics surrounding the budget's adoption, see Schick, *Congress and Money*; Shuman, *Politics and the Budget*; Dennis S. Ippolito, *Congressional Spending* (Ithaca, N.Y.: Cornell University Press, 1981); Joel Havemann, *Congress and the Budget* (Bloomington: Indiana University Press, 1978); Kenneth Shepsle, ed., *The Congressional Budget Process: Some Views from the Inside* (St. Louis: Washington University Center for the Study of American Business, 1980); and Aaron Wildavsky, *The Politics of the Budgetary Process*, 4th ed. (Boston: Little, Brown, 1984).

60. For an extended discussion of GRH, see Lance T. LeLoup, Barbara L. Graham, and Stacey Barwick, "Deficit Politics and Constitutional Government," *Public Budgeting and Finance* 7 (1987): 83-103; Penner and Abramson, *Broken Purse Strings*; Shuman, *Politics and the Budget*, chap. 10; Joseph White and Aaron Wildavsky, *The Deficit and the Public Interest: The Search for Responsible Budgeting in the 1980s* (Berkeley: University of California Press, 1989), chaps. 19 and 21; John B. Gilmour, *Reconcilable Differences? Congress, the Budget Process, and the Deficit* (Berkeley: University of California Press, 1989), chap. 5; Raphael Thelwell, "Gramm-Rudman-Hollings Four Years Later: A Dangerous Illusion," *Public Administration Review* 50 (1990): 190-198; and Sung Deuk Hahm, Mark S. Kamlet, David C. Mowery, and Tsai-Tsu Su, "The Influence of the Gramm-Rudman-Hollings Act on Federal Budgetary Outcomes, 1986-1989," *Journal of Policy Analysis and Management* 11 (1992): 207-234.

61. The estimation could not be perfect, given the many economic uncertainties on which it was based. In consequence, the drafters of GRH built in a "fudge

factor" of $10 billion. If the likely deficit was within $10 billion of the target (was less than $154 billion for fiscal 1987), the automatic cuts, the sequester, could be avoided.

62. That the law was a product of desperation is clear from the unorthodox process by which the bill was adopted. No committee in either house considered the bill. Rather, in debate on the Senate floor it was attached to a "must-pass" bill to raise the debt ceiling, thus permitting the government to continue to borrow money to meet its obligations. In a 75-24 vote, the Senate agreed to the amendment, virtually without having read it. Despite serious reservations about the GRH proposal, House Democrats could not stop its political momentum. They passed their own version, and it went to the House-Senate conference. The ultimate compromise version was more to the House's liking, but the basic outline of the automatic sequester procedure remained in the bill. The vote in the House was 271-154; that in the Senate, 61-31. See LeLoup, Graham, and Barwick, "Deficit Politics and Constitutional Government"; and Darrell M. West, *Congress and Economic Policymaking* (Pittsburgh, Pa.: University of Pittsburgh Press, 1987), chap. 7. Expectations about the success of GRH were low; Sen. Warren Rudman, one of the sponsors, called it "a bad idea whose time has come."

63. For details of the fiscal 1991 budget struggle, see Pamela Fessler, "Senate Plan Faces Uphill Fight; Exploratory Talks Set," *Congressional Quarterly Weekly Report,* May 5, 1990, 1329-1332; George Hager, "Defiant House Rebukes Leaders; New Round of Fights Begins," *Congressional Quarterly Weekly Report,* October 6, 1990, 3183-3188; George Hager, "One Outcome of the Budget Package: Higher Deficits on the Way," *Congressional Quarterly Weekly Report,* November 3, 1990, 3710-3713; and George Hager and Pamela Fessler, "Negotiators Walk Fine Line to Satisfy Both Chambers," *Congressional Quarterly Weekly Report,* October 20, 1990, 3476-3484. See also James A. Thurber, "New Rules for an Old Game: Zero-Sum Budgeting in the Postreform Congress," in *The Postreform Congress,* ed. Davidson, 257-278.

64. On the new law, see George Hager, "One Outcome of the Budget Package"; George Hager, "New Rules on Taxes, Spending May Mean Budget Standoff," *Congressional Quarterly Weekly Report,* January 26, 1991, 232-237; George Hager, "With Little Room to Maneuver, Bush Sets His Priorities," *Congressional Quarterly Weekly Report,* February 6, 1992, 332-337; John R. Cranford, "New Budget Process for Congress," *Congressional Quarterly Weekly Report,* November 3, 1990, 3712; Lawrence J. Haas, "Off Center," *National Journal,* December 8, 1990, 2971-2973; and Lawrence J. Haas, "Keeping the Score," *National Journal,* January 9, 1991, 189. For academics' commentary, consult Richard Doyle and Jerry McCaffery, "The Budget Enforcement Act of 1990: The Path to No-Fault Budgeting," *Public Budgeting and Finance* 10 (1991): 25-40; James A. Thurber and Samantha L. Durst, "Delay, Deadlock, and Deficits: Evaluating Congressional Budget Reform," in *Federal Budget and Financial Management Reform,* ed. Thomas D. Lynch (Westport, Conn.: Greenwood Press, 1991), 53-68; and James A. Thurber and Samantha L. Durst, "The 1990 Budget Enforcement Act: The Decline of Congressional Accountability," in *Congress Reconsidered,* 5th ed., ed. Dodd and Oppenheimer, 375-397.

65. On the congressional support agencies, see James A. Thurber, "The Evolving

Role and Effectiveness of the Congressional Research Agencies," in *The House at Work*, ed. Joseph Cooper and G. Calvin Mackenzie (Austin: University of Texas Press, 1981), 292-315; and Carol H. Weiss, ed., *Organizations for Policy Analysis: Helping Government Think* (Newbury Park, Calif.: Sage, 1992), chaps. 10-14. On committee staff changes and computer use in Congress, see Cooper and Mackenzie, *The House at Work*; Fox and Hammond, *Congressional Staffs*; Michael J. Malbin, *Unelected Representatives: Congressional Staff and the Future of Representative Government* (New York: Basic Books, 1980); and Stephen E. Frantzich, *Computers in Congress* (Beverly Hills, Calif.: Sage, 1982).

66. The Supreme Court's 1983 *Chadha* decision (see note 55 to this chapter) has called some of these legislative veto provisions into question.

67. See Morris S. Ogul, *Congress Oversees the Bureaucracy: Studies in Legislative Supervision* (Pittsburgh, Pa.: University of Pittsburgh Press, 1976); Joel D. Aberbach, *Keeping a Watchful Eye: The Politics of Congressional Oversight* (Washington, D.C.: Brookings Institution, 1990); Lawrence C. Dodd and Richard L. Schott, *Congress and the Administrative State* (New York: Wiley, 1979); John R. Bolton, *The Legislative Veto: Unseparating the Powers* (Washington, D.C.: American Enterprise Institute, 1977); and William West and Joseph Cooper, "The Congressional Veto and Administrative Rulemaking," *Political Science Quarterly* 98 (1983): 285-304. On the 1983 Supreme Court decision, see Joseph Cooper, "Postscript on the Congressional Veto: Is There Life after Chadha?" *Political Science Quarterly* 98 (1983): 427-429; and Joseph Cooper, "The Legislative Veto in the 1980s," in *Congress Reconsidered*, 3d ed., ed. Dodd and Oppenheimer, 364-389.

68. William P. Schaefer and James A. Thurber, "The Causes, Characteristics, and Political Consequences of the Legislative Veto" (Paper presented to the 1980 annual meeting of the Southern Political Science Association).

69. In the 103d Congress, the Steering and Policy Committee has 35 members: 10 official party leaders, 9 members appointed by the Speaker, 12 members elected from geographical regions, and the chairs of the Appropriations, Budget, Rules, and Ways and Means committees. The party leadership, quite obviously, continues to have considerable influence in the committee. In addition, in 1985, Speaker Thomas P. O'Neill, Jr., formed an informal group, dubbed the "Speaker's Cabinet," to advise him on various matters; its membership included "key committee leaders," party officials, and individuals representing differing ideological viewpoints. In 1993, this arrangement became formal with the creation of a "Speaker's Working Group on Policy Development," 31 members handpicked by the Speaker, including rank-and-file Democrats as well as committee chairs, to advise on policy and to promote party unity.

70. The voting record makes this clear: In the 93d Congress, the 15 Democrats on the Ways and Means Committee averaged 34.1 percent in support of the southern Democratic-Republican conservative coalition; in the same Congress, the 22 Democrats who were subsequently appointed to the Steering and Policy Committee in the 94th Congress (Speaker Carl Albert and freshman representative William Brodhead did not vote in the 93d Congress) averaged only 24.9 percent in support of the conservative coalition, a difference of 9.2 percent—nearly 1 vote in every 10. Similarly, in the 93d Congress, Ways and Means Democrats averaged 61.3 percent in support of the Democratic majority position, whereas the 22 voting members of the 1975 Steering Committee had cast 74.9 percent of

their votes in support of the Democratic majority position, a difference of 13.6 percent. In short, the reformers could reasonably expect the members of the Steering Committee, now empowered to make committee assignments subject to caucus ratification, to be decidedly less conservative and more inclined to back partisan majorities than the Ways and Means Democrats.

71. On the 1993 changes, see Donovan, "Busy Democrats Skirt Fights"; and Mary Jacoby, "In a Shocker, House Kills Narcotics Panel, Takes Aim at 3 Other Selects," *Roll Call*, January 28, 1993, 1, 17. In organizing for the 103d House, the Republicans made some modest adjustments in their leaders' authority. The minority leader was given control over the one preferential motion to which the party is entitled on pending legislation. The intent was to prevent senior members, who were assumed to be too close to the majority Democrats, from offering "sweetheart" motions that would preclude more forthright presentation of GOP opposition and alternatives to the Democrats' proposals. The new Republican rules also enjoined top committee members "to work closely with the leadership in drafting written plans for dealing with key issues." See Kuntz, "GOP Moderates Take a Hit in Caucus Elections." These changes would presumably enable the party leaders to rally party support more effectively to challenge the majority Democrats' policy initiatives.

72. See Bruce I. Oppenheimer, "The Changing Relationship between House Leadership and the Committee on Rules," in *Understanding Congressional Leadership*, ed. Frank A. Mackaman (Washington, D.C.: CQ Press, 1981), 207-225; Barbara Sinclair, *Majority Leadership in the U.S. House* (Baltimore: Johns Hopkins University Press, 1982); David J. Vogler, "Ad Hoc Committees in the House of Representatives and Purposive Models of Legislative Behavior," *Polity* 14 (1981): 89-109; Lawrence C. Dodd and Terry Sullivan, "Majority Party Leadership and Partisan Voting Gathering: The House Democratic Whip System," in *Understanding Congressional Leadership*, ed. Mackaman, 227-260; Lawrence Dodd, "The Expanded Role of the House Democratic Whips," *Congressional Studies* 7 (1979): 27-56; and Judith H. Parris, "The Senate Reorganizes Its Committees, 1977," *Political Science Quarterly* 94 (1979): 319-337.

73. Action against the Ways and Means Committee illustrates the diverse implications of reform. On one hand, the moves against the tax panel reduced that committee's independence; it could less easily go its own way, confident that the full membership of the House would defer to its expertise. The reforms increased the Democratic party's potential to bring the committee under its centralized control, to make it more responsible. On the other hand, dispersing committee authority—to more members, serving on independent subcommittees, meeting in open sessions—also had the potential to undercut control, to increase responsiveness to multiple points of view, at the expense of effective action. The need to respond to many participants could make it more difficult for Ways and Means to formulate and secure passage of workable financial programs.

74. In 1975, however, perhaps in the spirit of democratization, the caucus yielded its seldom-used authority to dictate the members' roll call votes.

75. Roger H. Davidson and Walter J. Oleszek, *Congress against Itself* (Bloomington: Indiana University Press, 1977).

76. See Parris, "The Senate Reorganizes Its Committees."

77. At the center of the reform controversy was the arcane question of whether the Senate can adopt new rules by simple majority vote at the start of each Congress. Despite Vice President Nelson Rockefeller's affirmative ruling on this issue, the defenders of the filibuster, led by James B. Allen (D-Ala.), outmaneuvered the reformers and salvaged the compromise, which not only imposed the 60-vote (rather than a simple majority) rule but reversed Rockefeller's ruling and established that a two-thirds vote is still required to end debate on changes in Senate rules.

78. *Congressional Quarterly Weekly Report*, December 13, 1975, 2721-2722, and February 24, 1979, 319-320. Here, too, the reforms promoted the goals of democratization (by letting smaller majorities invoke cloture) and responsibility (by permitting those majorities to act more easily).

79. On these changes, see Donovan, "Busy Democrats Skirt Fights."

80. *Congressional Quarterly Weekly Report*, September 3, 1977, 1855; September 17, 1977, 1973-1975; and October 15, 1977, 2183.

81. *Congressional Quarterly Weekly Report*, March 29, 1980, 886, and May 3, 1980, 1173-1174.

82. *Congressional Quarterly Weekly Report*, April 9, 1983, 695-696.

83. *Congressional Quarterly Weekly Report*, December 1, 1984, 3035.

4. The Impact of Congressional Reform

That substantial and significant congressional reform has occurred is incontrovertible. Congress in the 1990s is markedly
different from Congress in the 1960s. The legislature adopted
broad changes ostensibly to promote responsiveness, accountability,
and responsibility. These commonly cited justifications may have concealed electoral, policy, and power motives, however. In one sense, the
reformers have achieved their purposes. Congress is more democratic:
more members and concerned citizens can participate in congressional
deliberations. Congress is more visible: more of its operations, particularly in committee, are open to public scrutiny; more of its members'
campaign and financial dealings are matters of public record. And
Congress is potentially more effective: it is more capable of imposing
its policy preferences on the executive in foreign and domestic affairs
when it opts to do so.

Congress is to some degree more responsive, accountable, and responsible as a result of reform. But is it "better"? To answer this question, of course, requires a value judgment. Any analysis will reflect the
observer's views about what sort of institution the legislature should
be. Differing hopes and expectations will lead to varying assessments.
The proponents of executive dominance or congressional supremacy
may render different verdicts on congressional performance; they may
approve some results of reform and find others wanting, or may laud
different achievements of the postreform Congress. An unequivocal
answer to the query may also be impossible because postreform behavior cannot with certainty be attributed to the reforms themselves. Reform is, after all, part and parcel of broader change. Crises outside
Congress, new issues or the fundamental transformation of old ones,
and new members of Congress may contribute as much as or more than
specific reforms to the modifications of legislative activity.[1]

This chapter is an examination of the intended and unintended consequences of reform. Because reform was undertaken in response to many influences—both political and personal—and because it was not guided by any widely shared broad vision of desirable legislative organization and process, its effects seem inconsistent and uncertain. The evidence accumulated since 1977, when the reform impulse began to flag, suggests that the results of reform have been many and varied. Reformers' intentions have sometimes been realized, and sometimes not. Often quite unintended and undesirable consequences have resulted from reforms designed to enhance Congress's responsiveness, accountability, and responsibility.

Responsiveness and Fragmentation

Central to the reformers' efforts was a desire to democratize Congress. Their chief targets were the full committees, chaired by powerful, sometimes tyrannical, conservative lawmakers. By lessening the power of committee oligarchs, reformers hoped to make Congress a more responsive institution. Thus, they modified the seniority rule for selecting committee chairs; altered the committee assignment process, limiting the number of committee leadership positions any individual could hold; and delegated much committee power to subcommittees, newly provided with increased staff support.

Viewed narrowly, these changes may have accomplished their purpose, but from a broader, long-term perspective, their proponents may have won the battle but lost the war. Increased responsiveness may have exacted a high price. By slowing up the legislative process and requiring more elaborate bargaining to reach agreements among more participants, the changes may have made congressional decision making more arduous.

Modifying Seniority

With respect to seniority, in the House at least, the old order has been altered. Although the chairs of most committees, and those of the Appropriations and Ways and Means subcommittees, continue to be chosen on the basis of seniority, there have been a sufficient number of departures from the rule to restrain the chair's most arbitrary exercise of authority. On three occasions in 1975, one in 1985, two instances in 1991, and one in 1993, the Democratic caucus has removed a sitting committee chair. In three of those instances—the selection of Henry Reuss to head the Banking Committee (1975), Les Aspin to chair Armed Services (1985), and Charlie Rose to lead House Administration

(1991)—the new committee chair was not second in terms of seniority but farther down the list of senior Democrats. In addition, in a few cases junior members have challenged seniors for subcommittee chairs under the bidding procedures instituted in 1973 and have won. For example, in 1985, Democrats on the Science and Technology Committee rejected George E. Brown (Calif.), a frequent critic of the National Aeronautics and Space Agency, in favor of Bill Nelson (Fla.), a strong booster of NASA (the Kennedy Space Center is in the district he represented), for a subcommittee chair. Likewise, Judiciary Committee Democrats in 1989 chose Bruce A. Morrison (Conn.) over Romano Mazzoli (Ky.) to chair the panel's Subcommittee on Immigration, Refugees and International Law. In 1993, the Democratic caucus deprived Jamie Whitten not only of the Appropriations chair but of the top post on the Agriculture, Rural Development and Related Agencies subcommittee.[2] At the very least, senior committee leaders are on notice that the members of the caucus and their committee colleagues can vote to unseat them. The very real threat of sanctions probably has a similar restraining impact in the Senate, although to date senators have faithfully adhered to seniority in selecting committee chairs.

Changing the Committee Assignment Process

Another goal of the reformers was to democratize the committee assignment process, and to some extent they succeeded. Opportunities to compete for preferred assignments are clearly greater. The new rules of both parties in both chambers guarantee all members at least one major committee post. In the House, the Steering and Policy Committee, which now has the assignment responsibilities formerly held by the Democratic delegation of the Ways and Means Committee, is more representative of the full party membership. Steering and Policy tries to match members' requests and committee vacancies in order to accommodate as many members as possible.[3] In allocating assignments, the committee considers members' electoral needs (including regional and state political circumstances), support for the party leadership, policy views, and seniority.[4] Indeed, members often wage extensive and intense campaigns for particular seats, writing long memorandums and soliciting support from committee chairs, lobbyists, and state delegations to buttress their applications and improve their chances.

Yet members do not always succeed in winning the places they covet for two reasons. First, there are not always enough seats to go around, especially on the most desirable panels. Second, the party leaders may intervene when seats on particularly critical committees are at stake. The Speaker personally controls nominations to the Rules

Committee, and as leader and chair of Steering and Policy may influence who receives assignments to the Appropriations, Budget, and Ways and Means committees. The party leaders even calculate *leadership support scores* for incumbents who apply to change assignments, and Steering and Policy seemingly uses them in making decisions on transfer requests. The leaders seldom involve themselves in the assignment process, but when they do their influence may prove decisive. Thus, members have more opportunity to find congenial places on committees, but there is no certainty that they will succeed in doing so. Most of the time, the lawmakers get the committee posts they want, which can facilitate their pursuit of personal goals.[5]

Delegating to the Subcommittees

A major aim of committee reform was to create and sustain independent subcommittees, and here the reformers have succeeded admirably. The House moved a long way from full committee government to subcommittee government when it adopted the subcommittee bill of rights (see Chapter 3) and passed new rules granting more members subcommittee positions. House subcommittee reform "loosened the full committee chairs' stranglehold on subcommittee decision making." [6] But the subcommittees' power has not increased uniformly, and it is not clear that subcommittee influence over policy choice exceeds that of the full committees. In sum, subcommittees have assumed greater significance, but they still are not automatically the prime movers in the making of congressional public policy decisions.[7]

As retirements increased during the 1970s, junior members advanced rapidly and assumed subcommittee chairs. In the House, the subcommittee reforms did enable more (and junior) members to accede to positions of potential power. Limiting an individual to a single subcommittee chair initially opened up at least 16 leadership posts to members who had previously been denied them.[8] Moreover, because the number of House subcommittees grew—from 120 in the 92d Congress (1971-1972) to 151 in the 94th (1975-1976)—additional positions were available for still more majority members.[9]

The new subcommittee chairs are more liberal, more "typical" Democrats; thus committee leadership is more representative of the entire party.[10] Yet, as John Stanga, Jr., and David Farnsworth suggest, seniority, although wounded in principle, survives in practice, and much of the reform-induced change is concentrated in a few committees.[11] Exclusive House committees remain the province of senior members, and on other panels there has been only a modest reduction in the seniority of subcommittee chairs. Overall, however, it seems safe to say that in spite of the reduction in the number of subcommittees in recent years, more members have a subcommittee seat from which to seek influence than was the case in the prereform period.

More important, perhaps, is that most subcommittees are independent and active. In the 100th Congress (1987-1988), 84.6 percent of House bills sent to the full committee had been referred to subcommittees; 79.7 percent of the bills the full committee eventually reported to the floor had been referred initially to House subcommittees. In the prereform 91st Congress (1969-1971), the respective figures were 35.7 percent and 75.4 percent. Senate use of subcommittees, by contrast, remained unchanged in the same period. In the 100th Congress, House subcommittees conducted 52.0 percent of all committee meetings and held 95.1 percent of the hearings on bills initially referred to their parent full committees; the comparable figures for the prereform 91st Congress were 47.9 percent and 77.0 percent. In the Senate, however, subcommittees actually conducted a smaller proportion of meetings and hearings than subcommittees had in the prereform period. Another change is that House subcommittees control their own bills on the floor: subcommittee chairs managed 70.6 percent of the bills that reached the floor from their parent full committees in the 99th Congress (1985-1986), up from 49.0 percent in the prereform 91st Congress. Once again, no such increase in subcommittee activity is evident in the Senate. House subcommittee members have not become increasingly prominent in the chamber's conference committee delegations, however.[12] House subcommittees are much busier since adoption of their bill of rights. But in the smaller Senate, members have multiple committee assignments and, because they can exert influence in the full panel, they have little need to use subcommittees extensively.

In addition, subcommittees are often expert in their field of specialization (they have their own staffs), and they are protected from outside interference by guarantees of total jurisdiction, control over their own rules, and adequate budgets. Indeed, party leaders do not often seek to impose discipline on the subcommittees; most often they confer with subcommittee chairs on procedural matters, like scheduling, and only rarely lobby subcommittees with respect to the content of policy. In fact, committee leaders are more likely to initiate communications with party leaders than vice versa. Party leaders' demands are usually limited to issues of major significance, and they often are made after the subcommittee has already completed action. In general, the leadership "neither desires to influence nor is capable of influencing the specific legislative outcomes of the vast majority of subcommittee deliberations."[13]

Such subcommittee independence suggests that the impulse to democratize the committees, to give House members room to participate more fully in policy making, has increased legislative fragmentation.

There are today more individuals and power centers to deal with in coordinating congressional policy making. The legislature's ability to act at all, much less more forcefully, may have declined as decentralization has increased.

But independence (the ability to operate freely, without restraint) is not autonomy (the ability to make decisions stick at subsequent stages of the legislative process). Subcommittees may be independent but not autonomous. They control the conduct of legislative business only to a limited extent. For one thing, subcommittees remain subordinate to the full committees, which ultimately make policy recommendations. Indeed, Steven Smith and Christopher Deering find that the most independent and active subcommittees are often the least autonomous; the policy decisions of adventurous subcommittees may be challenged and reversed in full committee.[14]

Although House subcommittees now initiate consideration of more legislation, the number of bills originating there that the full committees actually report to the House floor has not risen appreciably. In the 91st Congress, 75.4 percent of reported bills were considered first in subcommittee; the figure for the postreform 96th Congress was 80.0 percent, and for the 100th, 79.7 percent.[15] Moreover, subcommittees—particularly those that deal with pork barrel, constituency matters such as rivers and harbors projects or agricultural subsidies—are regularly open to external group influences. As part of subgovernments, they may have to defer to the wishes of their policy-making partners. The broader range of participation in congressional affairs generated by the general movement toward democratization has led nonmembers to take a greater interest in committee and subcommittee operations, thus widening the range of opinions that subcommittees need to consider. In short, subcommittees are constrained by the full committees, by noncommittee members of Congress, and by outside interests. "Subcommittee chairs are dependent on the support of the full committee, which is often difficult to obtain."[16]

Variations on the Reform Theme

Not surprisingly, reform has not had consistent effects throughout Congress. As Richard Fenno has made clear, committee decisions are shaped by various influences: members' personal goals (reelection, power, policy influence), the external (environmental) forces to which the committee responds, the panel's "strategic premises" (decision rules or norms), and its decision-making processes (which reflect specialization, partisanship, and participation).[17] Because committees differ, change has had a different impact on each of them.

Norman Ornstein and David Rohde found that the reforms of the 1970s coincided with membership turnover in specific committees in distinctive ways, for instance. The House Agriculture Committee "implemented the full array of subcommittee-strengthening reforms," experienced major personnel change, and got a new chair, in the process becoming ideologically more moderate and regionally balanced. Despite these major alterations, because the new members' goals varied little from the motivations of the members they replaced, "little overt change in behavior or policy outputs occurred." [18] Ornstein and Rohde also found that reforms increased the independence and activity of many subcommittees of the House Commerce and Government Operations committees without significantly altering their policy-making behavior. The reforms, in fact, inhibited the policy activities of the former.[19] In the House Foreign Affairs Committee, the effect of new members and new rules was to put in prominent subcommittee positions liberal legislators who pressured the committee chair to join the more active panel members in attempting to place restrictions on presidential foreign policy leadership.[20] Overall, change and reform produced behavioral modifications in some committees but not in others.[21]

It may take wholesale change to jar a committee sufficiently that it alters its customary routines; the consequences are often unintended and, for some interests at least, undesirable. The case of the House Ways and Means Committee is illustrative. Although it had been a target of liberals' criticism during Wilbur Mills's lengthy and successful tenure as chairman, the committee was reformed only when circumstances were conducive—when Mills's personal problems made him and his panel vulnerable. Mills was forced from the chair in 1974, and Ways and Means was stripped of its committee assignment powers, required to create subcommittees, enlarged from twenty-five to thirty-seven members, and deprived of some procedural protection (the "closed rule") for legislation it reported. In consequence, the new chairman, Al Ullman, failed to sustain the committee's bipartisan consensus. The panel began to divide along partisan lines, and it suffered a series of humiliating defeats on the House floor.[22] Catherine Rudder concluded that the ability of Ways and Means to carry its proposals on the House floor was, in consequence of reform, seriously impaired.[23] Since 1981, under the leadership of Dan Rostenkowski (Ill.), Ways and Means has regained some of its earlier influence, but Randall Strahan has concluded that "the distinctive procedural autonomy of the prereform committee" has been "reduced through reforms that increased the authority of the majority party caucus and its leadership and established a new budget process." [24]

Planned reform and more general, unpredictable change mix in distinctive ways to influence the subcommittees' performance as well. David Price attributes changes in the House Commerce Committee's Subcommittee on Oversight and Investigations to the accession of John Moss (D-Calif.) to the subcommittee chair. Although replacement of the sitting chairman was only one aspect of a thoroughgoing reform—the parent committee rewrote its rules and reallocated its resources to accommodate its subcommittees—Moss was largely responsible for these changes. Price concludes that Moss's "goals and methods as a leader . . . made for alterations in the subcommittee's product and performance." Michael Malbin reaches a similar conclusion: subcommittee activity reflected Moss's legislative interests; reform per se was less critical.[25]

The moral seems clear: reform and more general change influence full committees and subcommittees in different ways. On balance, democratization has increased subcommittee members' opportunity to participate in congressional activity at the expense of the full committees, but it has not done so uniformly or with consistent effects on legislative policy making.

Nowhere is the variation in the impact of reform clearer than with respect to bicameralism. Reform and change moved the House some distance, if not all the way, toward subcommittee government. The Senate, in sharp contrast, changed very little. New members with new interests and a new spirit of member independence promoted decentralization in the House. But in the Senate, individual freedom had long been the order of the day; C. Lawrence Evans describes it as "rampant individualism."[26] The so-called Johnson Rule, dating from Lyndon Johnson's tenure as majority leader (1955-1961), guaranteed each senator a major committee assignment; the existence of 16 or more standing committees in a body of 100 members has made multiple assignments possible. Senators have been free to pursue their own interests since well before the reform era. With numerous and desirable assignments, they have had less need to seek subcommittee posts as a forum for influencing policy; they can achieve their purposes within the confines of the full committees.

In consequence, there has been a modest decrease in the number of Senate subcommittees: from 123 in the 92d Congress (1971-1972) and 140 in the 94th (1975-1976) to 103 in the 98th (1983-1984) and 87 in the 102d (1991-1992), after limitations were placed on members' committee assignments. Similarly, change was minimal in the overall importance of subcommittees in Senate deliberations during the 1970s and early 1980s. Throughout that period roughly 40 percent to 45 percent of the bills referred to full committee had been handled initially in subcommittee; the same percentages apply to bills reported by the full committees that had been the subject of subcommittee hearings. In fact, subcommittee meetings and hearings as a proportion of all such sessions actually declined, from 30.6 percent in the 91st Congress to 18.6 percent in the 100th Congress. The floor leaders in the Senate manage most of the routine bills when they reach the floor and, reflecting the members' individualism, bill sponsors handle more important legislation. Thus, the subcommittee chairs managed a small and decreasing number of bills.[27]

The role of subcommittees varies from full committee to full committee, but on balance subcommittees are considerably less significant in the Senate than in the House. The full committees continue to dominate committee politics, as they have for many years. Hard-pressed senators, short of time but not of influence in full committees and on the Senate floor, simply have less need to strengthen and use subcommittees.

Increasing Staff Resources

Another aim of the move toward democratization in Congress was to give members and committees more staff assistance and more access to it. On this front the reformers accomplished much of what they set out to do. Members' personal staffs have grown enormously. Representatives and senators can use staffers for legislative as well as for constituency service (reelection) purposes; for example, each senator is entitled to recruit a staff aide for each committee assignment. These resources, coupled with research assistance from the congressional support agencies—the Congressional Budget Office, the Office of Technology Assessment, the General Accounting Office, and the Congressional Research Service—give individual members access to substantial amounts of data that they can, of course, readily use to support their own policy goals and preferences.[28]

Dispersion of staff resources has proceeded apace in the House but has been restrained in the Senate. In both chambers the number of committee staff members has increased dramatically. House standing committees had 702 staffers on their payrolls in 1970 and nearly three times as many (1,970) in 1983. Since then, staff size has stabilized; standing committee employment was 1,986 in 1989. The Senate committee staff totaled 635 in 1970, peaked at 1,277 in 1975, and then declined slightly to 1,013 in 1989.[29] The reformed rules in the House permitted the subcommittees to have their own staffs. Not all subcommittees took immediate or full advantage of these provisions, but most did. In the 91st Congress (1969-1971), 23.2 percent of the House committee staff members were employed by subcommittees. A decade later, in the 97th Congress (1981-1982), the figure was 39.8 percent; by the 101st Congress (1989-1990) it had reached 45.2 percent. Senate sub-committees, in contrast, employed a fairly constant proportion of committee staff—42.1 percent in the 91st Congress, 32.5 percent in the 97th, and 38.7 percent in the 101st.[30] Full committee chairs retain considerable control over staff hiring in the Senate. Moreover, individual senators' committee-involved personal staffs offer a viable alternative to complete reliance on committee or subcommittee employees. Finally, new rules in both the House and Senate granted the minority party one-third of committee staff positions; by the 1990s most but not all panels had separate majority and minority party staffs. In short, reforms gave members of Congress more access to staff assistance in their own offices (Senate), in their subcommittees (House), or in both (House). Presumably, improved staff resources improve congressional responsiveness. Even if a 10 percent cut in congressional staffs, proposed in 1993 as one remedy for the federal deficit crisis, takes effect, the members' personnel resources will still be substantially greater than those available in the prereform era, thus enabling them to continue to respond to constituent requests for services and information.

The Impact of Democratization

These steps toward the democratization of Congress, combined with the new electoral realities of the reform era, have contributed to the increased potential for congressional responsiveness. Many members, particularly in the House, are regularly reelected with sizable vote margins, and they work hard to maintain their electoral security. They travel home on weekends; they maintain district offices and conduct extensive casework operations; they assign many of their staff members to "work the district." In general, they strive to earn and keep the goodwill, and the votes, of the "folks back home" by striving to serve their needs and interests.[31] Some view this acute sensitivity to constituents' sentiments as excessive responsiveness.[32]

In sum, the move toward democratization has dispersed authority more widely among members, especially in the House. The reforms of the 1970s have made the House more like the Senate.[33] Both chambers are decentralized: both afford individual members considerable freedom of action. Under the threat of ouster, committee chairs must share their authority with full committee majorities and more active and independent subcommittee leaders. On the whole, more individuals have influence, at least over a small square of the legislative turf. From these bastions they can attempt to shape policy and enhance their public image. Electorally more secure, fully staffed, and more assertive vis-à-vis the executive, contemporary members of Congress are in a position to respond to a wide variety of viewpoints. In this sense, the reformers have attained their purposes and made Congress more responsive.

The reformers' success in democratizing Congress has not been without cost, however. Dispersion of power has restricted Congress's ability to make public policy effectively and efficiently.[34] In the House, subcommittees have emerged as the chief culprits. Paradoxically, subcommittee growth and independence may make it more difficult for members to achieve their individual goals of electoral security and policy influence. One reason is that the increase in the number of subcommittees has increased the representatives' work load and responsibilities. Members have more places to be and more subjects to master; even with increased staff help, they may be unable to cope with the new demands on their time and energy. (Indeed, some believe that members depend too heavily on these "unelected representatives" on their personal and committee staffs.[35]) Congress as a whole has more specialization and expertise, as a result of increased staff and access to more and better data. But in the House, specialization and expertise may have declined; fewer members—only those on a given subcommittee—may be well enough informed to be considered specialists on certain topics and therefore more qualified to act decisively on particular policy issues. Fewer individuals take the lead within narrower policy domains, and when they leave Congress, or move to other full committee or subcommittee positions, the institutional memory of Congress is strained, possibly lessening the ability to draw on past experience in solving current problems.[36]

In addition, the existence of more House subcommittees may have made members more vulnerable to the pressures of interest group representatives. Lawmakers with responsibility for particular programs are fewer in number and thus more easily identifiable. Lobbyists know whom to approach with useful information and valuable electoral support; members have both opportunity and incentive to enter into mutually beneficial (in a narrow sense) relationships with group representatives and executive branch personnel having a concern for particular topics. The broader national interest may get less attention than it deserves in these circumstances. Finally, independent subcommittees add a new layer to the decision-making process. To have a chance of passage, programs must now clear subcommittee and full committee hurdles. Committee and party leaders must consult more members, particularly because subcommittee jurisdictions are not always clearly defined and several panels may insist on considering the same piece of pending legislation simultaneously. Indeed, jurisdictional struggles among subcommittees as well as among their parent panels are increasingly common. As noted in Chapter 3, the Bolling committee failed in its efforts to redefine and systematize committee jurisdictions; the 1977 Senate reforms improved but did not totally resolve the problem of overlapping committee jurisdictions. The 1993 Joint Committee on the Organization of Congress undertook, once again, to wrestle with the jurisdictional tangle. To deal with this organizational complexity takes time, and legislation may be slowed (if not sidetracked altogether) by the need to consider compromises and to construct coalitions from among so many participants.

In the Senate the story is different, but the result is the same. Individualism has long been the hallmark of senatorial behavior, and reform has not undercut individual members' freedom of action. The major impact of the relatively modest reform in the Senate was to provide members with augmented staff resources, which have contributed to their independence from committee and party discipline. Senators, like representatives, are able to pursue their policy predilections relatively unencumbered by any limitations. For Congress as a whole, then, reform has greatly increased the potential for individual participation in policy making, that is, for responsiveness. But the cost has been decreased ability to accelerate the movement of innovative public programs through the stages of the legislative process. More responsiveness may mean reduced responsibility. By multiplying the number of power centers, reform and change have increased the need for elaborate bargaining and compromise to reach agreement.

Accountability and Permeability

The second major thrust of the reform movement to create a more democratic Congress was the opening of legislative deliberations and legislators' finances to citizen and mass media consideration. The more the public knows about lawmakers' legislative activity and connections to pressure groups, economic interests, individual campaign contributors, and PACs, the greater its opportunity to hold members to account. In principle, sunshine laws, Federal Election Campaign Act disclosure provisions, and congressional codes of ethics have put legislators' accounts and activity on public display.

In practice, unless Congress decreed otherwise, the vast majority of congressional proceedings—in subcommittee, full committee, on the floor, and in conference—were public sessions; more than 90 percent of all such meetings were open. Members file their financial disclosure information with the Federal Election Commission and the media publicize it; the number of millionaires in the Senate (usually at least one-third of the membership) makes good copy. Citizens are in a much stronger position to evaluate the content and motivation of legislators' behavior and to hold them to account for it. To the extent that citizens make such judgments and act on them, they will participate more fully in legislative politics and the assembly will be more democratic. To the degree that lawmakers listen to and respect the public verdicts, Congress will be more responsive to public preferences.

Yet beneath the seeming success of these reforms lies a different reality. First, there is little if any persuasive evidence that citizens pay more attention to Congress than they did in the prereform era. Polls reveal that the electorate is not better informed about legislative action. Voters do not seem more able to name their incumbent representative, although many can recognize his or her name when it is presented to them.[37] There has been no detectable increase in issue-based voting in congressional elections; incumbency and partisanship, more than policy positions, still influence voters' opinions of Congress and congressional candidates.[38] Most incumbents continue to win reelection with relative ease. In 1990, however, possibly because of Congress's difficulty in passing a budget, a number survived with reduced pluralities. In 1992, when the public was allegedly fevered with anti-incumbent passion as a consequence of policy gridlock and the House banking and Post Office scandals, 88 percent of the sitting members (325 of 368) seeking reelection retained their seats in the House. As in 1990, however, many saw their majorities sharply reduced.[39]

Nor is there any sign that the public's assessment of Congress relative to other American political institutions has become more positive. In December 1984, 28 percent of the respondents in a Harris Survey professed to have "a great deal of confidence" in Congress. (The figure for the White House was 42 percent.) In June 1985, 32 percent expressed "positive" feelings about Congress (thought it was doing an "excellent" or "pretty good" job), while 46 percent harbored "negative" views of the legislature (rated its performance as "only fair" or "poor"). The scandals and difficulties of the late 1980s and early 1990s only made matters worse. By 1992, public confidence in Congress had reached an all-time low; in March of that year, only 18 percent of the population approved of the way Congress was doing its job. Citizens felt strongly that unethical behavior was rife on Capitol Hill and that the lawmakers were out of touch with ordinary people. Paradoxically, however, citizens continued to think well of their own senators and representatives. Two polls conducted in March 1992, at the height of popular disapproval of Congress as an institution, revealed that 56 percent and 54 percent of the respondents felt their own legislator merited reelection.[40]

Second, with committee proceedings and voting now matters of public record, lawmakers can no longer hide behind closed doors or enjoy the anonymity of unrecorded votes; they must act in the open.

With the media, ordinary citizens, and campaign contributors watching, they must take care to protect their electoral flanks. Increasingly, committees have resorted to "executive" or "informal" sessions, held prior to official meetings, where the members can talk freely and develop compromises without the intrusive presence of outsiders. In formal meetings, legislators may do little more than ratify agreements reached in private. Rep. Bill Frenzel (R-Minn.), who began his legislative service as a self-proclaimed "open meeting freak," observed that "since our meetings have been closed, our work has been less flawed . . . and our consensuses much stronger. I think it's the only way to fly." [41] The presence of lobbyists and administrative officials at public sessions—where they can monitor members' behavior, offer the texts of amendments, and notify their employers when and where to apply pressure—may have made it more difficult for committees to act decisively, to be responsible.

The rise of single-interest groups and PACs during the reform era may have made legislators less willing to risk offending any potentially decisive electoral force. Prudent lawmakers may feel obliged to resist party or presidential calls for support. Previously, members could affirm their support undetected, in the quiet of the committee room, or in a standing or teller vote on the floor, but at present there are dangers in doing so. Members may be loath to act at all, preferring to entrench themselves as ombudsmen and claiming credit for serving the district; or they may limit their policy making to "position taking"—choosing sides on substantive questions only when it is safe to do so. They may even obfuscate their stands to minimize the danger of being caught on the wrong side of a policy issue that turns out to be controversial.[42]

The financial disclosure requirement contained in the House and Senate ethics codes, first enacted in 1977, has not had much visible effect. There has been little if any diminution in the frequency or number of ethical problems faced by representatives and senators. The Senate "denounced" Herman Talmadge (D-Ga.) for campaign finance improprieties. The House Ethics Committee has been busy. As a result of its findings, the House censured Charles Diggs (D-Mich.) and Charles Wilson (D-Calif.) for improper financial dealings and expelled Michael Myers (D-Pa.) after he had been snared in the Abscam net. Others implicated in the Abscam scandal chose to resign, presumably to avoid expulsion. More recently, the Senate reproved Mark Hatfield (R-Ore.) and David Durenberger (R-Minn.) for financial irregularities and chastised the Keating Five for having used poor judgment or worse in attempting to influence regulators' treatment of a troubled savings and loan association. The Senate Ethics Committee investigated charges of sexual harassment against Brock Adams (D-Wash.), who declined to seek reelection, and Bob Packwood (R-Ore.).

But if there has been no reduction in malfeasance in the aftermath of reform, the future may be more promising. Voters, for their part, have not been particularly sympathetic to those legislators revealed as corrupt in some way or other. In 1980, Talmadge was denied reelection; the voters also delivered a resounding verdict (matched only by those in the criminal courts) that retired from office all save one of those accused in Abscam. In elections in Idaho, Republican representative George Hansen, convicted in 1984 of filing false financial disclosure forms, was narrowly defeated. In the 1990s, the electorate has been no kinder to legislators tarred in some way by scandal. "Abusers" of the House bank were prominent among the incumbent losers in 1992; voters also turned out Nicholas Mavroules (D-Mass.) after he was indicted on nineteen counts of fraud and bribery. These were dramatic cases—featuring videotapes of money changing hands and allegations of coat pockets stuffed with cash—conduct clearly offensive to many Americans' sense of morality. The effect of the ethics codes and financial disclosure requirements on more mundane conflicts of interest (for example, self-serving but legal behavior) remains unclear.

Campaign finance reform has had paradoxical results.[43] The new campaign election law—with its full disclosure provisions and its limits on contributions but not on expenditures—has seemingly helped to entrench incumbents, especially in the House. With presidential campaigns federally funded in full, private groups, particularly the newly legitimized PACs, have channeled their resources into congressional contests. Federal Election Commission data and Common Cause studies suggest that these donors have preferred the safe course of contributing to incumbents, many of whom hold potentially powerful committee or party positions in Congress, to the riskier strategy of funding challengers, who might someday hold prominent posts.[44] Incumbents start with sizable advantages accruing from the perquisites of office, and unless their opponents can raise and spend significant sums—often as much as a half million dollars—their prospects range from zero to nil. Gary Jacobson concludes that "any measure that limits the money available to candidates benefits incumbents." [45] Certainly, contribution limits appear to hinder financially needy House challengers; thus the members of the "out party," the Republicans, continue to oppose such limits. Senate contests, by contrast, tend to be more competitive.[46] Challengers are often more visible and attractive, better able to solicit the funds they need, and in consequence more likely to unseat the incumbent.[47]

To the degree that incumbent electoral security reduces personnel turnover in Congress, legislative accountability, however plausible in principle, will be inhibited. Old members espousing old points of view will continue to serve, even if they are out of touch, in policy terms, with their constituents, because they can fend off serious challenges. Only on those uncommon occasions when many voters become irate and let their legislators know about it will incumbents need to worry about being held to account. Most of the time, sitting lawmakers will continue to have considerable freedom to pursue their personal policy preferences.

This is not to say that the link between funding and votes is not well publicized. Specialized media and the large city dailies frequently note which groups contribute to which members of Congress and speculate about the possible effects of these donations on legislative behavior. For example, the Associated Press reported in 1985 that the PACs of the 20 largest defense contractors contributed more than $3.5 million to congressional and presidential campaigns in 1983-1984. They channeled their donations to key committee members. Sen. John Warner (R-Va.), a senior member of the Armed Services Committee, which has jurisdiction over the controversial MX missile, received $80,050 from defense industry PACs. Sen. Ted Stevens (R-Alaska), chairman of the Appropriations subcommittee that funds the MX, got $60,800 from the same PACs. In the House, the defense PACs gave Joseph Addabbo (D-N.Y.), chairman of the Appropriations subcommittee that considers the MX, $48,403; four other subcommittee Democrats got contributions in excess of $34,000 each. Overall, 13 of the 14 senators who received $30,000 or more from defense industry PACs, and 17 of the 20 House members to whom these PACs contributed at least $15,000, voted in March 1985 to build 21 more MX missiles.[48] It is difficult to know what to make of such contribution patterns. Do financial donations "buy" influence, or do PACs simply reward "friends" who already support group interests?[49] Citizens can find out who bankrolls the elected representatives and how those legislators vote, but the evidence, on balance, suggests that few engage in the complicated investigation and analysis necessary to hold their lawmakers to strict account.

Campaign finance and personal disclosure requirements have made life difficult for many members of Congress, however. During the latter half of the 1970s, record numbers of legislators chose to retire rather than risk the relentless exposure of their daily routines, and those of their families, to public scrutiny. Many left Congress at relatively young ages (in their fifties), having acquired substantial seniority and positions of some prominence and power. The increase in aggressive investigative reporting in the wake of Watergate no doubt accounts, at least in part, for this increased attention to the personal lives of legislators. Revelations that formerly were unreported—bouts with alcoholism, family problems, questionable financial transactions, even brushes with the law—became fair game for the media. Many lawmakers who found the rewards of legislative service not worth the long

hours and loss of privacy chose to pursue other careers.[50] In the four
elections from 1966 to 1972, an average of 18.5 representatives and 4.75
senators declined to seek reelection; in the reform era elections from
1974 to 1980, the figures were 43.3 and 7.5, respectively. The exodus
slowed appreciably in the 1980s; from 1982 to 1990, an average of 30.2
representatives and 4.4 senators retired. Members seemed increasingly
prepared to endure the attention that their positions in Congress at-
tracted.[51] In 1992, however, redistricting, scandal, and an expected
voter backlash against incumbents induced 67 House members to retire—an extraordinary departure.

The potential for citizen-enforced accountability is real, but unre-
alized. The public can, if it so chooses, hold members accountable, but
in reality it does not seem more aware of, or more sympathetic to,
Congress or its members, their activities, or their performance. In sum,
although congressional activity is certainly more accessible to citizens,
as the reformers hoped, the weight of the accumulated evidence suggests that the sunshine reforms have had limited effects. In fact, visibility may contribute to legislative inertia. Ever aware that they are, in a
real sense, on display, members may conclude that concern for constituents and policy caution, inaction, is the wisest course. Rather than risk
alienating constituents and groups whose reelection support they feel
is vital, they may avoid controversy and decline to act. Thus, by increasing the possibility for external actors to participate in congressional politics, the accountability reforms may have made Congress not
only more democratic but also more permeable—more open to pressures from voters and organized interests that reduce the institution's
ability to make effective public policy. Steps to increase accountability,
like those to promote decentralization (responsiveness), may have in-
advertently undercut congressional responsibility.

Responsibility and Centralization

Although reformers were eager to democratize Congress, to make it
more responsive and accountable, they were not unmindful of the
institution's shortcomings as an efficient policy maker. Consequently,
they moved to reduce congressional inertia. Flowing directly from the
legislative reaction to Vietnam and Watergate and impelled by the
Democratic sweep in the 1974 midterm elections was the effort to improve Congress's responsibility, the third fundamental thrust of the
reform movement. Specifically, the reformers aimed at increasing the
assembly's ability to assert and sustain legislative priorities even in the
face of determined executive opposition. They also sought to
strengthen the political parties in the hope of giving at least a modi-

cum of centralized, efficient direction to congressional policy making. To the same end Congress enacted a number of rules changes designed to ease the flow of legislation through a complicated legislative process. Once again, the reformers won some victories, suffered some setbacks, and occasionally produced results that they had not foreseen.

Battling the Executive

Nowhere is the difficulty in disentangling the effects of reform from those of more general political change more obvious than in evaluating the impact of the congressional assault on executive branch prerogatives. The War Powers Act and the Congressional Budget and Impoundment Control Act, the two most obvious manifestations of congressional revival, were passed in 1973 and 1974, respectively—a time of popular discontent, rapid turnover in Congress, and a scandal-ridden and politically vulnerable presidency. Rapidly changing events, new issues, and the election of new members converged to create the conditions in which Congress could launch a major challenge to the executive. External change, then, may have contributed as much as internal reform to the state of executive-legislative relations from the late 1970s to end of the 1980s. There has been no clear test of the war powers provisions and Congress has yet to establish a workable budget process. The available evidence suggests that, to date, Congress has not used its reclaimed authority to impose its will on the executive in a systematic way, especially in the military realm.

The War Powers Act. Overall, the available evidence concerning two decades of experience suggests a mixed set of outcomes. Congress has not had any appreciable impact on the president's commitment of troops to combat. But it has, from time to time, asserted its preferences using its constitutional authorization and appropriations powers. The president has felt obliged regularly to report to Congress in compliance with the War Powers Act, but most military adventures (Gerald Ford's recapture of the ship *Mayaguez*, seized by Cambodia in 1975; Jimmy Carter's abortive effort in 1979 to free the American hostages held in Iran; and George Bush's "arrest" of Panamanian General Manuel Noriega) were short-lived and were over before a decentralized Congress could formulate a meaningful response.

On two occasions, however, Congress played a visible role. In 1983, it forced Ronald Reagan to acknowledge his obligations under the War Powers Act and in return authorized sending U.S. Marines to Lebanon for eighteen months. On the eve of the 1991 Persian Gulf War, lawmakers voted, by a narrow 53-46 margin in the Senate, to permit George Bush to use force to end the Iraqi occupation of Kuwait. Even in these instances, the chief executive declined to recognize congressional assertion of war powers as legitimate. On decisions to use the military to provide humanitarian relief to Somalia and Bosnia, to which Congress acquiesced, the resolution was scarcely mentioned.

In most cases, the president complied with the letter if not the spirit of the statute. The law obligates the chief executive to consult with Congress, whenever possible, before committing U.S. troops to combat. Crisis situations make widespread discussion of military action difficult if not impossible, and presidents have limited their contacts with legislators to informing a select few (usually those expected to be sympathetic), rather than soliciting congressional opinion before making policy choices. The Iranian rescue mission is not a promising precedent for compliance with the consultation provisions of the War Powers Act. Given the long planning period that preceded the action, the Carter administration could easily have involved congressional leaders in its deliberations; it chose not to, and the members of Congress, although they voiced a few complaints, accepted the chief executive's behavior. The act also requires the president to report to Congress within forty-eight hours after he has ordered combat troops to face "hostilities" in the field. In a majority of cases, the president has sent appropriate messages, but he has asserted that he has done so as a courtesy, not in compliance with the act itself.[52] Ronald Reagan's use of marines as part of a multinational peacekeeping force in Lebanon in 1983 and 1984 illustrates the difficulties that can arise in such instances. The president claimed that since there were no real or imminent hostilities in the area, the act did not apply. But when violence escalated and the American forces suffered casualties, some in Congress protested Reagan's rejection of the act. The resulting compromise allowed Congress to claim a victory in winning the president's acceptance of the act, but he retained control over U.S. policy in the Middle East.

In reality, Congress has the opportunity to participate in military policy making only when U.S. troops remain in the field for extended periods. Under these circumstances, Congress can act decisively, ordering the troops home if it wishes, or it can make policy by default—by doing nothing and thus requiring the president to cease military operations after sixty days (see section on "Taming the Executive" in Chapter 3). The issue, of course, is whether the legislature will impose its preferences on the commander in chief, who will most certainly invoke the "national interest," the nation's prestige and honor, and the gravity of the situation. There is no reason to believe with certainty that members of Congress will be prepared in such circumstances to run the risk or assume the responsibility of overruling the chief executive.[53]

The War Powers Act may be more significant as a deterrent to pre-

cipitous or dubious armed intervention. Never entirely certain that
Congress will approve their actions, presidents may think twice before
committing troops abroad. For example, there was widespread specula-
tion that the Ford administration in 1974 was considering direct intervention in the Angolan civil war. The foreign policy committees of
Congress, especially the Senate Foreign Relations Committee, became
increasingly concerned, given what had happened in Vietnam, that
American commitment of money and weapons might escalate into military support of the faction favored by the United States. Such forthright expression of concern may well have contributed to executive
caution. No use of American troops was ever officially proposed.[54] Similar doubts about congressional reaction seem to have restrained the
Clinton administration's desire to commit troops to a U.N. mission to
enforce a cease fire in Bosnia.

Congress's success in imposing its military and foreign policy judgments on the executive has been uneven. To be sure, Congress has
flexed its institutional muscle frequently. The Senate refused to ratify
the second Strategic Arms Limitation Treaty (SALT II); repeatedly the
legislature has blocked or delayed (by threatening to use the legislative
veto) arms sales, the export of nuclear materials, and the ratification of
numerous treaties with neighboring nations (for example, maritime
treaties with Mexico and Canada failed in 1980). During the Reagan
administration, Congress regularly cut the defense budget below the
president's request (but allowed budget expenditures to rise dramatically above previous levels), imposed limits on production and deploy-
ment of the MX missile (but refused to eliminate the system entirely),
delayed production of new forms of chemical weapons, and reallocated military and economic assistance to foreign nations. Thomas
Franck and Edward Weisband view such actions as a beneficial reassertion of congressional foreign policy powers.[55]

Some signs point to a revival of legislative deference to the executive, however. Heightened international tensions increase risk to the
United States and incline legislators to accept the views of the professional military and the intelligence community. For instance, Congress
backed away from a comprehensive charter to regulate the activities of
the Central Intelligence Agency, and although it did assert its right to
prior notice of covert operations overseas, it reduced from eight to two
the number of congressional committees entitled to be informed about
CIA covert activities.[56] Fewer overseers, especially if they are carefully
briefed, may mean less intense legislative scrutiny of CIA operations.

Similarly, the fiscal 1981 foreign aid authorization bill, enacted in
response to the Indochina conflict, relaxed a number of constraints on
presidential discretion so that aid funds would be employed flexibly.
In 1985, after restricting intelligence operations in Nicaragua and bar-

ring all military involvement there, Congress reversed itself. It removed the restrictions and voted nonmilitary humanitarian aid to the rebel contras seeking to overthrow the Sandinista government. One widely touted explanation for this abrupt policy change was that members of Congress, especially Democrats, feared that constituents would fault them for being "soft on defense." A less cynical view is that the change was a sensible way to handle the difficult issue of dealing with an unfriendly government. Domestic problems with equally obvious electoral implications—the economy, taxation, social issues such as school prayer and abortion, or another energy crisis—may lead members to redirect their attention to the home front, leaving international matters to the chief executive.[57] In the early days of the Clinton administration, Congress was sharply divided about whether to push a reluctant president to act to counter Serbian aggression against Bosnian Muslims.

In sum, although presidents can no longer count on customary congressional acquiescence to their foreign policy initiatives, the legislature's assertiveness may be less a reflection of organizational reform than of more general, evolutionary change. Even without reform, new members with new ideas on new issues, eager to secure the support of their constituents, may be willing to use basic legislative prerogatives to challenge the administration. As membership and situations change, the old pattern of congressional subordination might reappear. Members' policy preferences and political purposes, more than institutional reforms, may be the decisive determinants of whether Congress challenges the chief executive.

The Congressional Budget and Impoundment Control Act. Assessment of the new budget process, as an example of legislative revival, yields a similarly cloudy picture: reform has intersected with other forms of change to produce unpredictable results. Here the situation is complicated by different budgetary procedures in the House and Senate. Moreover, the multiple motives of the reformers—recapturing fiscal power from the executive and pursuing liberal or conservative policy goals—inevitably lead to different views on the budget. From any vantage point, however, the revised procedures have produced a variable congressional record, one marked by both successes and failures.[58]

On the plus side, the 1974 act has clearly restored Congress's *potential* to assert its supremacy in fiscal matters. The Congressional Budget Office—which Aaron Wildavsky describes as "the best source of budget numbers in Washington"—provides Congress with reliable information with which to formulate independent budget proposals.[59] There is little doubt that if and when Congress wants to act decisively, it can invoke the provisions and procedures of the act to do so. On numerous occasions, congressional budget resolutions substantially reordered the executive's budget priorities. The new reconciliation process contained in the act presents the opportunity to impose discipline, to limit spending and deficits significantly. But promise is not performance; to date, Congress's willingness and ability to use the law to meet its proponents' aims have been limited. Indeed, continuing and accelerating discontent with the process has led to a series of efforts, largely problematic, to revise the way Congress creates the nation's budgets.

Early experience with the new process, however, produced some auspicious signs. Between 1975 and 1979, Congress observed the form of the new plan; for the most part, it formulated a coherent budget, specifying revenues, outlays, and the size of the deficit, although it did deviate somewhat from the prescribed timetable. The process thus looked as if it could produce the desired coherence and efficiency. This possibility was particularly evident in the Senate, where the Budget Committee worked well under the bipartisan leadership of Edmund Muskie (D-Me.), the chair, and Henry Bellmon (R-Okla.), the ranking minority member. It was careful to conform to the chamber's norms, individualism and reciprocity, and to avoid direct challenges to the other standing committees.[60]

The situation in the House was quite different. Motives beyond establishing a more rational budget process seem to have induced the chamber to limit the potential of its Budget Committee. House rules restrict service on that committee to three terms. Rotation of members reduces the long-term possibility of internal House influence and constrains the development of committee norms and expertise. House rules also mandate committee membership for representatives of the other revenue-related committees and the party leadership—Appropriations, and Ways and Means have five seats each on the Budget Committee; each party designates one member. In consequence, assignments went to liberal Democrats and conservative Republicans who, in pursuing their policy preferences, stressed partisanship and ideology; the result was a panel that was both polarized and volatile.[61] Partisanship, in fact, threatened the process, and the House was hard pressed to comply with the act, often passing the budget resolutions late and by slender margins.

Although the House did act more or less responsibly in passing a budget, those who had perceived budget reform as a way to alter the substance of policy found the record of the 1970s less promising— uneven at best, and disappointing in general. Conservatives hoped the process would enable them to spend less for domestic social programs and more on defense; liberals desired to reverse these priorities. Congress did depart substantially from the president's fiscal proposals for 1976 and 1977, favoring social spending over military spending. But this result may have reflected the natural enmity between the Republican White House and the Democratic Congress as much as the operation of the budget process itself. In contrast, some analysts have found the congressional impact on budgetary priorities in the period 1975-1979 as moderate to low.[62]

In short, between 1974 and 1979 the new process, as process, worked reasonably well. As a device to alter spending priorities, however, the process proved unsatisfactory to many observers. Reformers eager to slow the growth of federal expenditures and the national debt were particularly distressed, for the revised process slowed neither; both the budget and the debt continued seemingly inexorably on their upward spiral.[63] In fact, the new budget committees created by the act added another layer of participants in the budgetary routine, on top of the appropriations and tax panels. More interests had to be accommodated before a budget resolution could be adopted. In any case, in its early years the budget process did shift some influence to Congress and establish the basis for more efficient and informed congressional decision making; it did *not* always produce the substantive results its proponents would have preferred.

By decade's end, however, political and economic circumstances had changed dramatically; so, too, had the operation of the new budget process. Economic conditions deteriorated rapidly during the Carter administration. Inflation and unemployment soared, government revenues declined, and the deficit swelled. There was simply too little money available to fund the multitude of federal programs on the books. Congressional budgeting rested on the assumption that the legislature would have ample resources to distribute—an untenable premise by the late 1970s. An age of scarcity, of limited resources, had replaced the age of affluence. The conventional budgetary politics of distribution—dispersing funds to please the constituents and placate the special interests—no longer sufficed in a period of economic hardship.

Moreover, Congress itself changed during the 1970s. Its membership turned over rapidly, at least by conventional standards. Retirement rates rose rapidly in the latter half of the decade; seventy-five freshman Democrats had won House seats in 1974. New members took their places in a legislative system fundamentally altered by reform. The democratizing trend of 1970-1977 gave them positions of influence, particularly in subcommittees, from which to shape policy. To strengthen their support back home, new members had a strong incentive to continue distributive budget practices at a time when the economy was unable to provide the money to sustain the programs they desired. Budgetary processes collided with economic realities.

The 1980 elections were the catalyst for change. Ronald Reagan was not only elected by a landslide but the electorate gave him working majorities in both houses of Congress—clear control of the Senate and a revived conservative coalition of Republicans and southern Democrats in the House. Building on its political momentum, the new administration led the nation from a period of distribution to a period of redistribution. Reconciliation, used innovatively and in unforeseen ways, was the means by which to reorient the budget process.[64]

Post-1980 budgeting was consistent with the responsible parties and executive force theories (Chapter 1). Disciplined majorities in each chamber passed a budget that largely reflected the president's preferences: $100 billion in spending cuts and program reductions over a three-year period (1981-1983). Democratic alternatives, aimed at preserving the status quo, were turned aside.

The 1974 act intended *reconciliation*, which imposes a ceiling on total permissible expenditures, as a device to instruct committees to conform to the second binding budget resolution. Defining the fiscal "pie" in advance requires congressional budgeters to allocate available funds among numerous claimants without exceeding the mandated spending limits. Since there is not sufficient money to go around, there inevitably will be winners and losers; that is, redistribution will be the result of stringent reconciliation resolutions. The second budget resolution was due in September, but the Reagan administration, building on a precedent of the 1979 budget cycle, employed reconciliation in conjunction with the first resolution due in May, thus setting the terms of the budget debate entirely to its liking. Because the reconciliation instructions were passed early in the budget season, the issue was not whether to cut federal spending, but where and how much.

In 1981, the Reagan administration had the votes to impose severe (opponents said Draconian) reconciliation instructions on House and Senate committees. It achieved its purpose: "to limit the growth of . . . government by limiting the revenues available to be spent." [65] In practice, the reconciliation procedure culminates in a single bill, subject only to one take-it-or-leave-it, up-or-down vote.[66] It precludes individual votes on individual programs, proposed by numerous interests. In other words, reconciliation shifts discussion of the budget process from cuts in individual programs and their effects to a broader concern for the benefits that the total package of reductions will provide, consistent with the national interest.[67] The president proposed a budget and Congress, in the early days of Reagan's tenure, disposed of it consistently with his preferences.

The budget process, as it worked in 1981, did little to restore Congress's influence in financial matters; to the contrary, it subordinated the legislature to the administration, as the executive force theorists would have it. In one sense the process was efficient; a centralized procedure produced a budget with dispatch early in the legislative session. But in another sense efficiency declined. Beset by fiscal constraints and partisan conflict (the Democratic House battling the Republican Senate and White House), Congress became increasingly unable to pass appropriations bills. It therefore had to fund government programs by passing a *continuing resolution*, which permits spending to continue at the previous year's level until an appropriations measure clears Congress; in 1983, seven of the thirteen regular appropriations bills were funded under a continuing resolution for the entire fiscal year. In addition, Congress was unable to pass the second budget resolution; as a result, it decided in 1981 that the first resolution would automatically become binding unless a second resolution was passed. In sum, efficiency in terms of meeting the budget act's deadlines declined after 1980. Conservatives were relatively pleased with fiscal outcomes in the post-1980 phase of budget allocations: social programs received a decreasing share of federal funds, defense an enlarged portion. But total spending did not decline, and the deficits not only persisted but also soared to record heights. Liberals, conversely, took little solace in budget allocations under Ronald Reagan. From either perspective, it seems clear that the new economic and political conditions were conducive to a radical transformation of the budget process that the reformers has so adroitly crafted in 1974.

In the years following the 1981 Reagan "blitz," congressional budgeting took on a more "normal" cast. Individualistic members pursuing a multitude of personal economic aims fought vigorously in support of financial priorities consistent with their own values and those of their constituents. Congress used reconciliation to challenge at least some of the president's priorities. The House, where the 1982 and 1984 elections restored a working Democratic majority, forced the administration and the Republican-controlled Senate to back away from a proposal, passed in that chamber, to freeze the level of Social Security benefits for fiscal 1986. In addition, Congress made substantial cuts in the defense budget. Although the president requested an after-inflation increase of roughly 6 percent, the final defense budget figure reflected only a 3 percent increase to compensate for inflation. The president sought, with Senate support, to terminate more than a dozen federal programs, but the Democratic House successfully defended ongoing social programs; many were cut, but only one program (revenue sharing) was terminated. The complicated politics involved in reaching these settlements, which reduced the growth rate but not the size of either government spending or the deficit, delayed passage of the first resolution until August 1, 1985. Overall, many congressional priorities prevailed, indicating again that the legislature can, when it has the will to act, use the budget process to substitute its views for those of the chief executive.

Between 1982 and 1985, the budget process survived but did not achieve the purposes its proponents had envisioned. Resolutions were passed, reconciliation procedures were employed, but there was no budgetary discipline. There also seemed to be no agreement, in the nation as a whole or in Washington, on what the priorities should be financially. Some wanted tax cuts to stimulate the economy; others advocated cutting excessive social spending; many felt large defense expenditures were essential. Some believed that social programs, not defense, deserved priority; if tax increases were necessary to pay for these initiatives, they should be enacted. No middle ground, no basis for compromise, emerged. In Congress, the budget process proved incapable of producing majorities (as it had in 1981) that could devise a broad, coherent budget reflecting congressional priorities. Too many individualist lawmakers, acting within the highly decentralized system that reform had institutionalized, prevented Congress from realizing the goals of the 1974 act. Congress struggled to preserve the outlines of the process but was willing to bend the rules—waive requirements, ignore the timetables, reverse the order in which actions were taken, bypass the budget committees—in pursuit of more important policy goals. The deficit, spiraling upward, demonstrated the failure of congressional budgeting dramatically and incontrovertibly. By the end of 1985, it was obvious that only some radical reform could save the day.

In 1985, Congress acted forcefully to revise the budget process, at least temporarily, to deal with the deficit crisis. The Democrats seized the issue as one with which to challenge the Republican administration; poll after poll revealed that the public shared their concern about the deficit. Given the sensitivity of elected politicians to a potentially aroused electorate, it is not surprising that Congress decided to try once again to reform the budget process. With the reluctant endorsement of President Reagan, a coalition of House Democrats and Senate Republicans secured passage of the Gramm-Rudman-Hollings bill, a new scheme to balance the budget by 1991. The bill added another dimension to the regular congressional budget routine. If the usual process failed to reduce the deficit by a specified amount, the president is obligated automatically to "sequester" funds, that is, cut the budget to reduce the deficit to the required level. Some programs (Social Security, for example) are exempt from cuts, but the chief executive was given little discretion; the cuts are to be made equally in the domestic and defense portions of the budget, at a fixed percentage sufficient to lower the deficit to the mandatory target for each year. Substantively, then, Congress tried to force itself, and the president, to adopt policies that would eliminate the deficit over a six-year period.[68]

On balance, GRH had at best a moderating influence on deficits; it

sensitized members of Congress, as they pored over budget and reconciliation bills, to the need to restrain spending. Deficits, however, remained unacceptably high. The mandated levels were met on paper,
but breached when money was actually spent. The perennial problems—lack of agreement on levels of taxation and spending for military and domestic programs—led to stalemate. Majorities in favor of
budget discipline were not more likely to form under GRH than they
had been before 1986. The law did not compel members to make the
ordinary process work; rather it led to delay and obfuscation as the
lawmakers sought to protect their individual programmatic interests.
They resorted to a variety of gimmicks, "blue smoke and mirrors," to
comply with the letter of the law. For example, having made optimistic
economic assumptions—a high growth rate that would allegedly produce more revenue, low unemployment that would hold down government outlays for those without jobs, low interest rates that would
reduce the costs of servicing the national debt—they wrote resolutions
whose effect would be to produce higher income and lower spending,
and thus lower deficits, than might realistically have been expected.
They increased revenue by proposing one-time sales of government
assets—loans or resources such as oil from the Naval Petroleum Re-
serve. They moved items "off-budget" so they did not count against
the deficit. They moved one military payday from September 30 to
October 1, thus putting a multibillion dollar item in a subsequent fiscal
year and lowering the deficit for the current one. These dodges, coupled with some genuine revenue-producing and expenditure-reduc-
ing measures, enabled Congress to observe the form of the budget
process. The deficit, however, did not come down to the prescribed
levels; indeed, for fiscal 1990, it reached a near-record level of $220.4
billion. The GRH threat of severe automatic budget cuts did little if
anything to force individualistic members of Congress to abandon
short-run responsiveness in defense of favored programs for long-
term responsibility to control the deficit.

By 1990, it was readily apparent that GRH procedures were not going to bring the deficit under control. In fact, the process collapsed
during Congress's attempt to pass a budget resolution for fiscal 1991. In
passing the Budget Enforcement Act of 1990 directly after a summit
conference at which congressional leaders negotiated with officials of
the Bush administration, Congress abandoned the Gramm-Rudman-
Hollings effort to limit the deficit directly. The BEA seeks to control
separate categories of expenditures in order to hold down the deficit.
Although deficit targets are retained, separate binding budget ceilings
are set for discretionary spending for domestic, military, and international programs. Money saved in one area cannot be transferred to be
spent on another. A pay-as-you-go arrangement requires that the bud-

get be "deficit-neutral"; new expenditures must be offset by new taxes or cuts in spending on old programs. Sequesters in each expenditure category remain in place to enforce adherence to the spending caps. The new process is to guarantee compliance with a five-year budget plan intended to bring the deficit under control by fiscal year 1995.[69]

Overall, the BEA increases budgetary responsibility somewhat, but at the expense, from a congressional supremacy theorist's viewpoint, of subordinating a centralized budget process to increased presidential influence. The pay-as-you-go requirements essentially make budgeting a zero-sum game. The 1990 act, reflecting presidential as well as congressional priorities, sets expenditure totals for five years. Budgeting, in consequence, is not about how much to spend but about for what purposes to spend. To the extent that the spending levels reflect the views of the president and congressional leaders— party chiefs and the budget insiders on the appropriations committees—the process is more centralized. The fixed expenditure ceilings constrain the budget committees and the authorizing panels, which thus have considerably less freedom to shape the contours of the budget. Congressional leaders have more influence in a more centralized, "top-down" process, but they have had to negotiate with the executive branch the budget totals they seek to enact.

The leaders may have more authority to impose budgetary responsibility and rank-and-file legislators may have less opportunity to respond to personal and constituency interests; nonetheless, "specific policy outcomes are not likely to change dramatically as a result of BEA."[70] The leaders not only must negotiate with the president about spending priorities and revenue sources but must build coalitions in support of their budgets by appealing to election-conscious, constituency-oriented individual senators and representatives. Their leverage may have increased, but the members are far from powerless to resist. Moreover, the new rules and the complex process they create make budgeting more accessible to interest group fiscal specialists (if not to ordinary citizens) who may exert more pressure on individual legislators. In enacting budgets, lawmakers will, of necessity as before, have to sort out representative (responsiveness) and policy-making (responsibility) obligations. There is no guarantee they will act consistently with the latter. Indeed, such steps as removing Social Security surpluses from deficit calculations and exempting "emergency" spending from the mandatory spending caps may be an easy way to avoid making the hard political choices required to control the deficit.[71]

The possibility for responsible budgeting exists, but there is scant evidence to date that the BEA has either restored congressional parity with the executive branch or enabled the legislature to impose its own budgetary priorities. And the future remains problematic. The Democratic majority in the 103d Congress will have to define its relationships with the president in a period of unified rather than divided government. Budget issues are one of the public's chief policy concerns in the aftermath of the 1992 election, which restored the Democrats to the White House. The terms of the budget act of 1990 change for fiscal 1994. A single cap on total spending replaces the three separate ceilings that were in force; trade-offs among domestic, military, and international programs will be required and will certainly complicate the building of coalitions in support of any budget. Leaders, despite their seemingly enhanced position, are unlikely to have an easy time producing a responsible budget that successfully deals with the nation's deficit and other pressing policy problems.

With respect to impoundment, the budget act has had a pronounced effect: the president is now considerably less able to regulate the flow of federal funds. Impoundment for policy purposes, as Richard Nixon practiced it, is now virtually impossible without legislative acquiescence, and the burden has been transferred to the chief executive to win that approval.[72] When Congress appropriates, the funds are more likely to be spent.

Yet the anti-impoundment provisions have had unintended consequences as well. Traditionally, impoundment was a useful and noncontroversial device that promoted efficient administration. Now all matters concerning delayed expenditures, even the most routine deferrals, must be reported to Congress. Members have complained that many hours are wasted on relatively trivial items, a concern that bureaucrats share.[73] More seriously, the 1974 act appears to give the president an authority never previously acknowledged, namely, an opportunity to delay expenditures temporarily, at least for policy purposes. The chief executive can rescind funds (previously appropriated but not spent) for forty-five days, at the end of which congressional inaction compels their release.[74] On the whole, the impoundment provisions of the budget act improve the legislature's chances to impose its priorities if it is determined to do so. Whether its resolve will hold and what such decisiveness will accomplish will depend, of course, on future conditions inside and outside Congress.

Information and Oversight. There are similar uncertainties about the results of the "information revolution." It is incontrovertible that members of Congress have more access to more data than ever before. Increased staff resources, new agencies (Congressional Budget Office and Office of Technology Assessment), more effective old support facilities (General Accounting Office and Congressional Research Service), and improved computer technology enormously increase Congress's ability to engage in serious analysis that can sustain legislative alternatives to executive initiatives.

These developments are not necessarily entirely positive, however. Members of Congress may not have adequate incentive to seize the new opportunities. Fundamentally, senators and representatives are politicians, not objective analysts. They may well be searching less for optimal policies than for programs that will serve their political purposes. They want ideas that will satisfy their constituents, and they need solutions that will survive the bargaining and compromise of a decentralized legislature. In the late 1970s and early 1980s, for example, congressional committees tended to use OTA studies of railroad safety, nutrition, energy conservation, and other issues to support members' views rather than for purposes of enlightenment. In other words, members used analysis "strategically" more than "analytically"—to rationalize their presumably politically acceptable positions rather than to "seek the truth" about complex policy questions.[75] Policy analysts who do not recognize the political needs of their principals will find their advice ignored. When politics and analysis merge, the latter may be of considerable use to legislators; when they diverge, analysis is likely to receive a low priority.

Moreover, the information now readily available may actually distract lawmakers from programmatic activities. Overwhelmed by "information overload," members may be increasingly inclined to look to their staffs for substantive guidance.[76] Staff personnel who are prepared to be "entrepreneurs" rather than impartial "professionals" thus may come to play powerful roles.[77] Dependence on the experts may undercut the members' ability to make genuinely independent judgments. Finally, there is an information management problem; members may spend more time and energy administering their large staffs than they do using the data those staffs supply. Although many offices now employ professional managers,[78] the risk remains that organizational chaos will impede legislators' ability to delve into the substance of policy questions.

For all the increased attention Congress has paid to gaining control of a runaway bureaucracy, it is not certain how much has been accomplished. Increased oversight activity—more hearings, more reports, more legislative-bureaucratic contacts—has not necessarily meant more influence; at least it has not resulted in coordinated management of the executive agencies.[79] This probably suits most members of Congress, who, for policy or reelection reasons, prefer exerting power over some small segment of the bureaucracy to exercising broader institutional control.[80]

It is not that members lack the ability to maintain close, systematic oversight of the executive branch; in fact, there has been an increase in supervisory activity in recent years. The budget deficit has reduced opportunities for policy innovation; divided government and heightened partisanship stimulated congressional Democrats to look closely at the performance of the Republican administrations of Presidents Reagan and Bush. Increased information and staff resources have enabled independent subcommittees to undertake oversight activities if they choose to do so, and they have risen to the challenge.[81] Members still lack consistent incentives to conduct systematic oversight, however. They are reluctant to impair their cozy subgovernment relationships with executive agencies and interest groups, especially if those relationships further their electoral goals.[82] They seldom anticipate major gains—policy or political—from oversight and often prefer to devote their time and energy to other endeavors. In addition, with their party restored to the White House, congressional Democrats may be reluctant to challenge "their own" administration. As a result, members are "only episodically interested"; oversight continues to be "shortsighted"[83] and, despite its potential, affects policy only "at the margins."[84]

This point should not be overstated, however. Although selective in application, oversight, where it operates, is often an effective means of imposing congressional preferences on the executive branch. Channels exist by which lawmakers, within the limits of their attention to oversight, can and do make their views known to and enforce their will on agencies and bureaus. Bureaucrats find that it is desirable to consider legislative opinion carefully. Inevitably, those lawmakers who find rewards in the exercise of oversight will alert their less attentive colleagues to join them in watching agency activity.

Similar congressional caution has undercut forceful use of the legislative veto. Beginning in the late 1970s, Congress increasingly reserved for itself the right to block bureaucratic actions, but it vetoed few executive proposals. Its ability to do so, of course, probably induces administrative restraint, but there have been relatively few direct confrontations, particularly in domestic affairs. Congress did veto four Education Department regulations and blocked a Transportation Department rule that would have required used-car dealers to reveal known defects in the autos they offer for sale. But on balance, members seem content to protect and enhance their agency contacts rather than to risk causing serious interbranch conflicts.[85]

In 1983, in *Immigration and Naturalization Service v. Chadha*, the Supreme Court greatly restricted the form and use of the legislative veto as an unconstitutional violation of the lawmaking procedure. The Court concluded that because veto decisions are, in effect, policy decisions, their passage by concurrent resolution, which does not require the president's signature, was unconstitutional. One house of Congress cannot impose a veto; rather, the legislature as a whole must present veto resolutions to the chief executive for his acquiescence or disapproval. This requirement makes the veto more difficult to use: not only must majorities be mustered in both chambers to exercise the veto, but when the president rejects a legislative veto, two-thirds majorities are necessary in both chambers to override his veto. The ruling, in principle, vastly restricts Congress's ability to impose its will on the administrative apparatus. No longer can either house, without presidential approval, force bureaucratic compliance with legislative wishes.

In practice, however, the *Chadha* decision has not crippled the exercise of congressional oversight through use of the legislative veto. Alternative procedures are still available to those in Congress interested in supervising the bureaucracy. The lawmakers can enact, as they occasionally had done previously, "report and wait" provisions that require agencies to submit proposed decisions to Congress, where they must stay for a specified period before taking effect. During that time, Congress may approve the proposals by passing a joint resolution (which the president must sign), or indicate its disapproval by not acting at all, in which case the administration is barred from implementing the proposed decisions. Congressional leverage is highest when the law requires members who support agency proposals to pass joint resolutions to express approval; unless those in favor can assemble a winning coalition, the proposals lapse. Alternatively, Congress may impose a veto through the appropriations process. Funding measures can deny expenditures for the implementation of bureaucratic decisions to which congressional majorities object. Finally, because both the executive and legislative branches benefit from the congressional veto (the former receives discretionary power, the latter retains oversight control of the exercise of that discretion), they may reach informal understandings, reflecting congressional creativity and administration acquiescence, that are likely to preserve the legislative veto as a useful oversight device.[86] For instance, in 1989, the Bush administration and Congress agreed, informally, to suspend humanitarian foreign aid to the Nicaraguan contra rebels if any one of four congressional committees raised objections. Such accommodations, if written into law, would surely run counter to the *Chadha* decision.

In sum, the Congress of the 1990s is surely better equipped to wage war with the executive branch for policy leadership. Reform has given Congress new authority (the War Powers Act and the 1974 budget act) and increased analytic capability (expanded staffs and information resources), which have strengthened its ability to define and fight for its own priorities. But possession of a capability does not necessarily ensure its use. Whether Congress in fact challenges the executive branch depends on less predictable elements of political change—events inciting members to take up arms, and their willingness and determination to mount the attack. Only when broader change—new members, new external conditions, new policy issues—coincides with more effective legislative organizations and procedures is Congress likely to act as a forceful policy maker. Congress *can* be a more responsible institution in the postreform period: in its case, willingness is all.

Revival of the Fittest: Strengthening the Political Parties

Political parties are the chief centralizing mechanism in Congress; the extent to which they achieve unity determines whether the majority can work its legislative will. Thus, reformers eager to make Congress more responsible sought not only to rearm the legislature for its battles with the executive but to reallocate authority internally. The standing committees and their frequently autocratic chairs were the reformers' chief targets. One thrust of the attack aimed at the committee oligarchs was to strengthen the political parties. More cohesive, centralized parties would be more able to move a program through Congress efficiently and effectively, to reduce the opportunities to delay and defeat proposed legislation that were inevitable in a fragmented, pluralistic body. In reality, most legislators were unwilling to surrender more than a modicum of their individual freedom to the party leaders, and the movement to increase centralization proved to be halting at best, at least in the years immediately following the initial reforms. The party leaders remained hard put to achieve cohesion in the face of member individualism and institutional decentralization. In the long run, however, the forces of change—new members, new events, and a new policy agenda—allowed the party chiefs, with the approval (indeed at the insistence) of their members, to become more forceful players in the policy-making drama.

Even in the early prereform years and into the 1980s, there were some specific party successes. Using its newly won right to approve committee chairs, the House Democratic caucus did remove three elderly and supposedly arbitrary committee chairmen, but this action caused little or no change in committee factional alignments, leadership patterns, or policy outcomes. With more loyal, mainstream Democrats in place as leaders, these committees—Agriculture, Armed Services, and Banking—continued to function in their usual manner.[87] What can be said is that committee chairs are now on notice that they have no guarantee of retaining their positions, a fact that may influence the ways they use the powers available to them. The same seems true of subcommittee chairs. In fact, the message has not been lost on those who aspire to committee and subcommittee leadership positions. Sara Crook and John Hibbing find that the party loyalty of those near the top of the seniority ladder, in position to chair committees, increased markedly after the adoption of these reforms. Potential leaders recognize the necessity of voting with their party's majority to establish their credentials as reliable partisans worthy of responsibility.[88]

The Democratic caucus also won an occasional policy victory. In 1975, it voted to instruct the Rules Committee to permit an amendment repealing the oil depletion allowance, previously defeated in the Ways and Means Committee, to be offered on the floor. The amendment passed and eventually became law. But in general, the caucus was unwilling or unable to impose discipline on its majority, thus allowing individualism to flourish.

In the Senate, where little effort had been made to increase party power, members' freedom of action continued without restriction. Even so forceful a majority leader as Robert Dole (R-Kans.) struggled to keep his Republican colleagues in line. After 1984, when twenty-two GOP senators began to prepare 1986 reelection campaigns, Dole had a hard time finding common ground on budget, farm, international trade, and military issues. His troops marched to their own drummers on these matters. Like other leaders, he tried to curb members' independence, using only modest persuasion rather than sanction, and he did not always succeed in holding his party majority together.

The House Speaker, like the Democratic caucus, made successful but infrequent use of postreform powers. Although the Rules Committee, whose majority membership he nominates, usually supports the party leadership, even it balked from time to time.[89] For example, in 1980 the panel refused to comply with a request by Speaker Thomas P. O'Neill, Jr., for restrictions on amendments to the fiscal 1981 budget reconciliation bill. And in 1985, Rules Committee Chairman Claude Pepper (D Fla.) "vowed to kill" a banking bill promoting interstate, nationwide bank operations that the Commerce Committee had approved.[90] The Speaker used his newly granted power to establish ad hoc committees to gain passage of outer continental shelf legislation in 1975 and 1976 and President Carter's energy package in 1977. Committee conflict—five committees shared jurisdiction over major aspects of the energy program—had threatened to make concerted and comprehensive action impossible.[91] In most instances, however, such encroachment by the Speaker on standing committee preserves and authority seemed too risky, and unlikely to overcome the divergent and divisive preferences of individual party members.

The Speaker's increased bill referral powers may even have been counterproductive. He can refer a bill either to several committees at once (multiple referrals varied from 6 percent of all measures introduced in the 94th Congress to 14 percent in the 99th[92]) or sequentially, and impose time limits on committee consideration. Multiple referrals have greatly complicated the problem of coordinating congressional activity. Eric Uslaner reports that multireferred legislation lingered longer in committee, was more likely to be amended, and was less likely to pass if it reached the floor, than legislation referred sequentially.[93] Far from increasing centralization, the Speaker's referral power may encourage House committees to assert their authority; indeed, chairs of full committees have often made jurisdictional claims to compensate for their otherwise declining influence.[94] Multiple referral, as practiced into the 1980s, contributed more to lawmakers' responsiveness than to their responsibility. It allowed more members on more committees to become involved with particular pieces of legislation; slowed the lawmaking process to accommodate broadened participation; and forced bargaining and compromise among the committees with jurisdiction, often leading to incremental rather than boldly innovative policy making.

In the early days of reform, then, House leaders' new powers seemed inadequate to overcome the decentralizing forces that the reform movement unleashed. In the already individualistic Senate, party leaders' managerial ability also declined.[95] In neither house did reform produce significantly stronger parties that were more able to move their programs forward.

A decade after the major organizational reforms of Congress were in place, however, the parties began to play a more prominent part in legislative decision making and to take more advantage of the potential that the 1970s reforms had conferred on them.[96] Changes in the legislative environment led lawmakers in the House, though not in the Senate, to look to the party leadership for help in achieving their policy goals. The most significant change was the restriction of possibilities for policy innovation imposed by the massive federal budget deficits. There was little or no money available to undertake new programs, and reform-induced congressional decentralization made agreement on ways to spend what was available difficult to achieve. Any provisions that emerged from committee were vulnerable to attack on the floor, where members increasingly proposed amendments to pending bills.[97] Individual members could no longer count on easy passage of their favored legislative provisions.

Divided government exacerbated the problem; House Democrats needed discipline if they were to pass legislation over the strong opposition of the Republican minority supporting the programmatic preferences and the vetoes of a confrontational Republican president. At the same time, the composition of the Democratic majority changed, making the party ideologically more homogeneous. Its southern contingent became more like the northern contingent—that is, more liberal—thus facilitating agreement on policy matters and increasing partisan voting on the floor of the House. Under these circumstances, members came to see that strong party leadership could help them achieve their policy and personal aims. They enjoined their leaders to take advantage of the resources provided them by the 1970s reforms to move party legislation forward. In the 100th Congress (1987-1988) their leader, Speaker Jim Wright (Tex.), was more than ready to seize the opportunity to lead.[98]

Beginning in the mid-1980s, the Democratic party leaders in the House became more active, more forceful in moving party legislation forward. They have also made greater use of the party apparatus. The whip system has been enlarged; in the 103d Congress (1993-1994), more than one-third of the majority Democrats (90 of 258) are part of the whip organization. The Speaker has frequently used party task forces to organize support among rank-and-file Democrats for party policy initiatives. Enhanced communication among the members has enabled the leaders to articulate their views and to determine more readily what their followers will back. Speaker Wright and his successor, Thomas Foley (Wash.), used their opportunities to dole out rewards and punishments, to persuade members to support them more aggressively. Foley, for instance, declined to reappoint Dave McCurdy (Okla.), a persistent critic of the Speaker, to chair the Select Committee on Intelligence at the start of the 103d Congress. Failure to go along with the party, it seems, may have serious political costs. More generally, Democratic House leaders have more forcefully advanced a party legislative agenda and publicly advocated passage of particular bills.[99]

House party leaders have done more of late to structure the chamber's decision-making process. They have employed multiple referral to their advantage. Though the procedure may increase the number of members who must be accommodated and thus slow down the passage of bills, it may also bypass recalcitrant committees or force them to act lest they lose out to another panel promoting an alternative point of view. Imposition of deadlines for committee action may reduce the opportunities for delay or defeat in committees (or increase those opportunities if the leaders oppose the bill). The mere fact of referral to a particular committee that claims jurisdiction may earn goodwill for the leadership that may engender subsequent support. In short, though risks are involved, multiple referral can have strategic benefits for party leaders.[100]

Party leaders have also done more to influence decision making on the floor to their advantage. They have exploited their prerogative to schedule legislation, choosing times when the prospects for winning floor votes are greatest. They have increasingly packaged many programs in omnibus bills, forcing members to vote for some objectionable provisions in order to gain passage of a larger number of desirable items. Most important, they have used their control of the Rules Committee to manage floor proceedings in ways favorable to the party. Legislation commonly reaches the floor under restrictive rules that allow only a limited number of amendments, and that often require amendments to be voted on in a particular order, thus improving the chances of those whose passage the leadership favors. Leaders have often brought bills to the floor under a suspension of the rules procedure, which, although it requires a two-thirds majority to pass legislation, limits debate to forty minutes and precludes all amendments. Republicans have complained that the majority Democrats have abused the suspension procedure, which was intended to facilitate consideration of noncontroversial bills, in order to ease passage of more important legislation. In any case, these devices have been used, singly or in combination, to structure floor consideration of bills in ways that promote party interests.[101]

Senate party leaders, by contrast, have sought to enhance their ability to move legislation, but member individualism has for the most part thwarted any attempt to increase party cohesion. Leaders often involve themselves in policy making, make greater use of policy task forces, hold more frequent meetings of their party conferences, and offer more services to members. This increased activity, however, has not produced the cohesion needed to enact legislation incorporating party programs. Individual senators often resort to the filibuster or put a "hold" on a bill, thus blocking its consideration.[102] Leaders have had to negotiate more complicated unanimous consent agreements (often difficult to obtain) to avoid filibusters. They have frequently resorted to a tracking system that acknowledges a filibuster on one piece of legislation but permits the Senate also to consider other measures. They have sought to mobilize the sixty votes needed to invoke cloture and shut off a filibuster. But they have achieved only modest success in improving Senate policy-making responsibility; the chamber remains "a collegial body biased against ... the centralization of power to leaders." [103]

Stronger political parties are more apparent in the House than in the Senate, but even in the House it is not certain that centralization is either real or permanent. House members retain the upper hand in their dealings with party leaders. David Rohde defines the new partisan arrangements as "conditional party government": "party responsibility" would exist *only if* there were widespread policy agreement among House Democrats," that is, only on "policies on which there was Democratic consensus." [104] Barbara Sinclair makes the same point:

leaders are the elected *agents* of their members; their increased involvement in the legislative process is a response to the needs and demands of the Democratic membership.... Party leaders' capacity to affect legislative outcomes depends on almost continuous member *acquiescence and assent*.[105]

Party leadership appears to depend on rank-and-file willingness to accept it. When members' policy preferences and personal political goals are served by party cohesion and unity, they will voluntarily submit to party discipline. But leaders may not be able to produce such discipline when circumstances— policy interests or constituency pressures, for instance—incline individualistic members to exploit their own power bases in a still fundamentally decentralized legislature and to act at variance with leaders' initiatives.

Leadership also depends on the talents and skills of those who rise to the top party positions. But the Speaker and the floor leaders have few sanctions with which to compel their ostensible followers to vote the party line. Party leadership power is essentially psychological— members want to back their party when and if they can. Party leaders, in the last analysis, cannot force the rank-and-file to support their initiatives; they must entreat them to vote for party programs. Sinclair identifies two broad and often irreconcilable obligations of the party hierarchy: it must assemble coalitions to pass party bills and, at the same time, it must maintain "peace in the family." [106] Maintaining party harmony is an onerous duty, given the diversity of members' ideological positions, constituency commitments (including pursuit of electoral security), and vested interests. Leaders cannot readily induce their ostensible followers to rally in favor of party positions when the rank and file confront so many pressures to go their own ways. Centralization—through reform or on some voluntary basis—is hard to achieve in these circumstances, and without it, policy-making efficiency (responsibility) remains a will-o'-the-wisp. Individual member motives, more than formal leadership authority, determine whatever party unity exists at any moment in history.

Revising the Rules

Procedural reforms have produced only minimal and often unanticipated effects. Dilatory tactics are somewhat more difficult to use and legislation is less likely to become enmeshed in parliamentary thickets in the House, although this is hard to prove conclusively. Easing quorum call requirements and permitting voting by machine, clustering of votes, and more frequent committee meetings have all helped to expedite the flow of business, but the impact of these reforms on the substance of congressional policy making has certainly been marginal.

The major rules change accomplished by reform was the revision of the Senate cloture rule (Rule 22). Sixty votes (not the simple majority that the reformers preferred), rather than two-thirds of those present and voting, are now sufficient to terminate a filibuster. But the new procedures, including curtailment of the postcloture filibuster by means of amendment, do not seem to have facilitated more rapid processing of bills. This is not because cloture has not been invoked; in fact, it has been used more successfully in recent years. There were 103 cloture votes between 1917 (when the Senate enacted its first cloture rule) and 1975 (when the 60-vote rule was passed). Of these, 24 (23.3 percent) were successful, including 2 that concluded debate on altering the filibuster rule; 16 of these occurred between 1971 and 1975, indicating a marked decline in minority power. The filibuster claimed only one bill that would have passed under the three-fifths rule (a 1974 proposal to establish a consumer protection agency). In four other cases, 60 votes were cast for cloture, but subsequently the two-thirds majority needed to cut off debate was attained and the measures passed. Under the simple majority principle, 24 additional cloture votes would have succeeded.

From 1975 to 1990, there were 196 cloture votes. Of these, 82, or 41.8 percent, succeeded—almost twice the rate in the prereform era. Between 1976 and 1989, on 41 occasions, more than 67 members voted to end debate, suggesting that cloture would have been invoked even under the more stringent two-thirds rule. In 23 other instances, however, a filibuster was ended with fewer than the 67 votes that would have been required under the old rule (if all members were present); in these cases, the new procedure may have permitted the majority to prevail more readily.[107] In sum, under the revised Rule 22, there have been more filibusters (perhaps because senators have become more willing to employ the tactic on a wider range of issues), but majority efforts to terminate debate have also been more successful (perhaps because of the smaller number of votes needed to do so). Still, more than half of the post-1975 cloture votes failed.

Apparently, the norms concerning unlimited debate have changed in the wake of broader congressional change. Historically, the filibuster was reserved for major matters (particularly civil rights issues) about which a minority felt passionately. Now, by contrast, any topic seems fair game for extended discussion, led by a handful of senators (liberals as well as conservatives) or, on occasion, even by a single member. This acceptance of seemingly frivolous filibusters has undercut the intended effect of reform.[108] The Senate has agreed to restrict the use of the filibuster to facilitate consideration of the budget resolutions and reconciliation bills, but no serious effort has been made of late to reduce the opportunity for unlimited debate. In any case, even though the Senate invokes cloture more readily and has curbed the postcloture filibuster, a minority may still block the majority. The filibuster—conducted or merely threatened—continues to affect Senate floor action on a substantial amount of legislation.[109]

Summary

During the first half of the 1970s, members critical of Congress enacted sweeping legislative reforms. Motivated by policy inertia, personal powerlessness, public disapproval, and the desire for electoral security, they sought to democratize Congress (to make it more responsive and accountable) and to centralize its operations (to make it more responsible and to reclaim lost policy-making power, particularly that ceded to the president). In the 1980s, practices under the reformed regime were changed gradually and without drama, but the legislative landscape was rearranged nonetheless. Whether by revolution or evolution, Congress changes its institutional procedures in the same way that it makes policy in other areas—in piecemeal fashion. Therefore, it is scarcely surprising that the impact of reform has been uncertain. Reforms have often been incompatible; reformers have won some victories and suffered some setbacks, often discovering that their alterations have had quite unexpected or even undesirable results.

Certainly the changed Congress of the 1990s is better positioned to oppose the president, but given the changes in membership as well as the rapid turn of events, it is not clear that there will be steady pressure on members to use their potentially powerful weapons, especially with Democrats in control at both ends of Pennsylvania Avenue. The ultimate consequences of the War Powers Act and the 1974 budget act (as adjusted in 1985, 1987, and again in 1990), and of the increase in Congress's analytic capability, are impossible to predict. The legislature has been, on occasion, a more efficient, responsible decision maker, but in other instances, it has lacked the will to assert itself.

Centralizing reforms are in place—intended to increase party and leadership authority in the House and decrease minority use of dilatory tactics in both chambers—but they have seldom been employed decisively. Parties would seem to be stronger in the House, but whether partisan unity will endure, given the more buoyant economy and the influx of new members, remains to be seen. So long as leaders cannot impose discipline on electorally independent members, party cohesion remains problematic, dependent on member acquiescence. In the absence of more permanent, enforceable centralization measures, Congress may be hard pressed to act responsibly with any consistency.

The reforms have made Congress somewhat more responsive, however. A result of the attack on full committees has been wider dispersion of political influence; subcommittees have clearly become significant forces in House deliberations, if not those in the Senate. More members, with ties to more interests, possess the potential to affect public policy (and to oversee bureaucrats and represent their constituents more effectively). Junior members have secured advantageous legislative positions, but they have used them differently in different committees and subcommittees and on different policy questions.

In addition, since passage of the campaign spending, financial disclosure, and sunshine reforms, it is easier to hold Congress accountable. More can be known about congressional activity, but there is little reason to believe that more actually *is* known, at least by ordinary citizens. The legislature is certainly more accessible to the public, but that very permeability has increased legislators' vulnerability to external influences and has weakened an already fragile basis for centralized leadership. Most of the time, members of Congress seem to prefer decentralization, and they have protected it in the face of reform efforts. Even with the revival of political parties and partisanship in the 1990s, Congress is unquestionably more democratic—more participatory, more open to external messages and pressures—than it was in the 1960s, but at a price: it is less able to exert its institutional power and to enact innovative legislative programs efficiently. In short, reform prompted by mixed motives has produced mixed results.

The important lesson to be learned is unmistakable: reform is no panacea. As part and parcel of broad currents of change, congressional reform reflects a welter of societal and institutional forces. Altered circumstances inevitably undercut expectations and produce unforeseen outcomes; short-run success can evolve into long-term disappointment. Given the myriad of influences affecting legislative performance—new members with different values and aims; new economic, social, or political conditions and issues; and the organization and procedures of Congress itself—reformers often find that their best-laid plans have gone astray.[110]

Legislative history makes clear that reform has been both incremental and ephemeral. After 1977, members seemed to feel that enough had been done. To be sure, some conditions still demanded a response: the loophole in the Senate filibuster rule was quickly closed; ethical transgressions were punished; the use of riders on appropriations bills was restricted. But on the whole, the reform spirit flagged. After perfunctory consideration, proposals to clarify committee jurisdictions, to create an Energy Committee, to refine the budget process, and in general to improve legislative efficiency were brushed aside.[111] In the absence of strong facilitating conditions—supportive members, powerful public pressure for change, the stimulus of relevant national and international events—reform efforts foundered. Unresolved policy problems, public disenchantment with Congress in the wake of its perceived ethical lapses, and an influx of reform-oriented new members after the 1992 elections may have rekindled the reform spirit. Discussion of a multitude of specific reform proposals has begun, both within the Clinton administration and in the 1993 Joint Committee on the Organization of Congress. What, if anything, Congress will choose to adopt is uncertain.

Congress remains decentralized, responsive to a multitude of forces inside and outside its halls, and, as a result, hard pressed to formulate and enact legislation establishing coherent, responsible public policies. Organizational reform has increased the number of power centers involved in making policy, and party power is not sufficient to mobilize them readily in support of programs that either challenge or sustain the president. Sunshine reforms have exposed members to attentive citizens, most often belonging to organized interests. More independent members, faced with more difficult policy choices (the "politics of scarcity" requires allocation of sacrifice rather than dispensation of largess), often find it politically expedient to duck controversy: to defer to others, to delay, or to obfuscate. In consequence, Congress in the 1990s seems less willing and less able to frame and fight for its preferences. Restoration of unified government may offer the majority Democrats in Congress political cover; they may restrain their individualism and fall into line to support the programs of the Clinton administration. If they continue to assert their independence and to defend personal policy convictions and constituent interests against executive encroachment, policy making may prove difficult. Paradoxically, whatever course members choose, increased individual influence may add up to reduced institutional authority.

What observers make of these manifold changes in Congress and its mode of conducting legislative business depends, of course, on their values; what they see reflects what they want to see. To some, perhaps many, Congress is a "better" institution than it was two decades ago. After all, it is hard to quarrel with openness, accessibility, egalitarianism, and independence, and Congress as a result of reform has more of these admirable qualities. To others, however, Congress still comes up short. It seems less able to process legislation efficiently, to counterbalance a strong president, or to overcome the obstacles to efficiency posed by a decentralized institution. Two essential questions persist: Can a fragmented Congress do its job? If not, what reforms are still in order?

NOTES

1. For an imaginative (but largely ignored) plea to treat reforms as hypotheses to be tested scientifically and abandoned if disconfirmed, see Donald T. Campbell, "Reforms as Experiments," *American Psychologist* 24 (1969): 409-429.
2. On these cases, see *Congressional Quarterly Weekly Report*, February 9, 1985, 287;

Congressional Quarterly Weekly Report, September 30, 1989, 2567; and Elizabeth A. Palmer, "The Source of Whitten's Power," *Congressional Quarterly Weekly Report*, December 12, 1992, 3795. In 1974, John Moss (D-Calif.) successfully challenged full committee chairman Harley Staggers (D-W. Va.) for the top spot on the Commerce Committee's Subcommittee on Oversight and Investigations. Similarly, in 1981, Gus Yatron (D-Pa.) was deposed as chair of the House Foreign Affairs Subcommittee on Inter-American Affairs, presumably because he was too conservative; the seat went to Michael Barnes (D-Md.). On the Moss-Staggers contest, see David E. Price, "The Impact of Reform: The House Subcommittee on Oversight and Investigations," in *Legislative Reform: The Policy Impact*, ed. Leroy N. Rieselbach (Lexington, Mass.: Lexington Books, 1978), 133-147. On the ouster of Yatron, see *Congressional Quarterly Weekly Report*, February 7, 1981, 263. For three 1979 cases (two on the Commerce Committee, one on the Government Operations Committee), see *Congressional Quarterly Weekly Report*, February 3, 1979, 183-187.

3. Indeed, party leaders in pursuit of party unity have often increased the size of committees to make room for members seeking particular assignments. See Louis P. Westefield, "Majority Party Leadership and the Committee System in the House of Representatives," *American Political Science Review* 68 (1974): 1593-1604; David Whiteman, "A Theory of Congressional Organization: Committee Size in the U.S. House of Representatives," *American Politics Quarterly* 11 (1983): 49-70; and Steven S. Smith and Christopher J. Deering, *Committees in Congress*, 2d ed. (Washington, D.C.: CQ Press, 1990), 62-68.

4. Senate Republicans seem to be an exception here, in that they give more weight to seniority in resolving conflict over particular committee posts. See Smith and Deering, *Committees in Congress*, 2d ed., 71.

5. On committee assignments, see Smith and Deering, *Committees in Congress*, 2d ed., 68-75; Charles S. Bullock III, "House Committee Assignments," in *The Congressional System: Notes and Readings*, 2d ed., ed. Leroy N. Rieselbach (Belmont, Calif.: Wadsworth, 1979), 58-86; Steven S. Smith and Bruce A. Ray, "The Impact of Congressional Reform: House Democratic Committee Assignments," *Congress & the Presidency* 10 (1983): 219-240; and Heinz Eulau, "Legislative Committee Assignments," *Legislative Studies Quarterly* 9 (1984): 587-633.

6. Christopher J. Deering and Steven S. Smith, "Subcommittees in Congress," in *Congress Reconsidered*, 3d ed., ed. Lawrence C. Dodd and Bruce I. Oppenheimer (Washington, D.C.: CQ Press, 1985), 190.

7. See Roger H. Davidson, "Subcommittee Government: New Channels for Policy Making," in *The New Congress*, ed. Thomas E. Mann and Norman J. Ornstein (Washington, D.C.: American Enterprise Institute, 1981), 99-133; Richard L. Hall and C. Lawrence Evans, "The Power of Subcommittees," *Journal of Politics* 52 (1990): 335-355; Barry R. Weingast, "Fighting Fire with Fire: Amending Activity and Institutional Change in the Postreform Congress," in *The Postreform Congress*, ed. Roger H. Davidson (New York: St. Martin's Press, 1992), 142-168; and Smith and Deering, *Committees in Congress*, 2d ed., chap. 4.

8. Norman J. Ornstein, "Causes and Consequences of Congressional Change: Subcommittee Reforms in the House of Representatives, 1970-1973," in *Congress in Change: Evolution and Reform*, ed. Norman J. Ornstein (New York: Praeger, 1975), 88-114; John E. Stanga, Jr., and David N. Farnsworth, "Senior-

ity and Democratic Reforms in the House of Representatives: Committees and Subcommittees," in *Legislative Reform*, ed. Rieselbach, 35-47.

9. The House in 1981 adopted rules limiting each committee to eight subcommittees; those with fewer than six subcommittees at that time could create no more than six. In consequence, there were 130 subcommittees in the 98th Congress (1983-1984). Norman J. Ornstein, Thomas E. Mann, and Michael J. Malbin, *Vital Statistics on Congress, 1991-1992* (Washington, D.C.: American Enterprise Institute, 1992), Table 4-2, 111. At the start of the 103d Congress (1993-1994), the House limited major committees to six subcommittees and other panels to five (the exclusive committees—Appropriations, Rules, and Ways and Means—were exempt), thus eliminating 16 subcommittees and leaving approximately 121 in operation. Beth Donovan, "Busy Democrats Skirt Fight to Get House in Order," *Congressional Quarterly Weekly Report*, December 12, 1992, 3777-3780.

10. Smith and Deering, *Committees in Congress*, 2d ed., 131-134.

11. Stanga and Farnsworth, "Seniority and Democratic Reforms." On average, however, the length of time required for House Democrats to reach the top spot on subcommittees has declined with the adoption of the new rules, it takes longer to gain a subcommittee chair on the most prestigious panels. See Smith and Deering, *Committees in Congress* (Washington, D.C.: CQ Press, 1984), Table 6.1, 191.

12. These data are from Smith and Deering, *Committees in Congress*, 2d ed., chap. 4.

13. Christopher J. Deering and Steven S. Smith, "Majority Party Leadership and the Effects of Decentralization" (Paper presented to the Everett McKinley Dirksen Congressional Leadership Research Center-Sam Rayburn Library Conference, Understanding Congressional Leadership: The State of the Art, 1980), 36.

14. Smith and Deering, in *Committees in Congress*, 2d ed., 139, describe the distinction; as they forcefully put it: "Subcommittees are not autonomous creatures in the legislative process" (147).

15. Smith and Deering, *Committees in Congress*, 2d ed., Table 4-4, 140.

16. Ibid., 162.

17. Richard F. Fenno, Jr., *Congressmen in Committees* (Boston: Little, Brown, 1973).

18. Norman J. Ornstein and David W. Rohde, "Shifting Forces, Changing Rules, and Political Outcomes: The Impact of Congressional Change on Four House Committees," in *New Perspectives on the House of Representatives*, 3d ed., ed. Robert L. Peabody and Nelson W. Polsby (Chicago: Rand McNally, 1977), 186-269. For confirmatory evidence, see Joseph K. Unekis and Leroy N. Rieselbach, *Congressional Committee Politics: Continuity and Change* (New York: Praeger, 1984), chap. 4.

19. Ornstein and Rohde, "Shifting Forces," 237-252.

20. Ibid., 252-261. See also Frederick M. Kaiser, "Congressional Change and Foreign Policy: The House Committee on International Relations," in *Legislative Reform*, ed. Rieselbach, 61-71.

21. For additional evidence in support of this conclusion, see John Berg, "The Effects of Seniority Reform on Three House Committees," in *Legislative Reform*, ed. Rieselbach, 49-59; and Christopher J. Deering, "Adaptation and Consolidation in Congress's Foreign Policy Committees: Evolution in the Seventies"

(Paper presented to the 1980 annual meeting of the Midwest Political Science Association).

22. Glenn R. Parker and Suzanne L. Parker, "Factions in Committees: The U.S. House of Representatives," *American Political Science Review* 73 (1979): 85-103; and Unekis and Rieselbach, *Congressional Committee Politics*. In *Congressmen in Committees*, Fenno describes Ways and Means in the 1960s, at the height of Mills's influence. See also John F. Manley, *The Politics of Finance* (Boston: Little, Brown, 1970).

23. Catherine E. Rudder, "Fiscal Responsibility and the Revenue Committees," in *Congress Reconsidered*, 3d ed., ed. Dodd and Oppenheimer, 211-222; Catherine E. Rudder, "The Policy Impact of Reform of the Committee on Ways and Means," in *Legislative Reform*, ed. Rieselbach, 73-89; and Bruce I. Oppenheimer, "Policy Effects of U.S. House Reform: Decentralization and the Capacity to Resolve Energy Issues," *Legislative Studies Quarterly* 5 (1980): 5-30.

24. Randall Strahan, *New Ways and Means: Reform and Change in a Congressional Committee* (Chapel Hill: University of North Carolina Press, 1990), 164.

25. Price, "The Impact of Reform," 154; and Michael J. Malbin, "The Bolling Committee Revisited: Energy Oversight on an Investigative Subcommittee: (Paper presented to the 1978 annual meeting of the American Political Science Association). Committee leaders must act within the organizational requirements particular to individual committees, which reform may influence profoundly. See Strahan, *New Ways and Means*, esp. chap. 5, on Dan Rostenkowski; and more generally, C. Lawrence Evans, *Leadership in Committee: A Comparative Analysis of Leadership Behavior in the U.S. Senate* (Ann Arbor: University of Michigan Press, 1991).

26. Evans, *Leadership in Committee*, 2. See also Barbara Sinclair, *The Transformation of the U.S. Senate* (Baltimore: Johns Hopkins University Press, 1989).

27. Ornstein et al., *Vital Statistics*, Table 4-3, 112; Smith and Deering, *Committees in Congress*, 2d ed., Tables 4-4, 4-5, and 4-2, 140, 142, and 130. See also Deering and Smith, "Subcommittees in Congress."

28. Susan Webb Hammond, "Congressional Change and Reform: Staffing the Congress," in *Legislative Reform*, ed. Rieselbach, 181-193; and *Congressional Quarterly Weekly Report*, November 24, 1979, 2631-2638.

29. Ornstein et al., *Vital Statistics*, Table 5-5, 130.

30. Smith and Deering, *Committees in Congress*, 2d ed., Table 4-7, 152.

31. David R. Mayhew, *Congress: The Electoral Connection* (New Haven, Conn.: Yale University Press, 1974); Richard F. Fenno, Jr., *Home Style: Representatives in Their Districts* (Boston: Little, Brown, 1978); Glenn R. Parker, *Homeward Bound: Explaining Changes in Congressional Behavior* (Pittsburgh, Pa.: University of Pittsburgh Press, 1986); and Bruce Cain, John Ferejohn, and Morris Fiorina, *The Personal Vote: Constituency Service and Electoral Independence* (Cambridge, Mass.: Harvard University Press, 1987).

32. Morris P. Fiorina, *Congress: Keystone of the Washington Establishment*, 2d ed. (New Haven, Conn.: Yale University Press, 1989). The proponents of term limits believe that they will cause members of Congress to pay more attention to the "national interest" and less to the pleadings of parochial "special interests."

33. Randall B. Ripley, *Power in the Senate* (New York: St. Martin's Press, 1969);

Norman J. Ornstein, "The House and the Senate in a New Congress," in *The New Congress*, ed. Mann and Ornstein, 363-383; Smith and Deering, *Committees in Congress*, 2d ed., chap. 5; Steven S. Smith, "The Senate in the Postreform Era," in *The Postreform Congress*, ed. Davidson, 169-192; Norman J. Ornstein, Robert L. Peabody and David W. Rohde, "The U.S. Senate in an Era of Change," in *Congress Reconsidered*, 5th ed., ed. Lawrence C. Dodd and Bruce I. Oppenheimer (Washington, D.C.: CQ Press, 1993), 13-40; and Lawrence C. Dodd and Bruce I. Oppenheimer, "Maintaining Order in the House: The Struggle for Institutional Equilibrium," in ibid., 41-66.

34. Dodd and Oppenheimer, "Maintaining Order in the House"; James L. Sundquist, *The Decline and Resurgence of Congress* (Washington, D.C.: Brookings Institution, 1981); Walter J. Oleszek, "Integration and Fragmentation: Key Themes of Congressional Change," *Annals* 466 (1983): 272-290; and Smith and Deering, *Committees in Congress*, 2d ed., 159-162.

35. Michael J. Malbin, *Unelected Representatives: Congressional Staff and the Future of Representative Government* (New York: Basic Books, 1980).

36. Smith and Deering, *Committees in Congress*, 2d ed., 159-162.

37. See John A. Ferejohn, "On the Decline of Competition in Congressional Elections," *American Political Science Review* 71 (1977): 166-176; Thomas E. Mann, *Unsafe at Any Margin: Interpreting Congressional Elections* (Washington, D.C.: American Enterprise Institute, 1978); and Kent L. Tedin and Richard W. Murray, "Public Awareness of Congressional Representatives: Recall versus Recognition," *American Politics Quarterly* 7 (1979): 509-517.

38. See Thomas E. Mann and Raymond E. Wolfinger, "Candidates and Parties in Congressional Elections," *American Political Science Review* 74 (1980): 617-632; Barbara Hinckley, *Congressional Elections* (Washington, D.C.: CQ Press, 1981); and Gary C. Jacobson, *The Politics of Congressional Elections*, 3d ed. (New York: HarperCollins, 1992), chap. 5.

39. This was down slightly from the 93 percent to 98 percent incumbent reelection rate typical of the 1980s. And 9 of the 43 incumbent losses in 1992 were the inevitable result of redistricting that forced incumbents to run against one another in the same constituency.

40. The Harris Survey, release 1984, no. 112, December 17, 1984; release 1985, no. 47, June 13, 1985. Public assessment of Congress is volatile. In 1985, public sentiment shifted sharply. For the first time in twenty years, a popular majority (53 percent) gave Congress a positive rating; 46 percent of the respondents were negative about the legislature. The Harris Survey, release 1985, no. 46, June 10, 1985. On the paradox of public dislike of Congress as an institution and simultaneous citizen approval of the local legislator, see the sources cited in note 39 to Chap. 3. Data for the 1990s are given in "A Public Hearing on Congress," *Public Perspective* 4 (November-December, 1992): 82-92.

41. *Congressional Quarterly Weekly Report*, July 6, 1985, 1316.

42. On the political difficulties that acting in public may create, see Lewis A. Froman, Jr., and Randall B. Ripley, "Conditions for Party Leadership: The Case of the House Democrats," *American Political Science Review* 59 (1965): 52-63; Fiorina, *Congress: Keystone of the Washington Establishment*; and Mayhew, *Congress: The Electoral Connection*. Party leaders recognize that members give priority to local interests. As House Speaker O'Neill noted, "Members are more

home-oriented. They no longer have to follow the national philosophy of the party. They can get reelected on their newsletter, or on how they serve their constituents." *Congressional Quarterly Weekly Report*, September 13, 1980, 2696.

43. See Margaret L. Nugent and John R. Johannes, eds., *Money, Elections, and Democracy: Reforming Congressional Campaign Finance* (Boulder, Colo.: Westview Press, 1990); David B. Magleby and Candice J. Nelson, *The Money Chase: Congressional Campaign Finance Reform* (Washington, D.C.: Brookings Institution, 1990); and, more generally, Frank J. Sorauf, *Inside Campaign Finance: Myths and Realities* (New Haven, Conn.: Yale University Press, 1992).

44. In the 1989-1990 electoral cycle, for example, PACs contributed $108.6 million to House candidates. Of that sum, 80 percent went to incumbents, 6 percent to challengers, and 13 percent to candidates in open-seat races (where there was no incumbent on the ballot). The PACs also gave $41.3 million to Senate nominees—72 percent to incumbents, 20 percent to challengers, and 9 percent to open-seat candidates. Ornstein et al., *Vital Statistics on Congress, 1991-1992*, Tables 3-13 and 3-14, 100 and 103. In addition, PACs often make contributions classified as "independent expenditures"—funds spent without contact with candidates. Most often they are intended to support challengers or at least to oppose incumbents. Such contributions, from groups like the National Conservative Political Action Committee or the evangelical Christian movement's Moral Majority, may augur reduced group support for incumbents. Sorauf, in *Inside Campaign Finance*, 31, reports that independent expenditures totaled $4.7 million in 1990. On money and politics, see also Gary C. Jacobson, *Money in Congressional Elections* (New Haven, Conn.: Yale University Press, 1980); Herbert E. Alexander, *Financing Politics: Money, Elections, and Political Reform*, 3d ed. (Washington, D.C.: CQ Press, 1984); Michael J. Malbin, ed., *Money and Politics in the United States* (Chatham, N.J.: Chatham House, 1984); and Philip M. Stern, *Still the Best Congress Money Can Buy* (Washington, D.C.; Regnery Gateway, 1992).

45. Jacobson, *Money in Congressional Elections*, 194. See also Mayhew, *Congress: The Electoral Connection*, and Fiorina, *Congress: Keystone of the Washington Establishment*.

46. Mark C. Westlye, *Senate Elections and Campaign Intensity* (Baltimore: Johns Hopkins University Press, 1991); and Alan I. Abramowitz and Jeffrey A. Segal, *Senate Elections* (Ann Arbor: University of Michigan Press, 1992).

47. Barbara Hinckley, "House Reelections and Senate Defeats: The Role of the Challenger," *British Journal of Political Science* 10 (1980): 441-460. Gary C. Jacobson and Samuel Kernell, in *Strategy and Choice in Congressional Elections*, 2d ed. (New Haven, Conn.: Yale University Press, 1983), argue that attractive House and Senate challengers emerge and are more likely to win when conditions favoring their party (usually the one that does not control the White House) enable them to secure substantial funding sufficiently far in advance of election day to wage a strong campaign against the incumbent. Such conditions occur only rarely, and most often the incumbents triumph.

48. Robert Parry, "Defense Firms Increase Political Donations," *Louisville Courier-Journal*, April 1, 1985, A4.

49. Not surprisingly, only a few members, professing candor, acknowledge the impact of donations: "You can't buy a congressman for $5,000 [the maximum

PAC contribution to a single candidate in a single campaign]. But you can buy his vote. It's done on a regular basis" (Rep. Thomas Downey [D-N.Y.], quoted in *Time*, October 25, 1982, 20). The evidence produced by scholars, on balance, suggests that PAC contributions have only marginal effects on legislators' roll call votes. See John R. Wright, "PACs, Contributions, and Roll Calls: An Organizational Perspective," *American Political Science Review* 79 (1985): 400-414; John R. Wright, "PAC Contributions, Lobbying, and Representation," *Journal of Politics* 51 (1989): 713-729; Laura I. Langbein and Mark A. Lotwis, "The Political Efficacy of Lobbying and Money: Gun Control in the U.S. House," *Legislative Studies Quarterly* 15 (1990): 414-440; Janet M. Grenzke, "PACs and the Congressional Supermarket: The Currency is Complex," *American Journal of Political Science* 33 (1989): 1-24; and Janet Grenzke, "Money and Congressional Behavior," in *Money, Elections, and Democracy*, ed. Nugent and Johannes, 143-164. For evidence that PAC contributions most likely have a greater impact at the committee stage of deliberation than at the time of the floor vote, see John R. Wright, "Contributions, Lobbying, and Committee Voting in the U.S. House of Representatives," *American Political Science Review* 84 (1990): 417-438; and Richard L. Hall and Frank W. Wayman "Buying Time: Moneyed Interests and the Mobilization of Bias in Congressional Committees," *American Political Science Review* 84 (1990): 797-820.

50. For example, thirty-five-year-old Rep. John J. Cavanaugh (D-Neb.), well regarded in his district and in the House, retired in 1980 after two terms, in part because "the continuous campaigning is debilitating and campaign financing is corrupting" (quoted in *New York Times*, August 31, 1980, 20). See also the retirement speech of Rep. Otis Pike (D-N.Y.) in *Congressional Quarterly Weekly Report*, February 25, 1978, 528-529. On the retirement phenomenon in general, see Joseph Cooper and William West, "The Congressional Career in the 1970s," in *Congress Reconsidered*, 2d ed., ed. Lawrence C. Dodd and Bruce I. Oppenheimer (Washington, D.C.: CQ Press, 1981), 83-106; and John R. Hibbing, *Choosing to Leave: Voluntary Retirement from the U.S. House of Representatives* (Washington, D.C.: University Press of America, 1982). On service in the House, see John R. Hibbing, *Congressional Careers: Contours of Life in the U.S. House of Representatives* (Chapel Hill: University of North Carolina Press, 1991).

51. Ornstein et al., *Vital Statistics on Congress, 1991-1992*, Table 2-9, 60. See also Michael I. Moore and John R. Hibbing, "Is Serving in Congress Fun Again? Voluntary Retirements from the House Since the 1970s," *American Journal of Political Science* 56 (1992): 824-828.

52. Indeed, all presidents have argued that the act is an unconstitutional encroachment on the executive's constitutional powers as commander in chief. See Louis Fisher, "War Powers: The Need for Collective Judgment," in *Divided Democracy: Cooperation and Conflict between the President and Congress*, ed. James A. Thurber (Washington, D.C.: CQ Press, 1991), 199-217; Cecil V. Crabb, Jr., and Pat M. Holt, *Invitation to Struggle: Congress, the President, and Foreign Policy*, 2d ed. (Washington, D.C.: CQ Press, 1984); and the sources cited in note 53 to Chap. 3. Daniel Paul Franklin, in "War Powers in the Modern Context," *Congress & the Presidency* 14 (1987): 77-92, analyzes the impact of the act from 1973 to 1986.

53. Randall B. Ripley and Grace A. Franklin conclude pessimistically that "the War Powers Act is not likely to have much operational importance in the real world." See *Congress, the Bureaucracy, and Public Policy*, 5th ed. (Pacific Grove, Calif.: Brooks/Cole, 1991), 179.

54. Just to be certain, Congress added an amendment to the Department of Defense appropriations bill forbidding any expenditures for "any activities involving Angola directly or indirectly." Since CIA funds were hidden in the DOD appropriation, this action removed the legal basis for either overt or covert intervention in Angola. The amendment was repealed in 1985, however.

55. Thomas Franck and Edward Weisband, *Foreign Policy by Congress* (New York: Oxford University Press, 1979).

56. Loch K. Johnson, "Legislative Reform of Intelligence Policy," *Polity* 17 (1985): 549-573; Frank J. Smist, Jr., *Congress Oversees the United States Intelligence Community, 1947-1989* (Knoxville: University of Tennessee Press, 1990).

57. On the current state of executive-legislative relations with regard to foreign policy, see Thomas E. Mann, ed., *A Question of Balance: The President, the Congress, and Foreign Policy* (Washington, D.C.: Brookings Institution, 1990); and Cecil V. Crabb, Jr., and Pat M. Holt, *Invitation to Struggle: Congress, the President, and Foreign Policy*, 4th ed. (Washington, D.C.: CQ Press, 1992).

58. See John W. Ellwood, "Budget Control in a Redistributive Environment," in *Making Economic Policy in Congress*, ed. Allen Schick (Washington, D.C.: American Enterprise Institute, 1983), 69-99; John W. Ellwood, "The Great Exception: The Congressional Budget Process in an Age of Decentralization," in *Congress Reconsidered*, 3d ed., ed. Dodd and Oppenheimer, 246-271; W. Thomas Wander, F. Ted Herbert, and Gary W. Copeland, eds. *Congressional Budgeting: Politics, Process, and Power* (Baltimore: Johns Hopkins University Press, 1984); and the sources cited in note 59 to Chap. 3.

59. Aaron Wildavsky, *The Politics of the Budgetary Process*, 4th ed. (Boston: Little, Brown, 1984), 238.

60. Lance T. LeLoup, "Budgeting in the U.S. Senate: Old Ways of Doing New Things" (Paper presented to the 1979 annual meeting of the Midwest Political Science Association); and Shuman, *Politics and the Budget*. This is not to suggest that there was no conflict between the Senate Budget Committee and other committees. See Louis Fisher, "Congressional Budget Reform: Committee Conflicts" (Paper presented to the 1975 annual meeting of the Midwest Political Science Association); Catherine Rudder, "The Impact of the Budget and Impoundment Control Act of 1974 on the Revenue Committees of the U.S. Congress" (Paper presented to the 1977 annual meeting of the American Political Science Association); and Joel Havemann, *Congress and the Budget* (Bloomington: Indiana University Press, 1978). Rather, it is to suggest that the Senate panel sought accommodation not confrontation during the early phases of the new process. See also Wildavsky, *The Politics of the Budgetary Process*; and James A. Thurber, "New Powers of the Purse: An Assessment of Congressional Budget Reform," in *Legislative Reform*, ed. Rieselbach, 159-172.

61. Lance T. LeLoup, "Process vs. Policy: The U.S. House Budget Committee," *Legislative Studies Quarterly* 4 (1979): 227-254; and Unekis and Rieselbach, *Congressional Committee Politics*, chap. 2.

62. James P. Pfiffner, "Executive Control of the Congressional Budget" (Paper presented to the 1977 annual meeting of the Midwest Political Science Association); Allen Schick, "Whose Budget? It All Depends on Whether the President or Congress Is Doing the Counting," in *The Presidency and the Congress: A Shifting Balance of Power?*, ed. William S. Livingston, Lawrence C. Dodd, and Richard L. Schott (Austin, Texas: Lyndon B. Johnson Library, 1979), 124-142; LeLoup, "Budgeting in the U.S. Senate," and "Process versus Policy"; and Mark W. Huddleston, "Assessing Congressional Budget Reform: The Impact on Appropriations," *Policy Studies Journal* 9 (1980): 81-86.

63. Ellwood, "Budget Control."

64. Ibid.; and Allen Schick, "The Distributive Congress," in *Making Economic Policy in Congress*, ed. Schick, 257-273.

65. H. E. Shuman, *Politics and the Budget: The Struggle between the President and the Congress*, 2d ed. (Englewood Cliffs, N.J.: Prentice-Hall, 1988), 268.

66. Ironically, so powerful was the force behind the Reagan administration's 1981 reconciliation bill that it was "brought to the House floor in emasculated form.... The details were not available until the morning of the vote.... Figures were crossed out and substitute amounts penciled in. Some pages were misnumbered. Provisions were written by hand in the margins. To add insult to injury, one substitute amendment included the name and telephone number of . . . a staff member of the CBO." Ibid., 261. The bill passed anyway.

67. Ellwood, "Budget Control," 94.

68. On the mechanics of GRH, see Chap. 3, esp. notes 59-61.

69. On the 1990 Omnibus Budget Reconciliation Act, of which the Budget Enforcement Act was a part, see Chap. 3, esp. the section on "Taming the Executive," and the sources cited in notes 62 and 63 of that chapter.

70. James A. Thurber and Samantha L. Durst, "The 1990 Budget Enforcement Act: The Decline of Congressional Accountability," in *Congress Reconsidered*, 5th ed., ed. Dodd and Oppenheimer, 391.

71. On the impact to date and the potential impact of the BEA, see ibid.; and James A. Thurber, "New Rules for an Old Game: Zero-Sum Budgeting in the Postreform Congress," in *The Postreform Congress*, ed. Davidson, 257-278.

72. William G. Munselle, "Presidential Impoundment and Congressional Reform," in *Legislative Reform*, ed. Rieselbach, 173-181; and Shuman, *Politics and the Budget*.

73. Pfiffner, "Executive Control of the Congressional Budget"; Wildavsky, *The Politics of the Budgetary Process*.

74. Schick, "Whose Budget?" 112-113.

75. See David Whiteman, "The Fate of Policy Analysis in Congressional Decision Making: Three Types of Use in Committees," *Western Political Quarterly* 38 (1985): 294-311. See also Charles O. Jones, "Why Congress Can't Do Policy Analysis (or Words to That Effect)," *Policy Analysis* 2 (1976): 251-264; and Allen Schick, "The Supply and Demand for Analysis on Capitol Hill," *Policy Analysis* 2 (1976): 215-234.

76. Malbin, *Unelected Representatives*.

77. David E. Price, "Professionals and 'Entrepreneurs': Staff Orientations and Policy Making on Three Senate Committees," *Journal of Politics* 33 (1971): 316-336.

78. Hammond, "Congressional Change and Reform."

79. Lawrence C. Dodd and Richard L. Schott, *Congress and the Administrative State* (New York: Wiley, 1979); and Joel D. Aberbach, *Keeping a Watchful Eye: The Politics of Congressional Oversight* (Washington, D.C.: Brookings Institution, 1990), chaps. 2-3.

80. When some form of institutional control does seem warranted, Congress may resort to attaching "riders" to authorization or appropriations bills to prohibit spending for particular purposes (for example, to bar the Justice Department from committing money to institute any legal proceeding to require busing for desegregation). In 1983, the House Democrats adopted new rules that tightened party control over the use of riders, presumably to restrict their use by conservatives who oppose party positions. See *Congressional Quarterly Weekly Report*, January 8, 1983, 8.

81. Aberbach, *Keeping a Watchful Eye*; and Charles H. Foreman, Jr., *Signals from the Hill: Congressional Oversight and the Challenge of Social Regulation* (New Haven, Conn.: Yale University Press, 1988).

82. Dodd and Schott, *Congress and the Administrative State*; Morris P. Fiorina," Control of the Bureaucracy: A Mismatch of Incentives and Capabilities," in *The Presidency and the Congress*, ed. Livingston, Dodd, and Schott, 124-142; and Mathew D. McCubbins and Thomas Schwartz, "Congressional Oversight Overlooked: Police Patrols versus Fire Alarms," *American Journal of Political Science* 28 (1984): 169-179.

83. Foreman, *Signals from the Hill*, 15, 146.

84. Aberbach, *Keeping a Watchful Eye*, 198.

85. Richard E. Cohen, "Congress Steps Up Use of the Legislative Veto," *National Journal*, September 6, 1980, 1473-1477. For a detailed discussion of the legislative veto, see Chap. 3, esp. the section on "Taming the Executive" and the sources cited in notes 65 and 66. See also Louis Fisher, "Judicial Misjudgments about the Lawmaking Process: The Legislative Veto Case," *Public Administration Review* 45 (1985): 705-711.

86. On the legislative veto after *Chadha*, see Daniel Paul Franklin, "Why the Legislative Veto Isn't Dead," *Presidential Studies Quarterly* 16 (1986): 491-501; Louis Fisher, "The Administrative World of *Chadha* and *Bowsher*," *Public Administration Review* 47 (1987): 213-219; and Frederick M. Kaiser, "Congressional Control of Executive Actions in the Aftermath of the *Chadha* Decision," *Administrative Law Review* 36 (1984): 249-276.

87. Unekis and Rieselbach, *Congressional Committee Politics*, chap. 4. See also Berg, "The Effects of Seniority Reform."

88. Sara B. Crook and John R. Hibbing, "Congressional Reform and Party Discipline: The Effects of Changes in the Seniority System on Party Loyalty in the U.S. House of Representatives," *British Journal of Political Science* 15 (1985): 207-226. For corroborating evidence, see Smith and Deering, *Committees in Congress*, 2d ed., 131-134.

89. Stanley Bach, "Special Rules in the House of Representatives: Themes and Contemporary Variations," *Congressional Studies* 8 (1981): 37-58; and Bruce I. Oppenheimer, "The Changing Relationship between House Leadership and the Committee on Rules," in *Understanding Congressional Leadership*, ed. Frank H. Mackaman (Washington, D.C.: CQ Press, 1981), 207-225.

90. *Congressional Quarterly Weekly Report*, June 15, 1985, 1189.

91. Eric M. Uslaner, "The Congressional War on Energy: The Moral Equivalent of Leadership?" (Paper presented to the Everett McKinley Dirksen Congressional Leadership Research Center-Sam Rayburn Library Conference, Understanding Congressional Leadership, 1980); and Oppenheimer, "Policy Effects of U.S. House Reform."

92. Robert H. Davidson and Walter J. Oleszek, "From Monopoly to Management: Changing Patterns of Committee Deliberation," in *The Postreform Congress*, ed. Davidson, 129-141.

93. Uslaner, "The Congressional War on Energy," 12-13.

94. Oppenheimer, "Policy Effects of U.S. House Reform."

95. Robert L. Peabody, "Senate Party Leadership: From the 1950s to the 1980s" (Paper presented to the Everett McKinley Dirksen Congressional Leadership Research Center-Sam Rayburn Library Conference, Understanding Congressional Leadership, 1980). See also Roger H. Davidson, "Senate Leaders: Janitors for an Untidy Congress," in *Congress Reconsidered*, 3d ed., ed. Dodd and Oppenheimer, 225-252.

96. On the revival of the parties in the House, see David W. Rohde, *Parties and Leaders in the Postreform House* (Chicago: University of Chicago Press, 1991); and Barbara Sinclair, "The Emergence of Strong Leadership in the 1980s House of Representatives," *Journal of Politics* 54 (1992): 657-684. For a contrast with the Senate, see Steven S. Smith, "Forces of Change in Senate Party Leadership and Organization," in *Congress Reconsidered*, 5th ed., ed. Dodd and Oppenheimer, 259-290; and Smith, "The Senate in the Postreform Era."

97. Steven S. Smith, *Call to Order: Floor Politics in the House and Senate* (Washington, D.C.: Brookings Institution, 1989).

98. On Wright, see John M. Barry, *The Ambition and the Power: A True Story of Washington* (New York: Penguin Books, 1989); and Daniel J. Palazzolo, *The Speaker and the Budget: Leadership in the Post-Reform House of Representatives* (Pittsburgh, Pa.: University of Pittsburgh Press, 1992), esp. chap. 6.

99. According to Sinclair, in "The Emergence of Strong Leadership," leaders were involved to some extent in 83 percent of the measures on the congressional agenda in the 100th Congress (up from 46 percent in the 91st) and in a major way in 60 percent (up from 28 percent).

100. Davidson and Oleszek, "From Monopoly to Management"; Garry Young and Joseph Cooper, "Multiple Referral and the Transformation of House Decision Making," in *Congress Reconsidered*, 5th ed., ed. Dodd and Oppenheimer, 211-234; Roger H. Davidson, Walter J. Oleszek, and Thomas Kephart, "One Bill, Many Committees: Multiple Referrals in the House of Representatives," *Legislative Studies Quarterly* 13 (1988): 3-28; and Melissa P. Collie and Joseph Cooper, "Multiple Referral and the 'New' Committee System in the House of Representatives," in *Congress Reconsidered*, 4th ed., ed. Lawrence C. Dodd and Bruce I. Oppenheimer (Washington, D.C.: CQ Press, 1989), 245-272. The Senate has formal rules, never invoked, that permit multiple referral. Rather, unanimous consent agreements were negotiated on the relatively few occasions when the procedure has been used. See Smith, "Forces of Change"; and Roger H. Davidson, "Multiple Referral of Legislation in the U.S. Senate," *Legislative Studies Quarterly* 14 (1989): 375-392.

101. See Stanley Bach and Steven S. Smith, *Managing Uncertainty in the House of*

Representatives: Adaptation and Innovation in Special Rules (Washington, D.C.: Brookings Institution, 1988); Smith, *Call to Order*; Rohde, *Parties and Leaders*; and Sinclair, "The Emergence of Strong Leadership."

102. A hold allows an individual senator to demand advance notice of consideration of a bill; floor debate and decisions are delayed until the hold is removed.

103. Smith, "The Senate in the Postreform Era," 191; see also Smith, "Forces of Change."

104. Rohde, *Parties and Leaders*, 31, 34 (emphasis in original).

105. Barbara Sinclair, "House Majority Leadership in an Era of Legislative Constraint," in *The Postreform Congress*, ed. Davidson, 91-111 (emphasis added). David Price, a political scientist and student of Congress turned member of the House (D-N.C.), seconds this view, noting "an unmistakable fragility to leadership strength, which is now based less on 'strong parties external to the Congress' and more on the acquiescence of freewheeling individual members." See *The Congressional Experience: A View from the Hill* (Boulder, Colo.: Westview Press, 1992), 78-79.

106. Barbara Sinclair, *Majority Party Leadership in the U.S. House* (Baltimore: Johns Hopkins University Press, 1983).

107. Data on cloture votes are from *Congress and the Nation*, vol. 7 (Washington, D.C.: Congressional Quarterly, 1990), 1037-1039; Ornstein et al., *Vital Statistics on Congress, 1991-1992*; and the 1989 *Congressional Quarterly Almanac* (Washington, D.C.: Congressional Quarterly, 1990), 5.

108. See Raymond E. Wolfinger, "Filibusters, Majority Rule, Presidential Leadership, and Senate Norms," in *Readings on Congress*, ed. Raymond E. Wolfinger (Englewood Cliffs, N.J.: Prentice-Hall, 1971), 296-305; Patty D. Renfrow, "The Senate Filibuster System, 1917-1979: Changes and Consequences" (Paper presented to the 1980 annual meeting of the Southern Political Science Association): and Bruce I. Oppenheimer, "Changing Time Constraints on Congress: Historical Perspectives on the Use of Cloture," in *Congress Reconsidered*, 3d ed., ed. Dodd and Oppenheimer, 393-413.

109. For instance, in 1985 Senate conservatives led by Jesse Helms (R-N.C.) filibustered a bill to impose economic sanctions against South Africa in response to that nation's apartheid policy. The Senate invoked cloture, in an 88-8 vote, but the minority continued to use dilatory tactics and agreed to permit the chamber to vote on the bill only after liberal Democrats promised to drop amendments that would have made the bill even stronger. See *Congressional Quarterly Weekly Report*, July 13, 1985, 1364-1366. A subsequent threat to filibuster the conference report on the bill forced the Senate to postpone a final vote on the measure for a month, until after its summer recess.

110. One careful study found that reform "had no direct impact on . . . committee inputs and outputs once the effects of underlying trends attributable to complexity in the external environment" were considered. See Susan Webb Hammond and Laura I. Langbein, "The Impact of Complexity and Reform on Congressional Committee Output," *Political Behavior* 4 (1982): 237-263.

111. For more on the rejected proposals of the House (Obey) Commission on Administrative Review (1977), the House (Patterson) Select Committee on Committees (1979-1980), and the (Quayle) Senate Temporary Select Committee to Study the Senate Committee System, see Chap. 3.

5. The Reform Agenda in the 1990s

There are two lessons to be learned from the post-World War II reform experience. First, change tends to be gradual rather than the result of systematic planning for reform, and it comes spasmodically, not on schedule. Changing events, new issues, and changes in the membership of Congress conspire to create conditions that compel the legislature continually to alter the ways it conducts its business. Grand visions of an ideal Congress—such as the executive force and congressional supremacy theories—are seldom if ever invoked to justify procedural innovations. Rather, the legislators make changes pragmatically, in piecemeal fashion, in response to perceived needs to solve specific problems at particular times. Second, change and reform as often as not fail to resolve the difficulties targeted by their proponents; indeed, they may produce unforeseen and unintended consequences. Good intentions are no guarantee of desirable results. After nearly two decades of revising the budget process, Congress seems neither to have reclaimed authority from the dominant executive nor to have gained control of the federal deficit. In fact, in the view of some observers, the situation has deteriorated; the revised budgetary procedures may have made congressional budgeting less effective.[1]

Major reform efforts are rare in Congress; without strong incentives to effect significant changes, members are usually content to undertake marginal adjustments rather than wholesale reorganization. The need to refine congressional operations after World War II led to passage of the Legislative Reorganization Act of 1946. The "imperial presidency" of the 1960s and 1970s—symbolized by the Watergate scandals and the Vietnam War—impelled the major reform effort of the 1970s, which began formally with the Legislative Reorganization Act of 1970 and had reached its peak by the decade's end. After years of relative calm, the reform pot began to boil again in the late 1980s. Congress seemed unable to deal effectively with a number of pressing issues: the economy in general and the budget deficit in particular, health care, crime and drugs, education, and foreign aid. Divided government, with Republicans ensconced in the White House and the Democrats in command on Capitol Hill, seemed to contribute to policy gridlock that left most controversial matters unresolved.

Congress at this time was scarred by scandal. In the Senate, the Keating Five affair left the impression that members had difficulty distinguishing between private interests and the national welfare. Several other senators were also rebuked for personal misconduct or dubious financial transactions. The controversial Clarence Thomas Supreme Court confirmation hearings cast doubt on senatorial ability and objectivity. On the House side, the Post Office fiasco and the check kiting at the House bank brought the chamber into disrepute; a number of individual members were indicted for criminal conduct. Public approval ratings of Congress's performance plummeted to record lows. Many members chose to retire; 5 in the Senate and 43 in the House failed in 1992 reelection bids. For the convening of the 103d Congress, in January 1993, 14 Senate newcomers and 110 House newcomers had arrived in Washington, many of whom had campaigned on reform platforms. Reform became a hot topic.[2]

In 1992 Congress created a Joint Committee on the Organization of Congress (as it had prior to enacting the Reorganization Acts of 1946 and 1970) to study and assess reform proposals and to recommend appropriate revisions in the legislative process. The panel held a series of hearings over several months on a multitude of topics. As usual, little attention was focused on broad conceptions of the ideal Congress; most of the discussion concerned specific proposals that addressed particular matters. At the top of the agenda were steps to make Congress more accountable so that it would again be in the public's good graces. A legislature devoted to the public good, free from ethical taint, and acting "in the sunshine" could once again command citizen confidence. Given the widespread concern over Congress's alleged decision-making shortcomings, reforms to improve responsibility, to make the legislature an effective and efficient policy-maker, also stimulated substantial debate. A more responsible Congress could both make its preferences prevail over those of the executive and devise workable solutions to the nation's pressing policy problems.

Ironically (in view of the common criticism that Congress was out of touch with ordinary Americans), there was little consideration of proposals to enhance congressional responsiveness.[3] Reformers identified structural fragmentation, which accommodates responsiveness, as a prime source of policy inertia; they sought to find ways to increase centralization as a means to encourage responsible policy making. In general, as reform issues percolated through Congress, attention was given to a wide array of possible changes in congressional organization and procedure.[4]

Reforms for Accountability

"Sunshine" Reforms

As astute politicians who read the 1990 and 1992 election returns as well as the opinion polls, members of Congress, not surprisingly, thought seriously about ways to regain the public's respect, trust, and confidence. One issue of concern was how to make Congress more open to citizen scrutiny. Proposals to restrict closed committee meetings to consideration of national security matters, to require that committee reports include committee roll call votes, and to mandate on-the-record floor votes on tax increase bills would, if adopted, make legislators' actions more visible to outside observers.[5] Conducting question and answer sessions, in which administration officials would appear on the House or Senate floor to respond to legislators' inquiries, and "Oxford style" debates, in which teams of members from each party would debate major issues on the chamber floor, would allow the public to discover where the parties stood on the important controversies of the moment and to judge them accordingly.[6]

The minority House Republicans had their own suggestions. Debate less restricted by Rules Committee orders that limit the possibilities for presenting policy alternatives as amendments to pending legislation would allow them to present their views more specifically.[7] Conversely, they roundly denounced all efforts to restrict the use of "special orders" that permit them to make speeches at the end of the legislative day, which were broadcast on the C-SPAN network, and to give "one minutes" (short statements) while the House was in session, as efforts to restrict their ability to get the party's message to the voters.[8] In their view, any or all of these changes should make it easier for the electorate to inform itself more fully about what Congress is debating and where the parties to the discussions stand with respect to current controversies.

Ethics Reforms

The widespread feeling that members were overly beholden to special interests had contributed to the public's disenchantment with legislative performance. Senators and representatives, in response, sought ways to emphasize their freedom from undue pressure from special pleaders and their personal commitment to unbiased consideration of pending policy problems. The Senate struggled to find appropriate ways for members to serve their constituents (it is, after all, the duty of the legislature, as the "people's branch," to deal with citizens' legitimate claims) without exerting improper pressure on those in the executive branch charged with resolving those claims. The Keating Five affair was a classic example of the lawmakers' dilemma. The senators involved insisted that they had done no more for Charles Keating than they would have done for any constituent; their critics charged, and the Senate Ethics Committee concurred, that they had crossed the line of permissible representation to urge special treatment from bank regulators for a financial contributor. The chamber revised its rules to try to resolve the issue, but the effort produced little assurance that it would be easy to distinguish between proper representation and suspect activities. One proposal, a hardy perennial, is to create a congressional Office of Constituent Service to handle constituent requests for assistance. Members have been reluctant, however, to give up their casework activity, for which they believe they get much credit (and electoral support); in any event, it is not clear that such an office would deal with cases beyond the routine matters that are the most likely to require the legislators to make direct contact with administrators on behalf of their constituents.[9]

Members also considered the need to counter the belief, seemingly widely held in the electorate, that outsiders—lobbyists and political action committees—have excessive influence over Congress. Sen. Carl Levin (D-Mich.) introduced a bill, which the Senate passed, to compel more lobbyists to register, as well as to disclose their activities, the amounts of money they receive and spend to lobby members (gifts of more than $25 had to be reported), and the extent and nature of their contacts with them. Violators of the law would be subject to civil penalties of up to $200,000. Other proposals would make the offering of "gratuities" to lawmakers a crime—bribery. The intent here was both to reduce lobbyists' ability to influence members and to make their legitimate communications with members a part of the public record so that citizens would be able to ascertain the nature of lobbyist-legislator relationships and act accordingly.[10]

To allay the suspicion that Congress is incapable of keeping its ethical house in order, witnesses before the Joint Committee suggested a new procedure for investigating and resolving charges of senatorial misconduct. Worried that members of the ethics committees, serving simultaneously as investigators and jurors, were unable to make impartial judgments about their allegedly wayward colleagues, they proposed using special panels composed of outside experts, including former members or retired judges, to investigate specific charges of wrongdoing. Other proposals included the adoption of a written set of ethics guidelines that would apply to both chambers. The members resisted these changes, and indeed seemed more concerned with protecting themselves from unfair allegations; they indicated support for a statute of limitations on initiation of charges, asserted that sworn complaints should be required to trigger ethics cases, and urged provision of pro bono counsel for members accused of violations. Indeed, Richard Lugar (R-Ind.) went so far as to propose elimination of the ethics committees, arguing that the courts and the voters could deal effectively with ethical transgressions.[11] Ultimately, the Senate decided to establish a ten-member bipartisan task force, which was independent of the Joint Committee, to explore ethics issues and to recommend reforms aimed at restoring Congress's standing as an ethical institution.[12]

Campaign Finance Reform

A similar concern about the deleterious effects of money led to a renewed effort to reform the ways members finance their election campaigns, which congressional insiders and outsiders both recognized as a problem. The huge and constantly increasing costs of such campaigns forced members to commit substantial effort to fund raising, and many of these contributions came from organized interests, particularly PACs, seeking to advance their favored policy initiatives. Whether such contributions "buy" votes or merely ensure that groups will have the access to members that allows them to present their views directly remains an open question. Still, the ability to be heard confers an advantage, and even the possibility of an improper link between donor and recipient can arouse public skepticism about Congress's fairness. Most important, perhaps, current finance arrangements inhibit challengers eager to oust incumbents. The holders of powerful positions in the legislature receive the lion's share of PAC contributions, giving them a head start in any campaign. Accountability requires that voting citizens have an opportunity to replace lawmakers out of touch with their preferences with newcomers more responsive to popular needs (and possibly more attuned to public opinion); to the extent that financial advantages entrench incumbents, the voters are denied that opportunity.[13]

Recognizing the problems that arise from the ways campaigns are financed is one thing; deciding how to remedy those problems is quite another. Both partisan and interchamber differences colored and complicated reform prescriptions. Democrats, as the congressional majority and thus the recipients of most of the PAC money, resisted Republican calls for limiting such contributions. Reduced PAC money would make GOP challengers financially more competitive with Democratic incumbents. Democrats, for their part, proposed spending limits to hold down the spiraling costs of campaigns. Republicans rejected caps on total spending on the grounds that their challengers, less well known than incumbent Democrats, need to spend large sums to get their names and messages before the voters. The lower the limits, the more limited the challengers' prospects. Spending limits raise an additional, constitutional, problem. In *Buckley v. Valeo* (1976), the Supreme Court ruled that campaign contributions are a form of free speech and cannot be restricted. Thus, any reform would have to offer incentives—such as free or subsidized mail or vouchers for media advertising—to induce candidates to accept spending limits voluntarily. Moreover, if wealthy candidates declined to accept the limits, ways would have to be found to enable their less affluent opponents to fund competitive campaigns. Public funds, from tax revenues, are one way to replace reduced group contributions or to guarantee challengers adequate financing, but members of both parties, particularly Republicans, worried that the citizenry would see such expenditures as yet another example of legislators feeding at the public trough.

Senators and representatives had differing perspectives on campaign finance reform. The latter, less visible nationally and thus less able to solicit contributions from individual donors, were loath to give up PAC funds. Senators, more prominent in the media and on the national political scene, had more diverse sources of funds and less incentive to resist reduction in the availability of PAC funds. They were more prepared to respond to popular opinion, which seemed to them to demand that Congress "do something" about the evils of campaign finance. Given the wide-ranging and passionate differences about the nature of that "something," the prospects for meaningful reform seemed dim.

Ironically, the seeming intractability of the issue permitted the lawmakers to act during the second session of the 102d Congress (in 1992). President George Bush had announced in advance that he would veto any reform legislation that contained spending limits or public finance provisions and it was evident that congressional Republicans had the votes to sustain his veto. The majority Democrats thus felt free to act and they passed a wide-ranging reform bill. House candidates could spend no more than $600,000 per campaign; they could raise $200,000 from PAC contributions, solicit gifts of the same amount from individual contributors (in part matched by public funds), and receive another $200,000 in government money. An elaborate formula, reflecting state population, determined Senate spending limits. The bill strangely included no mention of the ways the public funds would be raised. To elicit the required voluntary compliance with the spending limits, the bill offered reduced mailing costs (candidates for both chambers) and free television time (candidates for the Senate).

It also contained chamber-specific provisions concerning PAC contributions: PACs could continue to donate $5,000 to House nominees but would be limited to $2,500 in gifts to Senate candidates. Permissible PAC contributions to state parties doubled, however, to $10,000. Finally, the bill limited candidates' personal contributions to their own campaigns to not more than 10 percent of the spending limit or $250,000, whichever was less. Knowing the bill would not become law, members had no qualms about striking a blow for reform. The president, as promised, vetoed the bill; Congress, as predicted, failed to override. The bill resurfaced in the 103d Congress, but with a Democratic president pledged to sign reform legislation, and given the controversy surrounding spending limits, PAC contributions, and public funding, its passage remains problematic.[14] Short of new legislation, some members have indicated support for giving the Federal Election Commission more funds and more staff to enforce existing regulations more rigorously.

The reformers' also addressed other campaign finance matters. They pushed to eliminate or severely limit so-called soft money contributions to political parties. Under a loophole in the Federal Election Campaign Act, large contributions (often as high as $100,000) to state and local party organizations are permissible for "party-building" activities such as voter registration drives and election day get-out-the-vote efforts. Such opportunities allowed large contributors, or fat cats, to have at least an indirect influence on federal elections, contrary to the intent of the FECA. Critics focused on the practice of "bundling," by which groups, including PACs, solicit the permissible $1,000 contributions from individuals and send them as a package to favored candidates. Although it is within the letter of the law, bundling of donations seemed to increase the influence of those who could present many checks to financially strapped candidates. "Independent expenditures" constituted another questionable practice. The FECA allows groups to spend funds in support of or opposition to candidates as long as there is no coordination or consultation with the candidates' campaign organizations.[15] In practice, it is difficult at best to demonstrate a lack of coordination with campaigns, and such expenditures seemed to permit circumvention of contribution limits. Reformers saw regulation of soft money, bundling, and independent expenditures as a means to overcome the appearance of corruption that undermines public confidence in its elected legislators. Future reform efforts will inevitably address these issues.

Other Reforms

As a further step to restore public respect for Congress, the reformers suggested additional cuts in the available perquisites of office. Many wanted to curtail the franking privilege, the sending of free mail to all "postal patrons" in a member's state or district, beyond the limits imposed in 1990 and 1991; to do so, their argument ran, would be to reduce incumbents' advantages and enable challengers to wage more competitive campaigns. Others were eager to eliminate privileges (such as free parking at Washington airports) that smacked of congressional arrogance and defiance of public opinion. Another idea was to require reductions of up to 25 percent in Congress's budget, especially for hiring staff; such an action would demonstrate the legislature's sensitivity to the deficit problem and its willingness to do its share to hold down costs. Rejection of cost-of-living salary increases for members and legislative branch employees would have the same effect. Critics argued that Congress should apply to itself various civil rights statutes (for example, the Americans with Disabilities Act and the Occupational Health and Safety Act) from which it (and the executive branch) is exempt.[16] A final possibility, unlikely to win much support, is to enlarge the House of Representatives. More districts, smaller in size and more homogeneous in composition, would ease the legislators' representational tasks and enable the citizens to hold them to account more readily.[17]

In truth, the value of these proposals is more symbolic than real; if adopted, they might foster a more favorable image of Congress, but it seems unlikely they would have a major effect on the ways the legislature does its work. The franking privilege has already been limited, and a strong case can be made that members need to retain a minimal ability to inform and educate their constituents about what Congress is doing in order to deal with the issues it faces. Members have already cut back on perquisites to the extent that they retain very few, certainly fewer than executives in the private sector. Staff cuts and other money-saving steps would save very little money; indeed, closing down Congress entirely would save only $2 billion (in a budget of more than $1 trillion), less than the cost of two B-1 Stealth bombers (of which twenty are on order). Few would quarrel with affording legislative branch personnel the same civil rights protections that ordinary citizens receive, but the direct impact of such action on congressional performance would surely be minimal. Nonetheless, these reforms, like those pertaining to congressional openness and visibility, ethics, and campaign finance, are likely to stimulate much discussion in the 1990s.

Reforms for Responsibility

An important charge leveled by critics was that the legislature was incapable or unwilling to face up to a host of policy issues that plagued the nation. The decentralized decision-making procedure of Congress, coupled with divided government, made it virtually impossible for the lawmakers to move meaningful programs through the legislative process: deadlock not decisiveness was the hallmark of congressional politics. Reformers, in consequence, introduced a wide variety of changes designed to make Congress a more effective, more responsible policy maker.

Countervailing the President

Some reformers, especially those inclined toward a congressional supremacy position, continued to search for ways to increase the ability of Congress to impose its will on the executive, or at least make its voice heard more clearly in the White House. As the Iran-contra affair and the debate in Congress over the American commitment of troops to the Persian Gulf demonstrated, the president continues to have the upper hand in the determination of the nation's foreign policy. The War Powers Act has not served its intended purpose, and pro-Congress members and observers continue to look for ways to increase Congress's contribution to the formulation of foreign policy, especially in the complex and uncertain post-cold war world. Some have proposed rewriting the War Powers Act to insist more forcefully on the president's obligation to consult with and report to Congress about decisions to commit U.S. troops and on Congress's option to compel withdrawal of such troops once they are committed to battle. The Congressional Research Service has suggested several less controversial ways for the legislature to make its views known more clearly to the president. It could issue a "statement of principles on sharing foreign affairs and war powers" that sets forth its claim for full participation in decision making that concerns international affairs; set up a permanent foreign policy consultation group and invite the chief executive to consult with it; or establish ad hoc committees to formulate the legislature's position on specific foreign policy issues as they emerge.[18]

Congressional assertion of power vis-à-vis the executive seems to also have come up short in the area of budgeting. Despite the almost continuous alteration of the budgetary process (in 1974, 1985, 1987, and 1990), Congress has not yet demonstrated the ability either to make its financial priorities prevail or to impose the discipline necessary to resolve the seemingly intractable deficit problem. Not surprisingly, then, proposals abound for another round of budgetary process reforms. The most extreme suggestion is to enact a balanced budget amendment to the Constitution. The details of the several proposed texts vary, but the basic thrust of the idea is to force the president and Congress to agree each year on an estimate of the government's total receipts and to prohibit expenditures that exceed the expected revenues unless Congress, by an extraordinary majority (perhaps three-fifths) roll call vote, authorizes outlays greater than receipts.

The idea raises many difficult problems. Drafting an amendment that defines the meaning of a balanced budget and incorporates all the contingencies that must be accounted for in the method of estimating federal revenues will be exceptionally difficult, and challenges to each year's decision will likely result in extended litigation. If an amendment were adopted, Congress and the executive might well evade its intent with the same sort of inventive, disingenuous budgeting that undermined the Gramm-Rudman-Hollings Act. An amendment would do no more than the previous statutory efforts at budget reform did to force Congress to take the politically difficult steps needed to control the deficit. Most important, a balanced budget amendment seems likely to reduce rather than increase congressional control of the budget. It would force the lawmakers to bargain with the president concerning the revenue estimate for any fiscal year. It would constrain Congress's right to appropriate money as it sees fit because it would preclude the option to fund important programs through deficit financing. Such concerns have made those members intent on preserving congressional independence and prerogative reluctant to consider such an amendment seriously.[19]

Reform ideas have focused on making the congressional process more manageable through institutional changes that do not cede budgetary power to the executive. A major impetus here is to simplify a complicated, multilayer process. Sen. Nancy Landon Kassebaum (R-Kans.) has proposed a radical change, one unlikely to pass. She would abolish the appropriations committees and distribute their powers to the authorizing committees. A leadership committee, composed of committee chairs, ranking committee members, and party leaders, would replace the budget committees; it would determine budget priorities and set spending limits for each of the authorizing panels, which would both authorize programs and appropriate the funds to pay for them.[20] Appropriations Committee members, needless to say, are less than enthusiastic about yielding their powers to determine government expenditure levels.

Ideas for less sweeping changes in the budget process abound. One suggestion calls for replacing annual budgeting with a two-year cycle. Authorization and appropriations decisions would be made in the first year; in the second year Congress would oversee how the money was spent. Supplemental legislation could be enacted throughout the period to deal with unforeseen contingencies. Another suggestion is to require that the president submit a balanced budget and that Congress vote on it, as amended. Making the budget process more coherent has also been suggested. Clear demarcation of stages would give all participants the opportunity to play their assigned roles in the process more effectively. After passage of the budget resolution, authorizing committees would have ample time to review the programs within their jurisdictions; only then would the appropriations committees make decisions about specific funding levels. Some members have proposed clarifying committee jurisdictions: only one subcommittee of one full committee would have responsibility for any program and for overseeing the agencies that run it. Some critics would either prohibit waiving of budget law requirements or require an extraordinary majority (perhaps three-fifths) vote to do so; more rigorous enforcement of the rules would curtail the possibilities for evading the budgetary discipline that the existing procedures seek to impose.[21] All of these ideas aim to make the budget process simpler and more coherent and thus more likely to represent a clear statement of Congress's budgetary priorities. Defenders of current procedures argue that institutional changes are neither the problem nor the solution. Rather, they assert, lack of agreement on the substance of policy, exacerbated by partisanship resulting from divided government, prevent members from using the existing mechanisms to enact a meaningful budget.

One set of proposed budgetary reforms aims directly at improving the legislature's ability to control the federal deficit. The simplest suggestion is to enact "sunset provisions" mandating periodic reexamination and reauthorization of all federal programs; those found to be ineffective or no longer necessary could be terminated. Separate operating budgets (covering the day-to-day costs of running the government) and capital budgets (funding long-term investments in roads and other infrastructure projects) could be required. New rules might require that the operating budget be balanced annually and that deficit financing be permitted only for necessary capital spending. Another possibility is to apply the reconciliation process, now limited to mandatory spending, to discretionary programs; to do so would give the budget committees another means to force expenditure reductions. More significant are proposals to control the growth of mandatory entitlements such as Social Security. These might have to be reviewed and renewed periodically, and reductions might be possible, or their growth might be limited to a fixed percentage determined by the inflation rate. (Most entitlements are indexed and rise proportionally with the Consumer Price Index.)[22] Such reforms, their proponents believe, could enable Congress to take forceful action on its own to reduce the budget deficit.

An important weapon in Congress's struggle to legislate effectively and without deferring excessively to the executive is information; well-informed lawmakers are better able to make expert, and thus convincing, arguments for their decisions to reject presidential initiatives and substitute their own views. In recent years, committee and members' office staffs have grown exponentially with the increase in size and complexity of the congressional work load. Congress has also drawn increasingly on enlarged support agencies: the Congressional Budget Office, the Office of Technology Assessment, the General Accounting Office, and the Congressional Research Service. Critics complain that these staffs have become too large and often create management problems for legislators that detract from their ability to focus on policy making.[23] To some reformers, the charges seem largely to be veiled efforts to challenge alleged congressional profligacy; these reformers often propose across-the-board staff cuts, sometimes as high as 25 percent, to demonstrate the legislature's commitment to lowering government expenditures.

More thoughtful observers, although recognizing the existence of some staff and information resource inefficiencies, defend Congress's need for accurate data. They focus on ways to make better use of current or slightly reduced information resources. Their suggestions include creating an Office of Congressional Staff Services to assist members in dealing with the mail and routine constituent requests for services; this would justify reducing the House office staff from eighteen to fifteen and would permit more effective allocation of the remaining staffers to important policy-related duties. Other suggestions include hiring more professional and fewer "political" staff members; linking member and committee staffs more closely with the support agencies (through expanded computer networks, for instance); and determining ways to improve the members' ability to use the support agencies effectively. The aim here is to provide Congress with a manageable but full range of pertinent information and with the incentives to use it productively to formulate sound public policy. Members themselves, of course, may be reluctant to give up some of the staff and informational assistance that serves their political as well as their legislative purposes. If they could be persuaded to do so, their improved information resources, along with a rationalized budget process, might allow Congress to play a more responsible role vis-à-vis the president in the making of domestic and foreign policy.

Strengthening the Parties

Discussion of improving congressional responsibility inevitably turns to the need to reduce structural fragmentation, to permit the legislature to act with dispatch and efficiency. The obvious starting place is to capitalize on the political party's potential as a centralizing agent. More effective parties, able to act cohesively, could move their programs ahead with fewer delays and less need to compromise on content with entrenched minorities. Reformers who desire more powerful parties promote changes to that end: to reduce the independence of committees and subcommittees and to strengthen the hand of the party leaders to smooth the passage of their initiatives through the legislative process.

Constraining the Committees. To limit the ability of recalcitrant committees and subcommittees to subvert party policy goals, the reformers advanced several suggestions.[24] One set proposes a streamlined, more coherent and logical committee structure. Committee jurisdictions could be rationalized. (They are now overlapping, with several committees claiming the right to consider particular policy areas.) Unneeded standing committees could be eliminated, as the House select panels have been; fewer committees, perhaps only one, would have jurisdiction over a given subject—energy or health matters, for example. If the House and Senate each had a parallel committee with the same basic responsibilities, more careful development of policy alternatives might be facilitated. Realigned and consolidated jurisdictions would also equalize congressional work loads, allowing more members to work on significant matters. Coupled with limits (already in effect) on the number of subcommittees per full committee and with proposed limits on member committee assignments—one plan calls for each member to have no more than two—committee restructuring might lead to a system of smaller, more expert panels in which lawmakers commit themselves more fully to policy making. In addition, term limits on committee service generally, or on service as a chair or ranking member, might discourage committee members from developing vested interests in committee matters; they would no longer have incentives to advance committee views at the expense of party considerations because they would soon be moving on to other committee assignments. The negative side of such term limits, of course, is that restricted tenure might well reduce member interest in developing policy expertise that would enhance the quality of committee policy making.

These reorganized committees could be responsible decision makers, but committee members might parlay their expertise to such an extent that they resist or ignore the wishes of their congressional colleagues. To avoid such a possibility, or to control maverick committees that exist under present jurisdictional arrangements, some reformers propose to make the Speaker of the House and the Democratic caucus better able to keep committee members, especially the chairs, in line with party positions. This is a difficult task: committee members should be more than mere ciphers doing the party's bidding; they need to use their special knowledge to produce effective policy and programs. The parties should harness, not undercut, committee strengths.

Still, the Speaker might do more with the powers already available. Influence over the Steering and Policy Committee, which flows from the power to make appointments to that body, allows him some say in initial committee assignments. The party caucus has assumed the right to oust sitting chairs at any time (not merely at the convening of a new Congress), and if given the chance to elect chairs in open competition (instead of voting first—up or down—on Steering and Policy's nomination of a single candidate, which is the present practice), the caucus might do more to place loyal partisans in committee leadership positions. In addition, the bill referral process could be simplified. The Speaker might resist making multiple referrals in the interest of reducing the number of committees that can delay or defeat legislation; or he might refer bills to some committees with authority to make recommendations only, not to amend or report bills. Limiting consideration to a single committee might put a bill in the hands of an unfriendly panel (multiple referrals do offer the opportunity to find a favorable forum for favored legislation), but if a hostile committee defies them, party leaders could bypass it by creating an ad hoc panel to consider a particular policy issue.[25] Such changes, along with those revising the structure of the committee system, might produce committees both expert and sensitive to party influence; the result, reformers hope, would be more responsible congressional policy making.

Enhancing the Party Leadership. More generally, party leaders might take on additional powers to promote legislative centralization and, in turn, effective policy formulation. One recurring problem is the lack of focus in congressional policy making—the absence of an agenda that concentrates members' attention on the most critical issues. Individualistic lawmakers tend to go their own ways, promoting policies that appeal to them and their particular constituents. In consequence, critics claim, the legislature does not use its resources effectively to resolve pressing policy problems. The newly created House Democrats' Speaker's Working Group on Policy Development (see the section on "Centralizing the Parties" in Chapter 3) may be able to develop a clear party agenda, especially if assisted by a skilled professional staff. If such a party program were developed in the period between the November elections and the convening of a new Congress the following January, the majority might begin deliberations on major matters early in the session and with advance commitment to party positions on the part of influential members, including committee leaders who had participated in formulating the program. The party leaders could make full use of the powers—over committee assignments, bill referral, scheduling, and floor consideration—that the 1970s reforms granted them to promote priority legislation. They might also take greater advantage of their access to the mass media to generate public support for these agenda items.[26]

Indeed, some observers suggest that party leaders already have the appropriate authority and that all that is really needed are changes in the operative legislative rules of the game, which presently hinder leaders' use of the available avenues of influence. Deference to the party rank and file prevents the leaders' forceful use of power. With a precise party agenda in place, the leaders could use their persuasive powers—their ability to advance a convincing substantive rationale for the priority programs as well as to confer political advantage on and provide protection for supportive members—to mobilize their partisan troops to pass the legislation they desire.[27] In any case, more forceful use of newly granted authority in support of party priorities might encourage more responsible congressional policy making.

Changing the Rules

The formal rules under which Congress considers legislation, especially those in the Senate, confer considerable advantages on a minority seeking to thwart the passage of bills. The rules establish a sequential decision-making process that enables a determined minority to block legislation in committee, on the floor of either house, or in conference committee. The process in a decentralized legislature has numerous "veto points" at which legislation may expire or at which significant compromise may be the only way to move a bill to the subsequent stage. Reformers, in consequence, look for ways to remove these procedural roadblocks to permit Congress to act responsibly, to enact legislation establishing meaningful programs.

The problem is less serious in the larger House of Representatives, where the majority, because of its control over the Committee on Rules, is able to have bills considered under favorable conditions. The committee's rules, which almost always reflect the leadership's wishes, may preclude many, if not all, hostile amendments, or may require roll call votes in a sequence that makes it probable that committee or party positions will prevail. The minority will have a hard time defeating the majority's proposals if the majority unites to support them. On the whole, dilatory tactics are insufficient to permit the minority to do much more than annoy the majority. Still, there have been some proposals to smooth the flow of legislation.

In general, reformers suggested, a more concentrated focus of attention would encourage responsible policy making. Many of the changes (noted in the section on "A Trend toward Responsibility" in Chapter 3) that would make Congress more accountable—fewer, more expert committees and subcommittees, with more equal work loads, for instance—might also improve policy formulation. More well informed members thinking seriously about a limited number of important bills might result in more creative policy solutions. Pruning the agenda of extraneous or unimportant measures might also give members more time to consider truly important matters. By some estimates, 40 percent of all legislation Congress enacts is commemorative—declaring April to be National American Legion Baseball Month or acknowledging the singular contribution of some ethnic group to American society. Such chores might profitably be given to an independent commission, or bills might be passed in more routine fashion. Similarly, less time might be given over to one minutes, brief speeches made at the start of the legislative day, or special orders, presented at the conclusion of the day's legislative business. Further increase in the use of the "suspension of the rules procedure"—under which relatively inconsequential bills are debated for forty minutes, but must pass by a two-thirds majority vote—might help clear the agenda of minor matters. Finally, the minority's ability to force quorum calls or require reading of the daily *Journal* in full, as delaying tactics, might be restricted.[28] Such modest rules changes could, in principle, permit the House to make policy with greater dispatch.[29]

Minority power poses a more serious threat to responsible policy making in the Senate. As a disciplined Republican minority demonstrated early in the 103d Congress (1993-1994), when it forced the majority to compromise on a major voter registration bill and defeated President Clinton's economic stimulus package, the filibuster can be a formidable weapon. To reduce the minority's opportunity to use extended debate to prevent the majority from acting, Democratic majority leader George Mitchell (Maine) proposed in 1993 a series of rules changes. He would limit debate on the motion to take up a bill (currently subject to a filibuster) to two hours; require a three-fifths majority vote to overturn the ruling of the presiding officer after cloture is invoked; make amendments introduced by the committee with jurisdiction automatically germane after cloture; and count the time used for quorum calls under cloture against the speaking time of the senator who insisted on the quorum call.

To the same end, Mitchell proposed to permit the majority to adopt a motion requiring that amendments to legislation be germane. He suggested ways to help conference committees reach agreement. The Senate should be able to send a bill to conference after passage of a single motion (rather than the three motions currently required in the absence of unanimous consent); fewer filibusters would then be possible. In addition, Mitchell wanted new rules to make it easier to dispense with a full reading on the floor of a conference committee's report. These changes would, he argued, make it possible for majority party and committee leaders to move their priority legislation past the minority with less difficulty. Given the strength of the Republican minority (forty-four votes) in the 103d Congress, Mitchell's proposals seem doomed to meet an untimely death.[30] No minority will eagerly surrender use of the rules as a delaying tactic.

Term Limits

Since the late 1980s, policy failures and unresolved major issues have been a major impetus for the assault on Congress. Limits on lawmakers' terms of office—from six to twelve years for members of the House and two terms for senators—have emerged as a popular remedy for congressional irresponsibility. By 1993, voters in referendums held in fifteen states had passed measures imposing such limits. The rationale for them was to free the legislators of a need, arising from aspirations for long careers in Congress, to cater excessively to the parochial constituency interests on which reelection depends. In the absence of such career concerns, members should be able to cast narrow interests aside in favor of the broader national interest—that is, become more responsible. Without the reelection incentive to curry favor from pressure groups, campaign contributors, or special interests, senators and representatives could "bite the bullet" and adopt effective programs even in the face of concerted opposition.

Many observers are unconvinced by this rationale, however. To serve the full time permitted still requires House members to win an additional five elections after their first electoral success; senators would have to win a second contest. To retain their seats, they would have to appeal to the voters in their states and districts, and it is doubtful that they would succeed if they simply declined to support programs that serve constituents' programmatic needs. Only in their final term, with no possibility whatsoever of reelection, would legislators be totally free to ignore constituency concerns—then they might act responsibly.

Moreover, term limits might have negative consequences. With only a short stint in Congress in their futures, members might feel it unnecessary to acquire the policy expertise required to be responsible policy makers; they might defer excessively to staff members; they also might devote their energies to finding favorable jobs to continue their careers after leaving the legislature. In addition, term limits would surely force some of the most experienced and knowledgeable lawmakers to leave office, inhibiting Congress's ability to formulate workable public policies. Beyond these substantive arguments against term limits, there are important political considerations. Members of Congress are career oriented; they should not be expected willingly to limit their political prospects, and they are highly unlikely to pass an amendment writing term limits into the Constitution. Some members, including Speaker of the House Thomas Foley, have begun legal action to have the state initiatives declared unconstitutional, claiming that the Constitution imposes only citizenship, age, and residence qualifications for legislative service that the states cannot alter.[31]

The Line-Item Veto

A reform proposal that has profound implications for congressional responsibility is the line-item veto. The Constitution, of course, allows the president to veto entire bills but not parts thereof. Chief executives, in consequence, must often accept some provisions they find objectionable to win approval of others, more numerous or more desirable. The line-item veto offers a partial remedy; it would let the president reject single items in appropriations bills. Under current law, the president may propose to rescind spending previously approved. That power is severely limited, however, for unless Congress votes in favor of it, the rescission expires after forty-five days and the chief executive must accept the expenditure; congressional inaction defeats the president. Under the line-item veto, Congress would have to override the president's veto by a two-thirds vote in each chamber, just as it does with respect to all legislation.

Variations on the line-item veto idea abound. One, "enhanced rescission," would give the president even greater control over expenditures. Presidential rescission proposals would go into effect unless both houses voted a motion of disapproval; if they did, the chief executive could veto the motion, forcing Congress to override by a two-thirds vote. Another variation, "expedited rescission," is less extreme. The president would propose to rescind a spending item and Congress would be forced to vote on the proposal, but the rescission would take effect only if simple majorities in both houses approved. Some have proposed extending the veto authority to single provisions in tax legislation as well as appropriations measures. All of these procedures would shift power from Congress to the president. Congress would have to insist more forcefully, and in public, on its spending priorities. Moreover, the president might use the item veto authority broadly to gain leverage over legislators with respect to other matters. Members opposed to presidential initiatives on any subject might face the unhappy prospect of a line-item veto of spending (or tax) items of vital concern to their constituents.

Presidents belonging to both parties, needless to say, have favored some form of line-item veto. More surprisingly, perhaps, so do many in Congress. In view of the significant public disapproval of pork barrel spending, the veto offers the legislators a chance to show that they are eager to control spending and hold down the deficit. Those inclined to favor the executive force theory (see Chapter 1) applaud a transfer of authority to the president; congressional supremacists deplore such an alteration in the balance of power between the branches. Those with vested interests in the current practice—such as members of the appropriations committees—or in constituency-oriented spending (liberals mostly) are less than enthusiastic about giving the president a line-item veto. Others are reluctant to adopt a change when the consequences are difficult to predict. Republicans in the 103d Congress, hopeful of regaining the White House, hold out for nothing less than powerful presidential line-item authority over both discretionary spending and tax bill provisions.[32] Agreement may be difficult to reach.

Reforms for Responsiveness

The bulk of the reformers' current criticisms of Congress focus on the lack of accountability and imperfect responsibility; responsiveness is not high on the reform agenda for the 1990s. Indeed, excessive responsiveness, undue deference to narrow interests, has been a major criticism of Congress. As a result, few specific changes have been proposed in the most recent reform debates to increase the legislature's responsiveness. The emphasis on finding ways to overcome congressional gridlock and to encourage innovative and effective policy making stimulated discussion of ways to centralize congressional decision making—limit committee independence, strengthen the political parties, change the rules of procedure. If adopted, these reforms would reduce responsiveness because they would speed legislative action and lessen members' opportunity to cater to parochial interests outside Washington.

If responsiveness was not a central concern in the renewed reform efforts, some of the ideas discussed still had potential, though indirect, implications for responsiveness. If campaign finance reforms permit challengers to unseat incumbents, the former may bring to Congress policy preferences more in tune with the electorates in their states and districts. Similarly, limits on the contributions of PACs may decrease their access to, and possibly their influence on, lawmakers, allowing the members to pay closer attention to the views of ordinary citizens. This is also (though not the only) rationale for limiting legislative terms: without the need to concentrate on ensuring their long-term careers in Congress, members would respond less to the special interests and more to basic citizen sentiments. Inside Congress, limiting tenure on committees or as committee leaders would bring different legislators, with different policy preferences, to the top spots on the committees. Broadly defining members' opportunities and obligations to serve constituents, not narrowing them as some proposed in the aftermath of the Keating Five affair, would tie senators and representatives more closely to their local electorates. In short, some of the reform proposals under discussion could have positive effects on congressional responsiveness as incidental by-products.

One set of developments has more immediate potential to increase a particular aspect of legislative responsiveness. House Democrats and Republicans have both been concerned with empowering the rank-and-file party members. The Democrats have enlarged their whip operations and established a Speaker's Working Group to advise on policy matters. Both steps increase the involvement of party caucus members in party affairs and give them the chance to shape the party agenda and determine party positions with respect to the items on that agenda. The Republicans are considering similar moves; Rep. Fred Grandy has proposed that the party create a broadly representative fourteen-member "executive council" to formulate party policy.[33] To the degree that the parties consider the views of a wide spectrum of their members, they may be more responsive to their full membership and, indirectly, to the diverse state and local electorates that send the lawmakers to Congress.

The minority House Republicans face a special problem. They suffer from the perception, not without some merit, that they do not count for much in the chamber's policy making. They propose reforms to permit their party to act more forcefully and with greater impact as the opposition. If adopted, the changes might make the House more responsive to minority party concerns. Specifically, the Republicans would like to see membership ratios on House committees accurately reflect the partisan balance in the chamber; currently the Democrats maintain dominant majorities on major committees. On the Rules Committee, for instance, there are nine Democrats and only four Republicans, enabling the majority to control the terms under which legislation reaches the floor. A "closed" or restricted rule may prevent the minority from offering significant amendments to pending legislation. More generally, the GOP would like fuller consultation with the majority Democrats about scheduling legislation for floor consideration. The Republicans propose that the House rules guarantee them the right to offer a motion to recommit any bill (to send it back to committee with instructions to alter its content) as a matter of course. They also insist that House rules that allocate one- third of committee staff to the minority—rules that the majority has ignored with impunity—be strongly enforced. All these steps would allow the minority to formulate its positions carefully and expertly, and to be sure that its views receive both publicity and consideration. The House, in consequence, would weigh Republican alternatives more seriously.[34] The Democrats retort that, as the majority, they have the responsibility to do everything necessary to pass their program. "Fairness or unfairness," as Joseph Moakley (D-Mass.), chair of the House Rules Committee, put it, "the majority has the prerogative to get legislation to the floor and subsequently enacted." [35]

Summary

The 1970s reform effort did not succeed to everyone's satisfaction in remaking Congress as a responsible policy maker. Neither passage of the war powers resolution nor several attempts to restructure the budget process enabled the legislature to reclaim fully its authority vis-à-vis the president. More forceful use of party mechanisms to overcome decentralization in the name of efficiency did not satisfy those eager to see Congress act with dispatch and effectiveness to write new and innovative public policies into the statute books. The minority remained entirely capable of exploiting the parliamentary rules to thwart the majority. Thus, when scandal and policy shortcomings brought Congress into disrepute at the end of the 1980s, the legislators were forced to face up to a new round of reform proposals. Numerous ideas surfaced to permit the legislature to challenge the executive (the line-item veto is the exception) and to streamline its internal operations—by constraining the committees, strengthening the parties, and eliminating procedural roadblocks—so that lawmakers will be better able to formulate responsible public policy. Term limits, in the view of some reformers, would focus members' attention on policy matters.

These items are "on the table"; which ones (if any) are adopted and whether they achieve their intended purposes are unanswered questions as the Clinton tenure begins. The history of previous reform efforts suggests that the members will do what they believe necessary to placate the critics. Beyond that, they will seek to preserve their freedom to act to attain their personal goals, whether concerned with policy, power, or constituency. The 110 freshmen in the 103d Congress face difficult reform choices. Many ran as avowed reformers; most are experienced politicians, not naive amateurs, eager to enact legislation and to launch careers in Congress. Initial indications are that most of them (especially the 67 entering Democrats) will stress policy making rather than reform.[36] In any event, whatever reforms they adopt are likely to be incremental, unrelated to broad executive force or congressional supremacy theories of the ideal Congress. Some observers, mostly outside the halls of the Capitol, continue to look for ways to make the legislature "better," to find the optimum blend of responsibility, responsiveness, and accountability. Their suggestions may offer a distinctive vision of the future Congress.

NOTES

1. See James A. Thurber and Samantha L. Durst, "The 1990 Budget Enforcement Act: The Decline of Congressional Accountability," in *Congress Reconsidered*, 5th ed., ed. Lawrence C. Dodd and Bruce I. Oppenheimer (Washington, D.C.: CQ Press, 1993), 375-397; and the discussion in Chap. 3.
2. For a fuller discussion of Congress's current problems, see the Introduction.
3. Campaign finance reform, widely touted as a way to improve accountability (disclosure of the sources and uses of campaign funds would expose candidates' potential conflicts of interest), would also benefit challengers, who are presumably more in touch with citizen concerns than entrenched incumbents, and as a result would increase legislative responsiveness.
4. For extensive compendiums of reform ideas, see Congressional Research Service, Library of Congress, *Congressional Reorganization: Options for Change* (Washington, D.C.: Congressional Research Service, 1992); Thomas E. Mann and Norman J. Ornstein, *Renewing Congress: A First Report* (Washington, D.C.: American Enterprise Institute and the Brookings Institution, 1992); and Mann and Ornstein, *Renewing Congress: A Second Report* (Washington, D.C.: Brookings Institution, 1993).
5. Karen Foerstel, "Members Threw Crowd-Pleasing Legislation into Hopper as First Session Drew to Close," *Roll Call*, January 9, 1992, 8; and Craig Winneker, "If I Were Speaker . . . ," *Roll Call*, January 30, 1992, 3, 14.
6. Sarah Cagle, "British-Style Q&A Idea Wins Support," *Roll Call*, February 17, 1992, 3; Mann and Ornstein, *Renewing Congress: A First Report*; and Beth Donovan, "Freshmen Show Little Unity in Shaping Reform Agenda," *Congressional Quarterly Weekly Report*, March 27, 1993, 728.
7. Winneker, "If I Were Speaker. . . ."
8. Karen Foerstel, "Fight over Speeches Heats Up," *Roll Call*, March 29, 1993, 16; and Mann and Ornstein, *Renewing Congress: A First Report*.
9. Glenn R. Simpson, "Post-Keating-5 Report on Constituent Service Awaits

Mitchell Action," *Roll Call*, February 24, 1992, 10; Glenn R. Simpson, "Senate Quietly OKs Constituent Service Rule," *Roll Call*, July 13, 1992, 18; and Congressional Research Service, *Congressional Reorganization*, 131-133.

10. David Masci, "Committee Moves to Tighten Registration Loopholes," *Congressional Quarterly Weekly Report*, June 27, 1992, 1858; Karen Foerstel, "Flurry of Congressional Reform Legislation Introduced on Opening Day of New Session," *Roll Call*, January 18, 1993, 16; Donovan, "Freshmen Show Little Unity"; and Michael Wines, "Senate Passes Stringent New Rules for Lobbyists," *New York Times*, May 7, 1993, A18.

11. Beth Donovan, with Chris Lawrence, "What's Wrong with Congress? Everybody Has an Opinion," *Congressional Quarterly Weekly Report*, February 8, 1993, 252-253; and Karen Foerstel, "Joint Committee Looks at Ethics Panels: Should Outsiders Be the Judges?" *Roll Call*, March 1, 1993, 11, 17.

12. Karen Foerstel, "New Ethics Task Force Set Up," *Roll Call*, March 8, 1993, 36.

13. On these matters, see Mann and Ornstein, *Renewing Congress: A First Report*, 61-64; and the discussion in Chap. 4, esp. notes 43-45.

14. See David B. Magleby and Candice J. Nelson, *The Money Chase: Congressional Campaign Finance Reform* (Washington, D.C.: Brookings Institution, 1990); Beth Donovan, "Overhaul Plan Readied as Tool to Blunt Scandals' Effects," *Congressional Quarterly Weekly Report*, April 4, 1992, 861-863; and Tim Curran, "This Time Around, It's for Real," *Roll Call*, January 18, 1993, sec. A, 14-15.

15. In 1993, President Clinton, goaded by third-party candidate Ross Perot, offered an administration reform plan that called for voluntary spending limits, some public financing, reduced PAC contributions to campaigns for elections (or reelections) to the Senate but not to the House, and limits on soft money contributions but not on bundling.

16. The House, in 1988, set up an Office of Fair Employment Practices to hear and adjudicate congressional employees' discrimination complaints. The Senate followed suit in 1991. The aim was to afford congressional workers the same protection that various civil rights statutes guarantee to citizens in the private sector. On the proposal to apply a number of civil rights laws directly to Congress, see Janet Hook, "House Changes Rules to Protect Its Workers," *Congressional Quarterly Weekly Report*, October 8, 1988, 2766; and Mary Jacoby, "Senate's Office of Fair Employment Practices Invites Public Comment on Final Regulations," *Roll Call*, March 15, 1993, 17.

17. For a discussion of the pros and cons of a larger House, see C. St. John Yates. "A House of Our Own or a House We've Outgrown? An Argument for Increasing the Size of the House of Representatives," *Columbia Journal of Law and Social Problems* 25 (1992): 157-196.

18. Congressional Research Service, *Congressional Reorganization*, 153-157.

19. Conservatives (mostly Republicans), who tend to be more concerned with controlling the deficit than with institutional issues relating to the separation of powers, have been the leading proponents of an amendment. On reform of the budget process, see James A. Thurber and Samantha L. Durst, "Delay, Deadlock, and Deficits: Evaluating Congressional Budget Reform," in *Federal Budget and Financial Management Reform*, ed. Thomas D. Lynch (Westport, Conn.: Greenwood Press, 1991), 53-88.

20. Craig Winneker, "Turn Authorizers into Appropriators, Too, Kassebaum

Boldly Asks Joint Committee," *Roll Call*, March 18, 1993, 12.

21. See Congressional Research Service, *Congressional Reorganization*, chap. 12; Thomas E. Mann and Norman J. Ornstein, Testimony prepared for delivery to the Joint Committee on the Organization of the U.S. Congress, mimeographed, February 16, 1993; and Karen Foerstel, "Even as House Votes on Budget, Members Slam Budget Process," *Roll Call*, March 22, 1993, 11.

22. Congressional Research Service, *Congressional Reorganization*, chap. 11; Mann and Ornstein, Testimony; and Foerstel, "Even as House Votes."

23. See the discussion in Chap. 4, esp. notes 75-78; also Mann and Ornstein, *Renewing Congress: A First Report*, 66-69; and Congressional Research Service, *Congressional Reorganization*, pt. 4.

24. See Congressional Research Service, *Congressional Reorganization*, pt. 3; Mann and Ornstein, *Renewing Congress: A First Report*, 21-44; Karen Foerstel, "GOP Game Plan Would Force Floor Vote on Term Limitations for Committee Chairmen," *Roll Call*, November 23, 1992, 7; Craig Winneker, "At First Meeting, Joint Committee's Broad Mandate for Hill Reform Gets Still Broader," *Roll Call*, January 28, 1993, 8, 18; and Donovan, "Freshmen Show Little Unity."

25. An additional set of committee reforms might have an indirect impact on legislative responsibility. Banning proxy voting (members authorize committee colleagues, usually the chair or ranking minority member, to vote for them when they cannot be present) and increasing the quorum (the number of members required to be present to conduct committee business) would encourage lawmakers to participate personally in hearings and markup sessions. These changes, coupled with fewer total assignments, might mean that more members would be better informed and might produce more carefully considered, and thus more responsible, public policy. See Congressional Research Service, *Congressional Reorganization*, chap. 6.

26. On these matters, see Mann and Ornstein, *Renewing Congress: A First Report*, 10-22; Congressional Research Service, *Congressional Reorganization*, pt. 2; David W. Rohde, *Parties and Leaders in the Postreform House* (Chicago: University of Chicago Press, 1991); and Barbara Sinclair, "The Emergence of Strong Leadership in the 1980s House of Representatives," *Journal of Politics* 54 (1992): 657-684.

27. Mann and Ornstein, *Renewing Congress: A First Report*, 12-15. Daniel J. Palazzolo, in *The Speaker and the Budget: Leadership in the Post-Reform House of Representatives* (Pittsburgh, Pa.: University of Pittsburgh Press, 1992), demonstrates that leaders' willingness to exploit aggressively the limited resources available to them enhances their ability to lead; R. Douglas Arnold, in *The Logic of Congressional Action* (New Haven, Conn.: Yale University Press, 1990), outlines the strategies leaders may use to build winning majority coalitions in support of favored bills.

28. On the leadership's control of House floor action, see Stanley Bach and Steven S. Smith, *Managing Uncertainty in the House of Representatives: Adaptation and Innovation in Special Rules* (Washington, D.C.: Brookings Institution, 1988); and Steven S. Smith, *Call to Order: Floor Politics in the House and Senate* (Washington, D.C.: Brookings Institution, 1989). For a general discussion of procedural change, consult Mann and Ornstein, *Renewing Congress: A First Report*, 44-52; and Congressional Research Service, *Congressional Reorganization*, pt. 5.

29. The minority Republicans vehemently oppose such rules changes, arguing that, given the majority's command over the agenda and floor consideration,

the minority needs every opportunity it can muster to present its alternatives to the Democrats' proposals.

30. Beth Donovan, "Mitchell Tilts at Rules Windmill," *Congressional Quarterly Weekly Report,* January 3, 1993, 205.

31. The argument against state-imposed term limits is that they would impermissibly add to the constitutional definition of the requirements for election to Congress. On this and other aspects of the term limits debate, see Gerald Benjamin and Michael J. Malbin, eds., *Limiting Legislative Terms* (Washington, D.C.: CQ Press, 1992); and the symposium on "Congressional Term Limits: Pro & Con," *The Long Term View: A Journal of Informed Opinion* 1 (1992).

32. On the merits and demerits of the line-item veto in its various forms, see Thurber and Durst, "Delay, Deadlock, and Deficits"; Vivica Novak, "Defective Remedy," *National Journal,* March 27, 1993, 749-753; and George Hager, "GOP, Black Caucus Force Delay in Line-Item Veto Debate," *Congressional Quarterly Weekly Report,* April 24, 1993, 1008-1009.

33. Timothy J. Berger, "Grandy Vows to Press for Major Changes in Organization of Republican Leadership," *Roll Call,* October 12, 1992, 5. Grandy's proposal, however, also calls for the minority leader to appoint five lower-level party leaders (currently elected by the full party conference) and to control the party budget. Such changes would centralize power in the hands of the top leaders and might reduce the ability of rank-and-file Republicans to influence party policy.

34. On these proposals, see Mann and Ornstein, *Renewing Congress: A First Report,* 54-60; and Winneker, "If I Were Speaker. . . ."

35. Quoted in Karen Foerstel, "Moakley Offers Rules Compromise of Sorts," *Roll Call,* May 24, 1993, 10, 44 (at 44).

36. Clifford Krauss, "Freshmen Run Afoul of the Status Quo," *New York Times,* April 4, 1993, 14; and Beth Donovan, "Fractures in Freshman Class Weaken Impact on House," *Congressional Quarterly Weekly Report,* April 3, 1993, 807-810.

6. The Future Congress

Congress has changed. The Congress of the 1990s has identifiable features that distinguish it from its predecessors. Most significantly, it is more responsive. A larger number of interests inside and outside the legislature are able to express their points of view. Member individualism still characterizes Congress. Delegation of the full committees' power to independent subcommittees has permitted more legislators, with relatively secure power positions, to influence at least some part of the congressional agenda. The new activists, who are largely intelligent, well informed, and independent-minded, forcefully express their own views as well as those of constituents important to them. In addition, the public has an increased ability (that it does not always use) to hold Congress accountable. Concerned citizens can, if they so choose, find out much about what Congress does; sunshine statutes enable them to find out whether and what financial stakes lawmakers have in what they do. In these ways Congress today is surely more democratic than Congresses of the recent past.

Responsiveness implies permeability; more openness and participation allow more interests to have access to Congress. This suggests a diminution in responsibility, however—a decline in the efficient formulation of policy. Although there is more firepower in their arsenals—new powers for the Speaker and House Democratic caucus, new rules to speed legislative action—the political parties, as the chief mechanism for centralizing legislative operations, still seem consistently incapable of developing coherent and workable programs. It is harder in the 1990s for Congress to face up to, much less resolve, the plethora of foreign and domestic crises. Responsiveness and accountability expose members to multiple pressures and make them accessible to many points of view. Permeability undercuts decisiveness, however; decentralization and fragmentation induce caution (some say cowardice). It often seems more profitable for members to avoid controversy, to minimize the political risks of addressing complicated and emotional issues, than to confront those issues and make hard policy choices. Constituency service, oversight, and other forms of nonpolicy representation afford some electoral protection; in-depth policy analysis and innovation are dangerous.

Needless to say, some observers view this more democratic (more responsive and accountable), less efficient (less responsible) Congress with alarm. The revival of the reform spirit in the 1990s, after its waning in the late 1970s and the 1980s, testifies to their renewed dissatisfaction with Congress; spurred by legislative policy-making failure and member malfeasance, they have offered a new set of reforms (summarized in Chapter 5). The nature and content of the contemporary reform agenda suggests, once again, that when change comes, it is guided less by broad visions than by narrower, pragmatic concerns. The recommendations the current reformers offer depend on their political perspectives and on which values—responsibility, responsiveness, accountability, or some combination of the three—are consistent with those perspectives.

An important lesson is that reforms designed to promote one value may have costs in terms of another. Reform occurs incrementally in response to political pressures and reformers' pragmatic motives. Piecemeal changes adopted over a number of years without benefit of a master plan do not always mesh well. The record of reform (see Chapter 4) is a record of anticipated and unanticipated results. Desirable outcomes may be followed by detrimental ones as political circumstances change.

A recalcitrant Congress that thwarts a liberal president's social or foreign policy initiatives may seem considerably more defensible when it blocks a conservative chief executive's efforts to decimate similar programs already on the books. A centralized budget process that allows the legislature to spend tax revenues for liberal purposes—despite a conservative administration's opposition—may seem much less defensible if it permits a conservative president to make drastic budget cuts. In short, political perspectives color assessments of reform. This chapter is an assessment of the future Congress based on the broader executive force and congressional supremacy theories (presented in Chapter 1); it proposes a new vision, *majoritarian democracy* that seeks an appropriate combination of congressional responsibility, responsiveness, and accountability.

A Responsible Congress

The pro-executive and pro-legislative views of Congress both propose to increase legislative responsibility. The two variants of the for-

mer—the executive force and the responsible parties theories—seek to
subordinate Congress to executive leadership. They advocate a centralized assembly that will promptly process the president's policy proposals. One version of the congressional supremacy ("Whig") theory also
endorses a hierarchical Congress able to act with dispatch. Reformers
of this school favor a centralized legislative process that will promote
legislative priorities rather than push through executive programs. (In
contrast, the literary theorists favor a responsive rather than a responsible Congress.) Each pro-executive view attributes the legislature's
inefficiency in formulating public policy to the fragmentation of
power in Congress. Each proposes reforms intended to permit Congress to act promptly and effectively. These reforms, however, would
reduce its political responsiveness.

The Pro-Executive View

The executive force theory, which (except during the Reagan and
Bush administrations) liberals have most often espoused, asserts that
the emergence of the president as chief policy maker and adminis-
trator is both inevitable and desirable. The separation of powers serves
to restrict the executive; Congress can and often does block valuable
presidential initiatives, particularly when government is divided—
when one party controls the White House and the other has a majority
in one or both houses of Congress.[1] Congressional reform since the
1970s has exacerbated the president's leadership problems. To obtain
winning coalitions in support of the administration's policies, the president must now court numerous power holders in Congress, rather
than only a few senior solons, as in the prereform period. In general,
the pro-president reformers would reduce the separation between the
branches by increasing the executive's ability to expedite movement of
its proposals through the legislative process.[2]

Congress, according to the executive force theorists, should devote
its energies to nonpolicy activities: overseeing the executive branch to
ensure that agencies conduct their operations honestly and in keeping
with policy goals, and providing services to link citizens more closely
with government. Congress, in effect, would concede lawmaking to
the president, occasionally modifying executive proposals but usually
only legitimizing them—stamping them with the congressional im-
primatur. In principle, Congress would be subordinate at all times to
the president, regardless of whether a conservative or a liberal sat in
the Oval Office. Efficient policy making, not development of particular
programs, is the goal of the pro-executive reformers. In its pure form,
this theory stresses efficient production of legislation; in reality, those

who favor executive power probably prefer a focus on particular programs—those that like-minded presidents propose. In either case, responsibility is central for the proponents of the executive force theory.

Frequently, the executive force theory goes hand in hand with the idea of the responsible two-party system, which would centralize the policy-making process by the agency of the disciplined political party.[3] Reformers who advocate this idea would incorporate into the legislative process some elements of the British parliamentary system.[4] As party leader, the president would have the unchallenged opportunity to win legislative approval for favored programs, as does the prime minister. Support from Congress would be virtually assured because the legislators, given their dependence on powerful political parties, could oppose the executive only at the risk of terminating their political careers. Popular accountability, not an independent legislature, is the control mechanism; the electorate would punish poor performance by voting the party in power out of office. According to the responsible parties theory, Congress would relinquish its lawmaking authority, concentrating instead on nonpolicy activities and becoming a part of the party "team."

Strengthening the presidency, whether or not within an invigorated party system, would entail altering both the internal operations of Congress and the system of electing legislators. With regard to congressional procedures, the pro-executive view supports reform intended to centralize congressional decision making, to reduce the ability of various minorities to block the president's program. Most important, perhaps, pro-executive reformers would curb the independence and autonomy of congressional committees. In theory, such reformers approve the 1971-1977 steps to reduce the powers of the panel chairs, thus enabling a majority of committee members to control the chairs' behavior; the trend toward stronger exercise of party leadership, at the expense of the committees, which has been evident since the mid-1980s; and the additional steps proposed by reformers in the 1990s (see Chapter 5).[5] A president who works with the legislative leaders, and who commands a committee majority, can move the administration's proposals through that committee. A more basic way to gain control of the committees would be to ensure that the chairs were party loyalists. The weakening of the seniority rule makes it possible for party majorities to select cooperative colleagues as committee leaders, using party loyalty as a central criterion. The record to date, however, suggests that personal power and policy, not party standards, have come into play on the few occasions when seniority has not proven decisive in the selection of committee and subcommittee leaders.[6]

Both methods of curtailing committee autonomy—replacing strict application of the seniority rule with an elective process and reducing the power and independence of committee leaders—increase the prominence of party leaders in Congress. Pro-executive reformers applaud such a change. Majority party leaders, they insist, should assume the role of their president's representatives on Capitol Hill rather than act as legislative emissaries to the White House (which is the current practice), thus committing themselves and their resources to advancing the administration's program. Party agencies, say these reformers, should pursue the same end. The caucus should be able to exercise power on behalf of the majority of its partisans. For example, it should control committee assignments, rewarding the faithful and punishing the disloyal. Reform has made this possibility a reality.[7]

The political party, loyal to the president, should set forth party positions, subject to review and ratification by the full party membership, and should be empowered to schedule party-sponsored bills for prompt floor consideration. The party caucus should be able to bind members to vote for major party-sponsored bills. In the House, the Speaker's new powers do afford some control over scheduling—authority Senate floor leaders have long enjoyed. But in reality, the unity of parties depends on their members' acquiescence; party leaders are still unable to compel their members' votes when party legislation is considered on the floor. In principle, a more centralized Congress—especially one with responsible parties able to punish dissenters through their control of the nominating process—would be able to enact bills incorporating executive programs with dispatch.

The reformers seeking to smooth the path of executive policies in Congress would change the rules of procedure as well. Here, too, the goal would be to reduce the ability of minorities, a decentralized system, to block administration programs at particular veto points. In the House, the majority exercises considerable control over the Rules Committee; by converting the committee to a reliable ally of the party leadership, it can substantially reduce one obstacle to the advancement of party programs.[8] Other minor rules changes lessening the incidence of dilatory tactics might also smooth the flow of legislation through the House.[9] The Senate reformers' main target has been unlimited debate, and they have made some gains. Sixty senators can terminate a filibuster, and time limits preclude an extended postcloture filibuster by amendment. But although it is still difficult to cut off debate, there has been little sign that the reformers will make a major effort to reduce the sixty votes now required to invoke cloture. Other suggestions to control Senate debate include eliminating various delaying tactics and distracting procedures. Such proposed changes could curtail a minority's ability to tie up debate on the House or Senate floor as a strategy to defeat specific bills.

The *line-item veto* is often proposed in this context. At present, the chief executive must accept or reject a bill in toto; a line-item veto would enable him to block enactment, subject to a congressional override, of single spending or tax provisions without having to reject the entire bill. The line-item veto would eliminate one popular strategy for asserting congressional policy-making initiatives: the inclusion of a few items opposed by the chief executive in legislation containing major programs he favors. Lawmakers assume the president will accept a few undesirable provisions rather than risk losing legislation on a matter of central concern to the administration. Pro-executive reformers see the line-item veto, and the more modest "enhanced rescission" alternative to it, as one way to strengthen the president's hand with regard to Congress.[10]

In addition, pro-executive reformers advocate electoral reforms to restrain the voting independence of members of Congress—in particular, reforms requiring members to back party-endorsed (most often, presidential) policy proposals. The election process, they argue, should ensure that the president has political support sufficient to pass his agenda, at least if he has a legislative majority. To this end these reformers continue to suggest lengthening lawmakers' terms of office to four years in the House and eight in the Senate. Thus, all members of Congress would be selected simultaneously with the president. Presumably, they would sense their obligation to him, attributing their victories at the polls more to his efforts than to their own. Another possibility is to schedule presidential elections shortly before congressional contests so that voters know who will be in the White House before casting their congressional ballots; this might encourage some voters to give the executive a legislative majority. Still another suggestion is to require all states to provide the electorate with an option to vote a straight party ticket; this might reduce the ticket splitting that seems to contribute to divided government.

These electoral reforms might encourage loyalty to the White House, but they would not compel it; there is no certainty that elections would no longer produce a president of one party and a Congress controlled wholly or in part by the opposition. For this reason, the responsible party reformers wish to guarantee party government and, in consequence, presidential government. They would have new, centralized national party committees control the fate of the party's congressional candidates. Public funding of campaigns—the channeling of tax dollars to nominees by the parties—would reduce dependence on individual or PAC contributors and eliminate one incentive to reject party leadership. The parties would manage a national campaign on national issues. If the ultimate power to control congressional nominations—to exact loyalty pledges in advance and to deprive recalcitrant legislators of their seats—rested with the president and the national committee, then the chief executive, like the British prime minister, could count on the support of a reliable legislative majority.

Finally, proponents of the pro-executive view advance some ideas that might break down the "we versus them" mentality so characteristic of divided government. One recommendation is to amend the Constitution to allow members of Congress to take cabinet positions without giving up their seats in the legislature. A more fundamental change would be an amendment permitting the government to "fall," as in European parliamentary systems, if deadlock developed or if Congress found the president to be weak, ineffective, or incompetent (but not necessarily impeachable). New elections would follow the fall of the government. Finally, some propose altering party rules to permit all congressional candidates, incumbents and challengers, as well as holdover senators, to sit as delegates at their party's presidential nominating convention.[11] Each of these steps would encourage cooperation rather than conflict between the executive and legislative branches, thus making programmatic action more likely. However desirable in principle, these reforms, especially those that require amending the Constitution, are not likely to win either congressional or public approval; they remain little more than a gleam in the eye of ivory tower visionaries.

All these suggestions, whether adopted wholly or in part, singly or in combination, would change the position of Congress in the national political process. Fragmentation of power would be diminished, centralization increased, committee independence restricted, the parties strengthened, and the rules altered to permit executive leadership to carry the day. According to the responsible parties theory, the chief executive would dominate the national party and, through it, the legislature. By controlling campaign finance, the parties would control congressional nominations and the legislative careers of the winners. The presidential candidate of each party would run on a clearly defined party platform, and the voters would select the candidate whose program best suited them. The victor would have a dependable legislative majority; the centralized, party-managed Congress would do the president's bidding.

This can be described as a responsibility-accountability scenario: lawmakers would be more responsible because they would obtain effective solutions to pressing problems promptly and efficiently, and more accountable because voters could replace the governing party with an opposition that they were convinced could do more and do it better.[12] Responsiveness would be the price. Subordinated to executive-dominated, disciplined political parties, lawmakers would be hard pressed to respond to citizen and group sentiments and to translate them into policy. Their appeals would focus on the president. Although he would have to calculate what public reaction to his initiatives might do to his party's fortunes, he would have broad authority to chart the nation's course for four years (or for a single, six-year term if that occasionally discussed proposal should be enacted).

The Pro-Legislative View

The less widely discussed congressional supremacy theory focuses to some extent on responsibility. This "Whig" view is, in a sense, the mirror image of the executive force theory. Congress would be the dominant force in national politics. The president would, of course, have considerably less initiative and would commit himself more to execution of congressionally determined policies than to advancement of his own agenda.[13]

Realization of the congressional supremacy theory would require many reforms. One would be to centralize legislative operations in ways not unlike those proposed by the executive force theorists. The power relations would be reversed, however: Congress would call the shots rather than respond to presidential leadership. James Burnham even proposes to dismantle the federal apparatus and turn most of its present duties over to the state and local governments.[14] Most observers discount the congressional-supremacy theory as hopelessly unrealistic, pointing out that the president—who can build on his power as commander in chief, his public image as the responsible political decision maker, and considerable precedent—has become too strong to be seriously challenged. The federal government has become too large, and too many citizens are too dependent on it, to be stripped of much of its authority and responsibility. "New federalism" proposals advanced during the Nixon, Ford, Reagan, and Bush administrations, which would transfer substantial authority from Washington to the states and localities, have won only modest support, even from the governors and mayors who would receive new powers, if not money, under such a plan.

Few critics of the pro-executive view have gone so far as to suggest that congressional supremacy is desirable or even workable. Even members of Congress, understandably opposed to subordination of the legislature to any branch, do not seek total mastery over the executive. Rather, those who favor a resurgent Congress have sought, and with some success, to redress the balance, to stem the historical flow of authority to the president. They have reasserted the necessity that congressional perspectives be heard and that they prevail when the nation indicates sufficient support for them. In short, the mainstream critics of executive force envision governmental decision making that is responsive to the sorts of interests only Congress is capable of representing adequately.

A Responsive Congress

The pro-legislative views, which energized the 1970s reforms, fell out of favor in the 1980s; critics of Congress blamed excessive decentralization for the legislature's inability to make responsible public policy. Yet there are still those (most often conservatives in the pre-Reagan period and liberals after 1980) who, although they do not seek to subordinate the executive, do value both responsiveness and congressional power. They prefer to obtain meaningful legislative participation in policy formation—a Congress able to assert its own priorities, despite executive opposition—without having to resort to excessive centralization. Their ideas, including many of those implemented in the 1970s, lead to even more dispersion of authority and to increased reliance on bargaining as the chief means of congressional conflict resolution.[15]

Reasserting Congressional Prerogatives

Proponents of legislative responsiveness and power have resisted efforts to reduce committee autonomy, to impose centralization by strengthening the political parties, or to foster both objectives by changing the rules. Thus, they opposed altering the seniority system and restricting the basic powers of committee leaders. Conceivably, election of committee chairs without regard to length of committee service could permit a disciplined majority to capture control of the panels. But such a result is unlikely unless chair selection is linked to centralization of legislative authority. The record since modification of the seniority rule seems to suggest a further dispersion of power. Although party majorities have, and may use, the ability to replace or control autocratic chairs, and thus promote responsiveness, they have rarely done so. Nonetheless, some of the pending proposals to strengthen the parties, if adopted (see Chapter 5), would curtail committee independence at the expense of legislative responsiveness. If the party leadership takes control of the committee assignment process or restricts subcommittee freedom of action, individual members, responsive to personal and constituency concerns, would find their influence reduced.

The pro-Congress reformers have suggested ways to strengthen the committees, both in general and in relation to the executive, without impairing their autonomy. Many observers, including members of Congress, have decried the confusion and overlapping of committee jurisdictions. Except for the modest 1977 Senate reforms, efforts to define or realign committee jurisdictions have accomplished little; too many members have vested interests in existing arrangements. The problem is compounded by the 1975 rule permitting the Speaker of the House to refer legislation to more than one committee. It is not unusual for two, three, or more panels to have jurisdiction over parts of particular pieces of legislation. Although such a situation may enhance responsiveness in the sense that it permits more points of view to be heard, it also impedes congressional policy making. Failure to enact legislation establishing sound programs may prompt citizens, interest groups, and even the members themselves to look to executive supremacy as the only way to overcome policy inertia. Moreover, committee work loads are unevenly distributed; some panels have many major responsibilities while others have far less important burdens. Clarified and redrawn committee jurisdictions might help Congress capitalize on its members' energies and expertise. Realigned committees and subcommittees, especially if well staffed and supplied with accurate information, might prove capable of both initiating effective public policies and responding to citizen concerns.

Whether or not the system is restructured, congressional committees could benefit from improved procedures. More open, less carefully stage-managed hearings, increased opportunity for deliberation, and fewer constraints on the participation of rank-and-file and minority party members should permit additional points of view to be aired. Improved hearings and extended consideration might also result in more useful reports, which, if circulated to the full chamber well in advance of floor consideration, might improve the quality of debate. Wider participation and fuller discussion could make Congress more responsive and more effective in opposing the executive.

The congressional supremacists' faith in open, autonomous committees is accompanied by a distrust of centralized political parties. Strengthened party caucuses or policy committees would reduce the chance for interests out of favor with party leaders to be heard; strong parties might run roughshod over the views of legislative minorities that deserve to have a say. Accordingly, the political parties in Congress should remain loose confederations that do little more than facilitate legislative organization. The Democratic Steering Committee in the Senate and the Democratic Steering and Policy Committee in the House—both of which assign Democrats to committees—could give the party leaders additional control. If these party panels responded regularly to the intervention of party leaders in the assignment process (the party leader chairs each committee), centralization might follow. Similarly, the new Speaker's Working Group in the House may seek to forge agreement on partisan positions and thus limit individual member discretion. If, however, these inclusive bodies were to represent more points of view, without leadership domination, the result could be to enhance responsiveness.

The pro-Congress forces seem as satisfied with the legislature's general procedures and organization as they are with autonomous committees and weak political parties. To be sure, they would prefer longer debate and fuller discussion in the House and more opportunity to propose amendments without restriction; such reforms would permit a wider range of views to find expression. But these reformers have resisted reforms that might alter the fundamental character of Congress, such as limits on the power of the House Rules Committee and changes in the Senate's rule of unlimited debate that might mute minority voices or minimize minority power. Decentralized authority, they believe, makes Congress more responsive.

Without making fundamental changes in legislative organization or procedure, the congressional supremacists seek to reassert legislative prerogatives in the face of what they see as a dramatic shift toward presidential domination of the policy-making process. To this end, they supported passage of the war powers resolution and budget reform bills. Their expectations have not been satisfied, however, and they continue to explore ways to revise the War Powers Act and the budget process to permit clear assertion of congressional priorities.

Improving Congressional Information Resources

Reforms providing lawmakers with more adequate staff resources and more information, thus improving their analytic capability, were welcomed by pro-Congress proponents. In principle, these developments should improve congressional responsiveness. Increased congressional staffs can generate and analyze new data, enabling lawmakers to make decisions based on reliable information. With its own independent staff, the minority party can now state its differences with the majority more clearly and persuasively. Beyond this, all members of the House might profitably use legislative assistants with specific policy responsibilities, comparable with those provided the senators. In theory, more assistance, data, and analysis should improve both the lawmakers' ability to draft legislation and their ability to challenge executive branch specialists.

Yet enlarged staffs, however attractive they seem in the abstract, may not have strengthened the legislature in relation to the executive. Indeed, some skeptics believe that the larger personal and committee staffs have created new burdens rather than alleviating or eliminating old ones. More employees highlight new areas for attention and, as a result, impose new demands on the legislators, already overcommitted in terms of time and energy. Moreover, large staffs risk converting the lawmaker into an office manager, with additional responsibilities that divert from policy making and other tasks. Without proper supervision, staffers, especially investigators, may be tempted, for personal or ideological reasons, to engage in unrestrained partisanship and to neglect data gathering and the generation of ideas.[16] Current proposals to cut staff allocations significantly are aimed at solving these problems (as well as saving money).

To the extent that increased staff support improves the quantity and quality of information that members of Congress actually use, it improves responsiveness. If provided with insufficient and unreliable data, legislators may feel obliged to defer to bureaucratic specialists presumed to "know better." The data available to them can also be limited by *executive privilege*—a doctrine justifying the president's withholding of information from Congress (and the public) in the "national interest"—and national defense requirements.[17] Interbranch competition and suspicion, especially in periods of divided government, prompt executive branch personnel to withhold information. Moreover, the executive branch is often able to orchestrate events in a way that minimizes legislators' opportunity to advance alternative proposals. Administration sources brief the media in off-the-record or "not for attribution" sessions, releasing only selective information that the media then interpret to suit their own purposes. In addition, news, appropriately structured, can be leaked to the media.

Beyond these impediments to full disclosure imposed by the executive, Congress contributes to its own information deficit. A decentralized institution with numerous centers of independent power, each with lines to different information sources, leads to fragmented, uncoordinated data; information collected by legislators in one place for one set of purposes is often inaccessible to other legislators in other locations with other purposes in mind. The computer revolution has alleviated the problem to some degree; office consoles give members access to centralized data banks. But individual lawmakers still must make many decisions about complex and controversial issues with minimal information. Installation of state-of-the-art computers and use of extensive data bases could permit lawmakers to retrieve information of interest to them. Legislators could choose what *they* want to know.

Their freedom to specialize, to follow their own inclinations, would be enhanced and the risk of being overwhelmed by information of no use to them would be reduced. The information system would become the lawmakers' servant, not their master.

The often arduous task of determining the existence, content, and location of bills of interest can be vastly simplified by modern computer facilities. The computer can store a legislative history; at any time, lawmakers can get an up-to-date status report on any measure. By working out their own position before they have to vote, they can reduce their dependence on word-of-mouth assurances from experts, party colleagues, or House leaders and avoid being caught off guard. Computers can help each legislator be in a far better position to interject personal views into congressional deliberations. Computerized information systems can also provide data on lobbyists (who they are, whom they represent, what legislation they support); on executive branch actions; on studies by congressional support agencies or various committee staffs; and on the content of present law. The ready information from these and other sources should enable members of Congress to make choices based on considerably more data than have traditionally entered their calculations.[18]

Another way to tackle the information deficit would be to increase opportunities for members to learn; for example, more funds and time for foreign travel and reading, more on-site visits to federal installations. Extended use could also be made of outside consultants or congressional task forces comparable to those the president uses, and of a "congressional institute of scholars" or similar university-type organization that might be established.[19] These steps, coupled with the growth of the General Accounting Office and the Congressional Research Service and the creation of the Congressional Budget Office and the Office of Technology Assessment, should improve Congress's information resources.[20]

All these reforms can strengthen Congress relative to the executive. The War Powers Act positioned the legislature to assert some control over military commitments. The 1974 budget act did the same with respect to fiscal matters. In the long run, creation of new resources— expert staffs and more reliable information—and a commitment to use them effectively may prove more fundamental in ensuring that Congress is permitted to have its way, even in the face of stiff executive opposition. Increased legislative power, reflecting views that differ from those of the president, would obviously contribute to more responsive policy making.

Protecting Member Independence

The congressional supremacists also have strong ideas about electoral politics. They stand firm against partisan redistricting and any effort to create disciplined national political parties. Indeed, the very localism (greater concern for constituency views than for national interests) deplored by proponents of the executive force theory is considered a positive virtue by those who support legislative power. Redistricting, even to reflect simple population equality, and party pressure to subscribe to a national party platform would limit the representation of diverse interests, especially those that are geographically dispersed or that otherwise cannot be represented on the basis of population alone.[21] Thus, an election system resembling the present one, in which candidates remain free to build their own organizations, raise their own funds, stake out their own issue positions, and appeal to whatever groups they deem appropriate, is highly desirable, according to proponents of the congressional supremacy theory. Such a system allows the widest possible range of viewpoints to find expression in Congress. In short, it increases congressional responsiveness.

Pro-Congress reformers envision a decentralized, representative legislature capable of making its public policy choices prevail despite executive opposition. As a responsive institution, a resurgent Congress should be able to listen to a diversity of interests and merge the sentiments of numerous power holders to formulate legislative programs that can compete on equal terms with executive proposals. Such competition, the interplay of roughly equal branches of government, should enhance the responsiveness of the entire policy process.

The more Congress is capable of frustrating the president, however, the greater the possibility of deadlock. The greater the need to reach agreements through bargaining, whether within the legislature or between Congress and the executive, the less likely that policy will be bold or imaginative. Moreover, the larger the number of interests that any policy settlement must accommodate, the slower the decision will be in coming. Thus a fully responsive legislature, open to all points of view and having multiple channels of communication, might produce policy of the "too little, too late" variety. It might find itself overtaken by future events and outstripped by history. The price of responsiveness may be less responsibility.

An Accountable Congress

Regardless of whether executive dominance or congressional supremacy is preferable, accountability is desirable; it complements both responsibility and responsiveness. As noted earlier, accountability sustains responsibility; there is a direct relationship between the two. The electorate chooses between two political parties and in so doing gives the winner both a mandate to govern and the majority to do so. In subsequent elections the voters decide, based on their assessment of the incumbent's performance, whether to renew that mandate or to put a new party in office. Retrospective evaluation by the electorate is the chief check on the administration's behavior; unless the citizenry is prepared to hold its rulers accountable, the government's power is unlimited because unchecked.

For those who place most value on a responsive Congress, accountability seems more difficult to achieve and perhaps less critical. A decentralized system is certainly hard for voters to fathom. When things go badly, and when the fateful decisions have emerged from elaborate bargaining among many decision makers at numerous stages of a complex process, it is difficult to know whom to blame. The voters must pay far more attention if they are to pin down who did what. The open channels of communication in a responsive Congress provide alternatives to accountability, however. Citizens can do more than judge ex post facto; they can, if they choose, use whatever means of access is available to them as individuals or as group members to present their views in advance. Thus, accountability is another way by which the electorate can set national directions. Accountability offers the ruled a way to manage those whom they have selected to govern them.

A first condition for accountability is that citizens be aware of their representatives' records. Several steps seem likely to generate more information about Congress, but not all of them are the responsibility of the legislature. First, the mass media can be encouraged to provide additional coverage. Admittedly, a 535-member, two-chamber institution does not have the aura and glamour of a chief executive. Nevertheless, television and the press could do a better job. They could give the kind of coverage usually reserved for dramatic events—for instance, the Senate Watergate hearings and the Senate Judiciary Committee's proceedings on the nomination of Clarence Thomas for a Supreme Court seat—to hearings on important issues such as national health insurance, entitlement program changes, defense procurement, abortion, school prayer, and the budget. As matters now stand, only the few events that the media deemed newsworthy receive extended treatment, and then only in the national press.[22]

Congress cannot compel media attention, but its sunshine reforms have simplified the media's task by exposing more of its activities to press investigation. Open hearings and committee meetings, recorded votes, and full disclosure of information about campaign funding and personal finances should help the citizenry determine where members of Congress stand with regard to public policy and perhaps why their actions were (or were not) taken.

Second, accountability requires informed, interested citizens capable of comparing their own views with those of their representatives and judging them accordingly. Little direct reform is possible, but some current trends seem promising. Polls show that the better educated citizens tend to be more knowledgeable about and interested in political affairs. As the nation's education level rises, more citizens should hold Congress accountable. If there is better media coverage of the less secretive Congress, these voters will be able to evaluate the legislature more carefully and more knowledgeably. The extended coverage of House and Senate debates by the C-SPAN cable television network allows interested people—a growing number if statistics on viewers are accurate—to watch the legislature in action. Candidates have also used more unconventional public relations tactics; their appearances on talk shows and at town meetings seem to attract wider audiences and should help educate the electorate.

A third prerequisite for effective accountability, that voters have clear choices among candidates within single states or districts, is more problematic, because little can be done to guarantee that voters will be able to select from among ideologically distinct nominees. A responsible order would make such a guarantee unnecessary. The individual candidates would be indebted to centralized parties, and the voter would merely have to evaluate the desirability of retaining the incumbent party. But under current electoral practices, which emphasize responsiveness more than responsibility, the parties remain decentralized. Whether the challenger is ideologically distinct from the incumbent depends on the uncertain operation of nominating politics in a given constituency.

Accountability, in short, will not be easy to improve. As noted in Chapter 4, the reformers' goals in this regard have not been fully realized: the public has not become better informed about Congress, despite the increased opportunity for it to do so. And reformers can do little to increase citizens' interest in legislative politics. Congress has taken steps to ensure that those who wish to inform themselves are not thwarted by unnecessary secrecy in the legislative branch. Current proposals for fuller disclosure of members' personal and campaign finances and stricter reporting requirements for lobbyists, if enacted, would make additional information available to attentive citizens. The possibility of a larger number of interested citizens monitoring a more visible Congress gives some hope for greater accountability.

More accountability, however, is not without costs. Increased openness, or permeability, may inhibit both responsibility and responsiveness. The need to deliberate and decide in public, in the glare of the media spotlight, may inhibit decisive decision making. Political fears of antagonizing voters or supportive interest groups may breed congressional caution. Rather than jeopardizing their reelection prospects, career-oriented members may evade hard choices, instead deferring to the president or delegating to the bureaucracy. Responsibility would surely decline under these circumstances. Conversely, accessibility to outside forces may undercut responsiveness. If senators and representatives worry about charges of unethical dealings with special interests, they may limit the access and influence of those interests. Here, too, efforts to maximize one value may interfere with realization of the other two.

Majoritarian Democracy in Congress

The pro-executive and pro-legislative views are, in a sense, unrealistic. The proposals made by their proponents are intended to help Congress achieve greater responsibility, responsiveness, and accountability, but they are not based on full-blown, widely accepted definitions of what constitutes a "better" political order. Rather, they emphasize tendencies—toward a more powerful executive or a revived legislature—that seem most likely to improve the political system. There is still considerable controversy about the wisdom and desirability of the specific reforms suggested by these broad visions. Those who advocate a more powerful president or a stronger Congress do not agree on the precise steps necessary to achieve their goals. There is unlikely to be widespread agreement on any package of fundamental reforms. Reform is more likely to come as it has in the past: incrementally, in response to societal change, specific crises, or electoral developments. The 1990s reform agenda and the discussions about specific items on it reinforce this conclusion.

This section presents a broader but still pragmatic vision of the future Congress. The majoritarian democracy model builds on the most successful reforms of the 1970s and the most promising proposals of the 1990s, and suggests a workable trade-off between responsibility and responsiveness, deliberation and decisiveness. This modest proposal may satisfy no one; it may present a policy-making process too slow to be responsible, too centralized to be responsive. Both values have advantages; they are sufficiently exclusive, however, that a gain in one is likely to bring about a loss in the other. The intent is to gain as much as possible of each value.

Such a mix is desirable because neither the pro-executive view nor the pro-legislative view is entirely tenable. Advocacy of executive force apparently grew out of a misplaced, perhaps naive faith in the inherent goodness of the president, but the events and personalities of the period since World War II have tarnished this view of executive nobility. Presidential domination of the nation's Indochina policy, the Watergate revelations about Richard Nixon (ironically demonstrating a thirst for power in a chief executive publicly committed to reducing the scope of federal government authority), and the behavior of the Reagan White House in the Iran-contra affair have made clear the extent to which presidential power has grown. Few liberals approved of such exercise of executive supremacy. It appears equally doubtful that conservatives would be eager to see such strength exerted by a liberal in the White House. Thus, no matter whose ox is gored, there seems good reason to avoid an undue concentration of authority in the hands of the chief executive.[23]

Yet the congressional supremacy arguments are no more promising. Neither a highly centralized Congress, independent of the president and capable of taking responsible action, nor a largely fragmented institution, broadly responsive, is a pleasing vision. The first possibility is both unrealistic (there are simply too many matters to be handled with dispatch) and undesirable (the same arguments that apply to a powerful presidency militate against a concentration of authority in the legislature). Discontinuing some federal programs to facilitate congressional dominance of those that remain seems impractical. There are too many programs, each targeting a different group, to allow easy termination. In addition, it is by no means certain that state and local governments could or would take up the responsibility devolved from the federal government. The second possibility, the fragmented institution with minority interests protected at each stage of the decision-making process, invites paralysis. In short, there is little reason to expect beneficial results from converting Congress to a body that is either exclusively responsible or exclusively responsive.

The answer, clearly, is some combination of features that advances to some degree both responsibility and responsiveness. Majoritarian democracy would combine an open, responsive, deliberative stage of legislative policy making with a more decisive, responsible, decision-making stage. The former is democratic: it seeks open avenues of participation for all. The latter is majoritarian: it endeavors to permit majorities, having been given sufficient time for deliberation, to prevail at the point of decision.

This vision in no way discounts the importance and desirability of public accountability. The steps to achieve more effective accountability, noted in the previous section, should be pursued. Admittedly, not all legislative activity can or should take place in public. "Open covenants, openly arrived at" is not totally valid with regard to Congress any more than it is in diplomacy. Topics such as national security demand secrecy. Compromise settlements on many matters can be worked out more easily in private. What is important is that the public be able to ascertain what has been done and who supported the actions taken. To the extent that Congress operates openly and the citizenry is attentive to its actions, accountability is enhanced, the bond between rulers and ruled is tightened, and the opportunity for popular control of government is improved.

Responsiveness in the Deliberative Stage

The policy process should be most responsive in the early stages of lawmaking, especially during committee consideration. Citizens should have ample opportunity to present their views. (Citizens can hold Congress to account later, when they render at the polls a verdict about whether their views were heard.[24]) The pro-legislative reforms are intended to democratize Congress in order to foster its responsiveness: the aim is to get responsive individuals into the legislature and to let them speak there for the widest possible diversity of interests.

In electoral terms this means the continuation of present practices. Current districting methods, which reflect population equality, are satisfactory; so is localism, with its constituency-based, individualized campaigns. Campaign reforms that favor incumbents are undesirable, however. With their vast campaign advantages (incumbents' congressional perquisites are estimated to be worth more than $500,000 a year), they need little additional help. Some fear that the Federal Election Campaign Act and its amendments have made it harder for challengers to compete. The legislation permitted the rise of PACs, which tend to support incumbents. Even though the Supreme Court struck down the FECA limits on the amount that candidates can spend on their own behalf, challengers may simply be unable to raise sufficient funds to mount effective campaigns against entrenched members. Public financing of congressional elections, which would equalize the money available to incumbent and challenger, would have the same effect. The perquisites of office would still give incumbents an advantage that challengers could not overcome by spending larger sums. Reduction of incumbents' perquisites, restriction of PAC contributions, and provision of equal access to mass media—all ideas currently under discussion as part of campaign reform—might help level the electoral playing field. In any case, the electoral process should operate to allow as wide a latitude as possible for candidates who speak for local interests and voice divergent concerns.

Inside Congress, majoritarian democracy calls for a moderately paced deliberative stage that promotes the expression of multiple points of view. Members should be assigned to the committees that will enable them to serve their constituencies best. The changes in Senate and House committee assignment procedures and the limitations on the holding of subcommittee chairs disperse power, giving junior legislators greater opportunities to achieve positions of significance. More important, perhaps, is that committee majorities firmly control the conduct of committee business, which was one goal of the 1970 reorganization act. Under such conditions there is less concern about the method of selecting committee chairs. It is not seniority per se that has given rise to most complaints, but rather the fact that the seniority rule automatically elevated the most senior majority member to a powerful position. Now that the committee leaders are on notice that they may be removed for cause, they will probably be more attentive to the views of rank-and-file members of the committee, and their selection may be less of a problem. The real virtue of the seniority rule—an automatic, impersonal, noncompetitive method of choosing committee chairs is preserved when the committee leaders and their committee colleagues are more equal in power.

Such democratically governed legislative committees should be able to consider more fully the available options with regard to each bill, especially given the increased information and research resources now available to Congress. An expansion of staff, but not to the extent that the members become office managers rather than policy makers, seems likely to help; the addition of minority staff members should certainly facilitate the airing of diverse points of view. So, too, should the use of computerized information systems that permit legislators to develop, promote, and sustain their own policy proposals. Finally, responsiveness might be better served if committees with clear jurisdictions scheduled and announced open hearings well in advance, gave witnesses ample notice, and, most important, invited and encouraged the less well-organized interests to appear (and perhaps subsidized their appearance).

In short, majoritarian democracy envisions the survival of a fragmented Congress, with independent, specialized committees and subcommittees as the basis for the division of labor. The suggested reforms are designed to make sure that the widest possible range of opinion finds its way into legislative deliberations. Norms acknowledging specialization of, and reciprocity among, committees should continue to be observed. Likewise, political parties should retain their nonideological, noncoercive roles as facilitators of election and managers of legislative organization. Under these conditions, legislative committees—composed of expert lawmakers, adequately staffed, and open to the views of all interested parties—should generate responsible policy proposals.

Responsibility: Facilitating Policy Making

However responsive the process by which legislation is formulated, bills must have a chance not only to pass Congress but to survive executive branch opposition. Otherwise, of course, the legislative process is an exercise in futility. Unless the national legislature can act, and act in ways that resolve problems, it is not likely to serve as an effective counterweight to executive authority. Majoritarian democracy requires a decisive decision-making stage in which the legislature can approve or reject bills that address the nation's problems. Two reforms are needed: measures to help majorities to act and statutory restraints on presidential power.

With respect to the first requirement of majoritarian democracy, reform should permit Congress to deal expeditiously with committee proposals, the product of the responsive deliberative stage. This requires removal of several procedural devices that protect minorities and delay or block congressional action. The main focus here is on changing the rules to facilitate majoritarian action. Several reforms would help guarantee prompt action on committee recommendations in the House. Extended panel consideration of proposals, often intended to bury the legislation permanently, could be prevented by a more readily usable discharge rule. After allowance of sufficient time for full study and deliberation—say, 90 or 120 days—a discharge petition bearing 150 signatures would enable bills to move to the floor for a vote.[25]

Although the Rules Committee has been tamed (it is largely under control of the party leadership), it is still capable of blocking legislation that a majority favors. The committee, in theory at least, might hold up, or impose unfavorable conditions on, action on a bill that the Speaker opposes but that an authorizing committee, or a bipartisan majority on the floor, wishes to see passed. To eliminate this possibility, adoption of a variant of the twenty-one-day-rule, enacted twice and later rejected, would guarantee the full chamber a chance to act on reported legislation. If Rules caused a three-week delay in getting the bill to the floor, the chair of the committee reporting the legislation could move to force Rules to act, and if supported by a majority of the full House, could in effect discharge that panel. Such a step would obviate the need to rely exclusively on party leaders to move legislation. Other minor changes aimed at eliminating the use of delaying tactics—such as making excessive quorum calls or requiring the reading of the *Journal* in full—could marginally improve in the House's ability, already superior to that of the Senate, to deal decisively with pending bills. In general, the Speaker's more aggressive use of his existing power to manage matters on the floor would smooth the path of legislation once the committees reported bills out.

As noted, the major target of reform in the Senate has been the filibuster. A revision of the cloture rule—especially if coupled with elimination of the "morning hour," which would make debate more germane and focused and limit the opportunities to filibuster—should accelerate floor proceedings so that a decision point can be reached more quickly. Curbs on *holds*, the informal practice that permits a single senator to block consideration of legislation or nominations by the executive for extended periods, would also speed Senate action. So would rules that allow measures supported by majorities to reach the floor, even in spite of the leadership's opposition. Senate leaders can manipulate the chamber's schedule to thwart a majority of members, although it is not clear that they often use this tactic. These innovations are subject to possible abuse—easier access of bills to the floor might clutter the agenda and prevent action—but they could increase the likelihood that determined majorities would carry the day on behalf of the bills they favor.[26]

Of course, bills would still have to be approved by the president, who could veto measures and prevail unless Congress mustered a two-thirds majority in each house to override the veto. Some reforms already enacted may eventually strengthen Congress's competitive position. Despite all the uncertainties about and problems with the revised budget process, Congress can, if it is determined to, assert its own fiscal priorities by means of that process. The imposition by Congress of a spending ceiling in line with anticipated revenue, and the allocation of that sum to various budgetary categories, could make legislative budget decisions serious competitors with those the executive proposes. The 1990 Omnibus Budget Reconciliation Act included a variant of this proposal; whether Congress will continue to cap spending in fiscal year 1994, when the act's limits expire, is uncertain.

In addition, Congress might reconsider a proposal made by David R. Obey (D-Wis.) for an "omnibus budget" that would merge all authorizations, appropriations, and revenue measures in a single bill. The result would be to speed up the process, give the budget the force of law, and centralize budget making. If the budget were formulated independently of the executive, the efficiency of financial decision making by the legislature might also be increased.[27] Some of the items on the 1990s reform agenda—a two-year budget cycle and a simplified budgetary process, for example—might serve the same purposes. Finally, the 1974 Congressional Budget and Impoundment Control Act, requiring the president to release funds unless the legislature agrees to his action, has enabled congressional fiscal priorities to prevail more often. Granting the president the line-item veto or increasing his rescission authority would, of course, make it more difficult for the legislature to assert its will.

Legislation defining and regularizing the claim of executive privilege and requiring agencies to divulge information would reduce the information deficit under which Congress continues to operate. The War Powers Act has the potential (again if Congress makes clear its determination to use it or threatens to use it) to make the chief executive take congressional concerns seriously in decisions about the use of military forces in undeclared wars or for purposes of police actions; it can restore congressional influence on the determination of foreign policy. All these steps could correct in favor of Congress the executive-legislative imbalance of power; all could contribute to a policy process in which both branches are forces to reckon with. Its renewed strength would enable Congress to make effective policy decisions more efficiently.

Needed: A New Congressional Image

Statutory and structural changes, however much they would strengthen Congress in relation to the president, are not enough to create an effective majoritarian institution. Subtler change, more difficult to achieve, is necessary. Congress must enhance its reputation as a body committed to placing national interests above local concerns. It must become an institution whose integrity is beyond suspicion and that can rise above "politics as usual" to make contributions to the national welfare that are consistently equal, if not superior, to those made by the executive. Congress suffers in this regard, for the public seems to view it more as an appendage than as a rival of the president. When the citizenry holds the chief executive in high esteem, it usually values the legislature as well; when the president suffers a loss of prestige, so does Congress. Congress's public image also suffers whenever it appears to thwart presidential leadership.

Competing for public respect with the unitary executive is not easy for the pluralistic legislature. Yet some of the reforms proposed and already adopted may enhance Congress's reputation. If the legislature gets more media attention, has less internal secrecy, and is more assertive in policy making, more citizens may realize that it is an important feature of the political landscape. A major cause of public skepticism is a sense that lawmakers are not entirely ethical. Doubts about the detachment of legislators have prompted efforts to uncover possible conflicts of interest and to ensure that they seek to promote the public good, not their own financial positions. The reputation of Congress and popular support for its views are eroded by persistent fears that legislators are still guilty of self-serving behavior.

Members' illegal or unethical actions over three decades, despite adoption of the House and Senate ethics codes in 1977, have sustained the public's concern about congressional ethics. The pressures of legislative life make ethics a continuing issue. On the one hand, public expectations are high; citizens want their elected representatives to be beyond reproach. On the other hand, to put it bluntly, legislators need money. They must engage in virtually nonstop campaigning, which is costly. Some maintain residences both in their home district and in Washington. Some are caught up in the expensive and demanding social life of the capital. In addition, the lawmaking task itself has inherent difficulties. To be responsive and stay in touch with the populace, lawmakers must listen to the requests and petitions of many groups and organizations. It is not surprising that some citizens with policy concerns exploit their access to legislators to further their own goals; in so doing they sometimes offer inducements that are somewhere between corruption—graft and bribery—and legitimate campaign contributions.

In recent years, criminal indictments and major scandals—such as the Abscam affair and the House bank and Keating Five scandals— have made the headlines. Far more pervasive than these dramatic events, however, are conflict of interest situations where lawmakers render judgments in matters in which they have a personal stake What should citizens make of the lawmakers who accept sizable sums from PACs with major interests in programs whose contents the legislators determine? The frequent posing of such questions has led to the sunshine statutes and financial disclosure laws currently on the books. Each chamber, in addition, has an ethics committee charged with policing the ethical conduct of its members. According to critics, however, neither committee has accomplished much; both incentives and enforcement powers have been lacking.

Some remedial steps have been taken. Members can no longer accept honoraria from private groups; there are now limits on the outside income they can earn. In addition, the current reform agenda contains numerous proposals—more stringent codes of ethics, more thoroughly enforced; strict limits on gifts from lobbyists with legislative interests in matters before the legislature; and fuller disclosure of personal and campaign finances—that aim both to control and to publicize potential conflict of interest situations. Reformers find Congress's self-policing in this regard inadequate, and they are unwilling to rely exclusively on the electorate to punish transgressors. It is extremely difficult to establish the existence of genuine conflict of interest; legislators may share the viewpoints of certain constituents and act on behalf of those interests without engaging in improper conduct. The line between public interest and private interest is not easy to draw; the reformers want to ensure that senators and representatives avoid having, or at least reveal having, any stakes in the issues they must decide.[28]

In short, if Congress is to compete with the executive, and to make its policy determinations prevail, it must have the support of the public; it must be recognized as a non-self-serving body whose priorities are not suspect. To this end, strict and well-enforced codes of conduct, conflict of interest statutes, and disclosure laws should help convince the citizenry that the legislature has nothing to hide and is worthy of the public esteem that is necessary for an effective Congress.

A last, and perhaps most important, requisite for a Congress capable of independent policy making is the determination to assert its preferences. Critics often charge, with some justice, that many lawmakers are unwilling to run the political risks of making a serious commitment to policy making; they prefer to concern themselves with local interests and to let the president define the legislative work load. Congress has often been less than forceful in promoting its own initiatives. Until recently at least, Congress tolerated internal norms of reciprocity and courtesy that placed minority power and inaction above majority rule and decisiveness. Congress has stressed self-protection: it can then take credit for what goes right and avoid the blame for unsuccessful policies. If the legislature is to make headway toward more effective policy making, it must overcome its tendency to dodge risk and to defer to the executive branch or other experts rather than to stand and fight for its own preferences.

What is required is a Congress coequal with the president in more than just a theoretical sense, a legislature willing to assert its views and to accept the consequences when its actions prove unsuccessful. This necessitates more political courage; legislators must be prepared to state publicly the nation's position on issues even when local conditions suggest some other course of action. They must eschew a legislative culture that puts a premium on something for everyone and that condones the achievement of this goal through reciprocity and logrolling; rather they must be prepared to say "no" to a colleague and, more difficult, to have "no" said to them. Members of Congress must be willing to match their best efforts against the ideas of the executive and to stand or fall on the quality of those efforts. Such a show of determination will not come easily, and there will unquestionably be electoral casualties along the way. Yet only if Congress demonstrates such an exercise of will can it hope to achieve parity with a powerful executive.

Conclusion

Majoritarian democracy envisions an operative system of checks and balances—more precisely, a system of separate institutions, legislative and executive, with overlapping powers. According to this view, the traditional, now seemingly naive, faith in the beneficence of the president is untenable, and some executive-legislative cooperation in policy making is desirable. Such cooperation, from the legislative point of view, has three major components.

1. *A responsive deliberative stage of policy making.* Policy formulation would be a democratic, participatory process. A strengthened and more accessible legislature, with an enlarged staff and improved information resources, would sift proposals and draft legislation designed to serve the nation's needs. Because such a careful, reflective, and open deliberative stage would take time, there might be intervals during which problems would intensify or opportunities for solutions would be lost. But this is a price that must be paid if politicians are to be responsive, if their solutions are to reflect citizens' needs and desires. Moreover, the costs could be minimized if the deliberative stage was not allowed to extend beyond reasonable necessity.

2. *A responsible decision-making stage of policy making* The deliberative stage, during which committees produced legislation to be considered by the full chamber, would be followed by a decisive, action stage of decision making. At this point Congress should be organized to permit majorities to make decisions. Easier discharge of bills from committees; simpler access of bills to the floor; more germane debate, especially in the Senate; and less use of delaying tactics, particularly the Senate filibuster, could permit simple majorities to act. After due deliberation and careful formulation of bills, lawmakers should judge them on their merits and vote them up or down without delay.

Costs would be incurred at this stage as well. To move legislation with dispatch means limiting opportunities for minorities to stall. Minorities can and should have a full say during the deliberative stage, but at the point of action they must not be permitted to make policy by blocking decision making. At this stage the need to be responsible must override the need to represent, to be responsive. Lawmakers must first listen carefully and then act decisively.

3. *A Congress that is strengthened relative to the executive.* Congressional policy making, reflecting a satisfactory mix of responsiveness and responsibility, must produce decisions that have a reasonable chance of prevailing despite the president's exercise of power. Majoritarian democracy envisages a Congress with increased statutory authority; an improved public reputation; and, most important, a stronger will to assert legislative priorities. Continued reform in these directions would go far toward demonstrating the existence of such determination on the part of Congress.

Even though these proposals can be adopted incrementally, without changing the Constitution, the prospects for additional reform are uncertain. The executive will resist such changes, and some in the legislature may be reluctant to yield powers they presently possess. Majoritarian democracy is a vision of Congress and the presidency— each with its own constituency and independent power base—working together to make responsible and responsive public policy. If citizens have more access to and information about Congress, they will be more able to hold their elected representatives accountable. If the vision suggested seems workable, Congress can continue to build on the reforms of the 1970s and the proposals of the 1990s. The essential reinvigoration of the legislature depends on such action.

Summary

During the 1950s and 1960s, numerous critics of Congress found the institution wanting. When conditions were conducive, particularly between 1970 and 1977, Congress enacted a series of broad reforms designed to promote legislative responsibility, responsiveness, and accountability. When Congress was confronted by changed circumstances—unexpected events, new issues, and new members—in the late 1980s, a new reform agenda began to emerge. Although reformers then and now have seldom advanced pure, theoretical visions of an ideal Congress, their proposals tend to reflect two contrasting and often incompatible perspectives. For the most part, those who put a premium on prompt, efficient solutions to policy problems (that is, who favor responsibility) emphasize the need for a centralized Congress, as advocated by the executive force and responsible parties theories. They are prepared to sacrifice openness and multiple channels of communication—that is, responsiveness—for effective resolution of policy issues. They propose additional reforms to strengthen the executive's policy-making position, and they are prepared to rely on citizen-enforced accountability to keep the powerful president in check.

On the other side are those reformers, equally committed to achieving results, who value most a free and open deliberative process. As the price for responsiveness, they are ready to accept a decentralized system advocated by the pro-Congress (literary and Whig) theories. They view favorably a legislature, however irresponsible, that reaches decisions slowly and only after considerable negotiation and compromise. The reforms they propose to achieve their goals rely less on the assessment of accountability after the fact, at the polls, than on the ability of individual citizens and organized groups to present their views prior to policy formulation. Pro-legislative reformers promote a Congress ready to restrain, even to impose its own views on, the executive branch, including the president.

There is, of course, no right or wrong way to choose between these alternative visions of Congress and its future, whether one relies on definitive evaluation criteria or on empirical evidence. The choice ultimately rests on normative values, on the relative weight assigned to the competing values of responsibility and responsiveness. Indeed, in the real world no one vision has dominated the reform movement: decentralization and fragmentation (promoting responsiveness) seemed more predominant during the 1980s than in the previous decade; in the 1990s, the tide seems to have shifted toward centralization (promoting responsibility). Because reforms were adopted piecemeal over a period of years—in the same way that Congress makes substantive policy—there was no overall consistency in the pattern of reform; proponents of each vision won some victories and suffered some setbacks. Realistically, this is all that reformers should reasonably expect, but no group is satisfied, and each continues to advance its particular reform agenda. Others, less philosophically inclined, look for some middle ground, some optimum mix of responsibility, responsiveness, and accountability that will permit Congress and the president to play their respective roles in the policy-making process. Majoritarian democracy is only one manifestation of this search for a better legislature.

There are obviously clear limits to what reform can accomplish. One lesson of the reform experience is that societal change—events and elections—may stir the reform impulse; without such outside pressures the reform effort may wane. A second lesson is that reforms reflect different values and motivations, and in consequence, fail to meet fully some of their proponent's goals. Reformers should not expect that short-term success will inevitably continue over the long haul. As the world of Congress changes, and the people who serve in the legislature enter and leave, reformed organization and processes may cease to produce acceptable results and may require additional adjustment. Incremental solutions (the institutional tinkering so attractive to pragmatic reformers) may help, at least temporarily, but they are likely to prove impermanent as widespread change impinges on them.[29]

In the absence of any widely shared vision of what the legislature should be, reform is likely to be episodic and incremental. Congress remains fundamentally a representative institution sensitive to political pressures and public preferences. When there is a national consensus, Congress is likely to reflect it; no institutional organizations or processes can keep a determined majority of members from acting. When agreement is lacking, as it often is on controversial matters, reform cannot induce action; conventional congressional politics—decision making through bargaining and compromise—is likely to come into play.

Barring a major policy disaster or a constitutional crisis, reform will continue to be problematic. Congress, for lack of a viable alternative, may well continue to "muddle through," true to the classic pattern of American politics and policy making. The reformed Congress of the 1990s will most probably be different from the legislature of the 1980s, which is unquestionably quite distinct from that of the 1970s—but it is not clear in what specific ways. It is in this context that the quest, perhaps quixotic, for the quintessential Congress will continue.

NOTES

1. Divided government prevailed for twenty-eight of the forty-six years between 1946—when the Republicans won control of the Senate and House and Harry S. Truman was president—and 1992.
2. (Solon was an Athenian statesman of the late seventh and early sixth centuries B.C. who instituted legal reforms.) For arguments supporting a strong presidency, see Robert A. Dahl, *Congress and Foreign Policy* (New York: Harcourt, Brace and World, 1950); James M. Burns, *Congress on Trial* (New York: Harper, 1949), and *The Deadlock of Democracy* (Englewood Cliffs, N.J.: Prentice-Hall, 1963); Walter Lippmann, *The Public Philosophy* (Boston: Little, Brown, 1954); and Clinton Rossiter, *The American Presidency*, rev. ed. (New York: Harcourt, Brace, and World, 1960). On the pro-president position in the proposals of the Committee on the Constitutional System, see Dom Bonafede, "Reform of U.S. System of Government Is on the Minds and Agendas of Many," *National Journal*, June 29, 1985, 1521-1524. For more wide-ranging proposals to reform the American constitutional system, see Burke Marshall, ed., *A Workable Government* (New York: Norton, 1985); Donald L. Robinson, ed., *Reforming American Government* (Boulder, Colo.: Westview Press, 1985); and James L. Sundquist, *Constitutional Reform and Effective Government*, 2d ed. (Washington, D.C.: Brookings Institution, 1992).
3. See American Political Science Association, Committee on Political Parties, *Toward a More Responsible Two-Party System* (New York: Rinehart, 1950); E. E. Schattschneider, *Party Government* (New York: Rinehart, 1942); Austin Ranney, *The Doctrine of Responsible Party Government* (Urbana: University of Illinois Press, 1962); Davis S. Broder, *The Party's Over: The Failure of Politics in America* (New York: Harper and Row, 1972); Evron M. Kirkpatrick, "Toward a More Responsible Two-Party System: Political Science, Policy Science, or Pseudo-Science?" *American Political Science Review* 65 (1971): 965-990; and Gerald M. Pomper, "Toward a More Responsible Two-Party System: What Again?" *Journal of Politics* 33 (1971): 916-940.
4. In reality, British parties scarcely resemble the image of them held by the responsible parties school. See David Butler, "American Myths about British Political Parties," *Virginia Quarterly Review* 31 (1955): 45-56; and Robert T. McKenzie, *British Political Parties* (New York: Praeger, 1964).
5. The pro-president reformers, of course, are less than elated by the delegation of the full committees' powers to subcommittees. This additional decentralization makes it all the more difficult to induce Congress to act; more participants must

be mobilized to support presidential policy proposals.

6. See Barbara Hinckley, "Seniority 1975: Old Theories Confront New Facts," *British Journal of Political Science* 6 (1976): 383-399; and Glenn R. Parker, "The Selection of Committee Leaders in the House of Representatives," *American Politics Quarterly* 7 (1979): 71-93.

7. House Democrats deprived Phil Gramm (Texas) of his seat on the Budget Committee after he cooperated with the Reagan administration's 1981 budget blitz by sponsoring the Republican alternative, which was adopted in lieu of the Democratic plan. After his ouster, Gramm resigned from the party, ran for reelection as a Republican, and won easily. See Ross K. Baker "Party and Institutional Sanctions in the U.S. House: The Case of Congressman Gramm," *Legislative Studies Quarterly* 10 (1985): 315-337. In general, however, using committee assignments as a plum to encourage party discipline is still the exception, not the rule.

8. The Speaker's control over the Rules Committee and the Democratic caucus's ability to instruct the committee have lessened the need to reintroduce the twenty-one-day rule, under which the Speaker could, over committee objection, call up measures for floor consideration after the bill had been in the Rules Committee more than twenty-one days. The rule was adopted on two occasions—most recently in the 89th Congress (1965-1966)—and did facilitate the movement of legislation to the floor. But in each instance it did not survive renewed conservative strength in the subsequent Congress and was stricken from the rules.

9. Another proposal, applicable to all committees, would alter the discharge rule. The number of legislators' signatures required to extract a bill from a committee unwilling to report it would be reduced from the present 218, a majority of the full chamber, to some more readily attainable number, such as 150. This idea, popular in the earlier reform period, has received scant attention from recent reform advocates.

10. The line item veto fight neatly illustrates the continuing interplay of politics and principle in reform proposals. During the Reagan presidency, some reformers, recognizing that they could not muster a two-thirds vote to amend the Constitution, proposed to give the president the line-item veto for a two-year trial period. The experiment would expire before the end of the Reagan administration, permitting its supporters, mainly Republicans, to reassess their position should the Democrats win the presidency in 1988. Some line-item veto supporters saw the issue as a matter of principle, however. Sen. Edward Kennedy (D-Mass.), hardly a close ally of the Reagan administration, supported the proposal, arguing that "the fundamental issue . . . is fiscal responsibility, and it has little to do with the partisan politics of the moment. . . . A larger principle and a long perspective are at stake" (quoted in the *Boston Globe*, July 24, 1985, 3). In the Clinton administration, the issue has resurfaced and a similar mix of positions has emerged. Some Democrats favor giving a president of their party the line-item authority; others, notably the members of the Congressional Black Caucus, oppose it on the grounds that it undercuts Congress's authority. Some Republicans have rejected a two-year experiment with the line-item veto because it would confer an advantage on the opposition party's chief executive; others have supported the idea as a matter of principle. See Mary Jacoby, "Un-

likely Coalition of Blacks, Republicans Keeps the Line-Item Veto Bottled Up," *Roll Call*, April 28, 1993, 3, 28; and George Hager, "Arm-Twisting Yields House Win for Spending Control Bill," *Congressional Quarterly Weekly Report*, May 1, 1993, 1069.

11. On all these suggestions, see the sources cited in note 2 to this chapter.

12. Of course, this system requires that the electorate have thorough knowledge of the political issues in presidential (and congressional) campaigns, and there is some doubt that present-day voters are capable of rendering the policy mandates that this level of accountability requires. See Herbert B. Asher, *Presidential Elections in American Politics*, 4th ed. (Homewood, Ill.: Dorsey Press, 1988); and Gary C. Jacobson, *The Politics of Congressional Elections*, 3d ed. (New York: HarperCollins, 1992).

13. James Burnham, *Congress and the American Tradition* (Chicago: Regnery, 1959); and Alfred de Grazia, *Republic in Crisis: Congress against the Executive Force* (New York: Federal Legal Publications, 1965).

14. Burnham, *Congress and the American Tradition*.

15. Dispersion of authority is highly compatible with legislators' career aspirations, as has been noted. In a stable institution such as Congress, many lawmakers aspire to long-term congressional service. Thus, organizational and procedural reforms that enable them to exert influence, even over small segments of legislative business, have been attractive. Such reforms have allowed legislators to make a mark and to find a niche for themselves early in their congressional careers.

16. See Michael J. Malbin, *Unelected Representatives: Congressional Staff and the Future of Representative Government* (New York: Basic Books, 1980).

17. In *U.S. v. Nixon* (1974), the Supreme Court required the defendant to turn over to the special prosecutor Watergate tapes that Nixon asserted were protected by executive privilege. Although not applicable in situations involving possible criminal misconduct, executive privilege did have many useful purposes, the Court seemed to say. The implication was that the doctrine might well apply in other, more ordinary circumstances. The end of the cold war has virtually eliminated controversy over executive privilege, but legislation has been proposed from time to time that would (1) require executive personnel to appear before legislative committees, if only to claim executive privilege; (2) require a formal, written statement by the president to invoke the privilege; and (3) enforce the request for information by mandating an automatic cutoff of funds for a noncomplying agency. Such a bill, if enacted, would force the executive to justify withholding information from Congress.

18. See Stephen E. Frantzich, *Computers in Congress: The Politics of Information* (Beverly Hills, Calif.: Sage, 1982).

19. On the information problem in general, see John S. Saloma III, *Congress and the New Politics* (Boston: Little, Brown, 1969). Other useful sources include Joseph Cooper and G. Calvin Mackenzie, eds., *The House at Work* (Austin: University of Texas Press, 1981); *Congressional Quarterly Weekly Report*, July 13, 1985, 1379-1382; and Charles R. Dechert, "Availability of Information for Congressional Operations," and James A. Robinson, "Decision-Making in Congress," in *Congress: The First Branch of Government*, coord. Alfred de Grazia (Washington, D.C.: American Enterprise Institute, 1966), 167-211, 259-294.

20. An increase in information resources will be of little value if members do not use them or use them unproductively. Some observers fear that the legislators' use of computers to win reelection—to answer the mail or solicit campaign funds rather than to promote programs or conduct oversight—will detract from legislators' ability to be responsive in policy terms. They remain free to use data as they see fit—for their personal purposes, political or programmatic; if they decide to pursue undesirable (from the observer's standpoint) goals, no amount of data will improve responsiveness to public interests.

21. When the Supreme Court, in *Baker v. Carr* (1962) and *Wesberry v. Sanders* (1964), mandated population equality for House districts, there was a fear that reapportionment would cause conservative rural areas to lose representation to liberal urban areas. In fact, the dozen or so seats that rural areas lost in the redistricting process triggered by these decisions in the 1960s and 1970s wound up being controlled by suburban conservatives rather than by big-city liberals. (The cities also lost population.) More recent redistricting, reflecting 1980 and 1990 Census figures, has redistributed the seats regionally. The industrial Frost Belt (the Northeast and Midwest) has yielded seats to the southwestern Sun Belt. Overall, the effect of court-enforced reapportionment has been minimal. See Richard Born, "Partisan Intentions and Election Day Realities in the Congressional Redistricting Process," *American Political Science Review* 79 (1985): 305-319; Larry M. Schwab, *The Impact of Congressional Reapportionment and Redistricting* (Lanham, Md.: University Press of America, 1988); and David Butler and Bruce Cain, *Congressional Redistricting: Comparative and Theoretical Perspectives* (New York: Macmillan, 1992). Following the 1990 Census, in accordance with amendments to the Voting Rights Act of 1964, several states created House districts specifically designed to elect minority—black and Hispanic—members. These actions have been challenged in the courts as impermissible racial gerrymandering, but should the courts approve them, or (as some have proposed) impose some standard of proportional representation (a party winning a certain proportion of votes gets the same proportion of seats), the fears of the pro-Congress reformers might prove to be well founded. In June 1993, in a challenge to North Carolina's congressional districting, the Court ruled, 5-4, that "bizarre" districts drawn to increase the election of minorities to Congress *might* violate whites' civil rights, and returned the matter to the district court for further consideration.

22. On the media and Congress, see Robert Blanchard, ed., *Congress and the News Media* (New York: Hastings House, 1974); Stephen Hess, *The Washington Reporters* (Washington, D.C.: Brookings Institution, 1981); Michael J. Robinson, "Three Faces of Congressional Media," in *The New Congress*, ed. Thomas E. Mann and Norman J. Ornstein (Washington, D.C.: American Enterprise Institute, 1981), 55-96; Charles M. Tidmarch and John J. Pitney, Jr., "Covering Congress," *Polity* 17 (1985): 464-483; Peter Clarke and Susan H. Evans, *Covering Campaigns: Journalism in Congressional Elections* (Stanford, Calif.: Stanford University Press, 1983); Timothy E. Cook, *Making Laws and Making News: Media Strategies in the U.S. House of Representatives* (Washington, D.C.: Brookings Institution, 1989); and Stephen Hess, *Live from Capitol Hill* (Washington, D.C.: Brookings Institution, 1991).

23. As a practical matter, the reforms necessary to implement a presidential-domi-

nance arrangement, especially with the creation of responsible parties, would require amending the Constitution and making numerous statutory revisions. Congress can hardly be expected to enact legislation calling for the dissolution of its own claims to policy-making influence.

24. In this section, voting is treated as a means of transmitting views on political issues. Voting fosters accountability and responsiveness simultaneously. As a retrospective judgment, it holds incumbents to account for their past performance. As to the future, it offers suggestions about what should be done—at least it does so if policy sentiments shape voters' choices.

25. One of the chief reasons for the relative infrequency with which discharge petitions (requiring 218 signatures, a majority of the full House) are signed is the reluctance of rank-and-file representatives to risk the wrath of powerful committee leaders and experts. Easier discharge requirements, coupled with a decrease in the chair's control over the committee, should increase the prospect of getting legislation to the floor. But these changes would make it possible for a minority to force floor consideration of bills unacceptable to the majority. Such legislation presumably would not be passed; to force floor consideration could complicate the schedule and, in delaying action on priority bills, would retard the achievement of congressional responsibility.

26. These majorities would, in all probability, continue to be similar to those existing at present—they shift from issue to issue and are the result of a negotiation process. Rules changes would enhance a majority coalition's ability to get a floor vote and pass its measures.

27. *Congressional Quarterly Weekly Report,* November 24, 1984, 2983-2984. The Democratic caucus rejected the Obey proposal at the start of the 99th Congress (1985-1986); see *Congressional Quarterly Weekly Report,* December 8, 1984, 2054-2055.

28. On ethics, see New York City Bar Association, Report of the Special Committee on Congressional Ethics, *Congress and the Public Trust* (New York: Atheneum, 1970); Robert S. Getz, *Congressional Ethics* (New York: Van Nostrand, 1966); Robert Sherrill, "Why We Can't Depend on Congress to Keep Congress Honest," *New York Times Magazine,* July 19, 1970, 5ff.; Task Force on Broadcasting and the Legislature, *Openly Arrived At* (New York: Twentieth Century Fund, 1974); Edmund Beard and Stephen Horn, *Congressional Ethics: The View from the House* (Washington, D.C.: Brookings Institution, 1975); Hastings Center, *The Ethics of Legislative Life: A Report by the Hastings Center* (Hastings-on-Hudson, N.Y.: Hastings Center Institute of Society, Ethics, and the Life Sciences, 1985); and Vera Vogelsang-Coombs and Larry A. Bakken, "The Conduct of Legislators," in *Ethics, Government, and Public Policy: A Research Guide,* ed. James S. Bowman and F. A. Elliston (Westport, Conn.: Greenwood Press, 1988), 79-102.

29. For a major effort to develop a theory explaining congressional change and reform, see Lawrence C. Dodd, "A Theory of Congressional Cycles: Solving the Puzzle of Change," in *Policy Change in Congress,* ed. Gerald C. Wright, Jr., Leroy N. Rieselbach, and Lawrence C. Dodd (New York: Agathon Press, 1986), 3-44.

Appendix: Major Congressional Reforms, 1970-1993

Reforms Promoting Responsiveness

Redistributing Committee Power

1970 If a House Democratic committee chair declines to call a committee meeting, a majority can vote to meet anyway, with the ranking majority member presiding.

Any House committee member having the support of a committee majority can move for floor consideration of a bill if the chair fails to do so within seven days after a rule is granted.

1971 House Democratic and Republican committees on committees need not follow seniority in nominating committee chairs.

Ten House Democrats can force a vote in the party caucus on the committee on committees' nominations for committee chairs.

1973 At meetings of the House Democratic caucus, one-fifth of those present and voting can force a vote on each nominee for committee chair.

Senate Republicans on each committee can elect their ranking member without regard to seniority.

1975 Senate Democrats can vote in caucus for committee chairs without regard to seniority.

The House Democratic caucus can select chairs of the Appropriations Committee subcommittee using the same procedures used to pick chairs of the full committee.

Strengthening the Subcommittees

1973 House Democrats designate their members on each full committee as the committee caucus, with power to choose subcommittee chairs and set subcommittee budgets.

The House "subcommittee bill of rights" mandates that legislation be referred to subcommittees; that subcommittees be able to meet, hold hearings, and report legislation; and that each subcommittee have adequate staff and budget.

1973-1975 House Democrats establish a "bidding" procedure, based on seniority, for determining subcommittee assignments.

1974 Each House full committee (Rules Committee and Budget Committee excepted) is required to have at least four subcommittees.

1976 The committee caucus of each House full committee is empowered to determine the number of its subcommittees and to define their jurisdictions.

1977 House subcommittee chairs are selected by secret ballot.

Democratizing Reforms

1970 Senators are limited to service on two major committees and one minor committee.

No senator can chair more than one full committee or more than one subcommittee of a major committee.

1971 Each House subcommittee chair is allowed to hire the subcommittee staff.

No House Democrat can serve on more than two legislative committees or chair more than one legislative subcommittee.

1973 No House Democrat can serve on more than one exclusive committee, one major committee, or two nonmajor committees. Each member is entitled to one exclusive or major committee assignment.

1975 The chair of an exclusive committee or a major House committee is barred from chairing any other committee or serving on any other exclusive, major, or nonmajor committee.

1977 House Democrats cannot chair more than one subcommittee.

The House Speaker is obligated to appoint conferees from among those with basic responsibility for the legislation and to include, to the greatest extent possible, supporters of the bill's major provisions.

1978 House members can attend any meetings of committee or subcommittee (except those of the Ethics Committee), even if it is a closed session.

House Democrats who chair a full committee can chair a subcommittee only on that committee.

1979 House Democrats are limited to service on five subcommittees of standing committees.

Other Reforms

1970 The minority party in the House is guaranteed a minimum of ten minutes of debate on any amendment printed in the *Congressional Record* at least one day prior to the debate.

The minority party in the House is permitted to call its own witnesses on at least one day of committee hearings on a bill.

The minority party in the House is given at least three days to file minority views on committee reports.

1971 One-half of a Democratic state delegation in the House can nominate candidates for committee assignments in opposition to the choice of the Committee on Committees.

1975 The minority party in the House can hire one-third of committee staff.

Participation in House floor debate on conference reports must be divided equally between majority and minority members.

1977 The House Democratic caucus can elect the chair of the Democratic Congressional Campaign Committee. (Previously, the chair was elected by the committee itself.)

Reforms Promoting Accountability

"Sunshine" Reforms

1970 House allows television and radio coverage of committee hearings.

House teller votes are recorded.

House and Senate committee votes are recorded and made available to the public.

1973 All House committee sessions are open to the public. A separate roll call vote is required to close sessions.

1975 House committee sessions can be closed only with a separate roll call vote each day.

All Senate committee sessions are open to the public.

1977 Only the full House, by recorded roll call vote, can close a conference committee meeting.

1978 House permits television coverage of floor sessions.

1986 Senate permits television coverage of floor sessions.

Campaign Finance Reforms

1974 Federal Election Campaign Act amendments limit individual and organization contributions to congressional campaigns.

Additional FECA amendments require congressional candidates to report source and use of campaign funds.

Ethics Reforms

1977 House limits use of franked mail.

1977-1978 Senate and House adopt codes of ethics requiring disclosure of members' income and financial holdings, barring unofficial office accounts, and limiting outside income from honoraria to 15 percent of congressional salary.

1985 Senate raises permissible level of outside income to 40 percent of congressional salary.

1989 Ethics in Government Act limits size of gifts members may accept from lobbyists.

1990 Senate rewrites Rule 42 in an effort to define legitimate member representation of constituency interests.

1990, 1992 House adopts further limits on use of franked mail.

1992 House establishes position of director of non-legislative and financial services to manage its fiscal affairs.

Reforms Promoting Responsibility

Challenging the Executive

1970 Enlargement of the Congressional Research Service of the Library of Congress.

1970, 1974 Enlargement and strengthening of the General Accounting Office.

1972 Creation of the Office of Technology Assessment.

1973 Passage of the War Powers Act.

1974 Passage of the Congressional Budget and Impoundment Control Act, which establishes the Congressional Budget Office.

1985, 1987 Passage and revision of the Balanced Budget and Emergency Deficit Control Act (Gramm-Rudman-Hollings Act), which alters budgetary procedures.

1990 Passage of Budget Enforcement Act, which revises budgetary procedures.

Strengthening the Political Parties

1973 House Democratic leaders (Speaker, majority leader, and whip) are made members of the party Committee on Committees.

House Democrats establish the Steering and Policy Committee, with the Speaker as chair.

1974 House enacts legislation requiring a modest revision and clarification of committee jurisdictions.

House Speaker is empowered to refer bills to committees jointly and sequentially and to create ad hoc committees to expedite treatment of legislation.

1975 House Democratic Steering and Policy Committee is given the powers of the party's Committee on Committees.

House Speaker is authorized to nominate Democratic members of the Rules Committee.

1977 House Speaker is allowed to set time limits on joint and sequential committee consideration of legislation.

Senate leaders are given enlarged powers over bill referrals and scheduling.

Senate significantly revises its committee jurisdictions.

1993 House Democratic caucus assumes power to remove committee chairs at any time, not just at start of a new Congress.

House limits major committees (Appropriations, Rules, and Ways and Means excepted) to six subcommittees and limits minor committees to five subcommittees.

Changing the Rules

1970 House committees are permitted to meet while House is in session, except under special circumstances.

House establishes an electronic voting system.

House is allowed to dispense with reading of the *Journal*.

1970, 1977, 1979 Limits are placed on the use of quorum calls in House for dilatory purposes.

1975 Senate revises cloture rule: sixty senators can cut off debate.

1977, 1979 House can cluster roll call votes to expedite voting. Subsequent votes in a series are limited to five minutes.

1979 Twenty-five (rather than twenty) House members are required to demand a roll call in the Committee of the Whole House.

Senate is required to vote on a bill within 100 hours after cloture is invoked.

1986 Senate limits post-cloture debate to 30 hours.

1993 House permits "rolling quorum" in committee to facilitate consideration of legislation.

House restricts use of privileged motions as a dilatory tactic.

Selected Bibliography

General Views, Reviews, and Overviews

Theoretical Orientations and Perspectives

American Political Science Association, Committee on Political Parties. *Toward a More Responsible Two-Party System.* New York: Rinehart, 1950.

Bolling, Richard. *House Out of Order.* New York: Dutton, 1965.

Burnham, James. *Congress and the American Tradition.* Chicago: Regnery, 1969.

Burns, J. M. *The Deadlock of Democracy.* Englewood Cliffs, N.J.: Prentice-Hall, 1963.

Congressional Research Service, Library of Congress. *Congressional Reorganization: Options for Change.* Washington. D.C.: Congressional Research Service, 1992.

Cooper, Joseph. "Strengthening the Congress: An Organizational Analysis." *Harvard Journal on Legislation* 2 (1975): 301-368.

Davidson, R. H., D. M. Kovenock, and M. K. O'Leary. *Congress in Crisis: Politics and Congressional Reform.* Belmont, Calif.: Wadsworth, 1966.

Davidson, R. H., and W. J. Oleszek. "Adaptation and Consolidation: Structural Innovation in the House of Representatives." *Legislative Studies Quarterly* 1 (1976): 37-65.

de Grazia, Alfred. "Toward a New Model of Congress." In *Congress: The First Branch of Government*, coordinated by Alfred de Grazia, 1-22. Washington, D.C.: American Enterprise Institute, 1966.

Dexter, L. A. "Undesigned Consequences of Purposive Legislative Action." *Journal of Public Policy* 1 (1981): 413-431.

Dodd, L. C. "Woodrow Wilson's *Congressional Government* and the Modern Congress: The 'Universal Principle' of Change." *Congress & the Presidency* 14 (1987): 33-49.

Jones, C. O. "How Reform Changes Congress." In *Legislative Reform and*

Public Policy, edited by Susan Welch and J. G. Peters, 11-29. New York: Praeger, 1977.

_____. "Will Reform Change Congress?" In *Congress Reconsidered*, edited by L. C. Dodd and B. I. Oppenheimer, 247-260. New York: Praeger, 1977.

Mann, T. E., and N. J. Ornstein. *Renewing Congress: A First Report*. Washington, D.C.: American Enterprise Institute and the Brookings Institution, 1992.

_____. *Renewing Congress: A Second Report*. Washington, D.C.: Brookings Institution, 1993.

Oleszek, W. J. "A Perspective on Congressional Reform." In *Legislative Reform and Public Policy*, edited by Susan Welch and J. G. Peters, 3-10. New York: Praeger, 1977.

_____. "Integration and Fragmentation: Key Themes of Congressional Change." *Annals* 466 (1983): 193-205.

Patterson, S. C. "Conclusions: On the Study of Legislative Reform." In *Legislative Reform and Public Policy*, edited by Susan Welch and J. G. Peters, 214-222. New York: Praeger, 1977.

Rohde, D. W., and K. A. Shepsle. "Thinking about Legislative Reform." In *Legislative Reform: The Policy Impact*, edited by L. N. Rieselbach, 9-21. Lexington, Mass.: Lexington Books, 1978.

Saloma, J. S. III. *Congress and the New Politics*. Boston: Little, Brown, 1969.

Shepsle, K. A. "The Changing Textbook Congress." In *Can the Government Govern?*, edited by J. E. Chubb and P. E. Peterson, 238-266. Washington, D.C.: Brookings Institution, 1989.

Change and Reform in the 1970s and 1980s

Bailey C. J. "Beyond the New Congress: Aspects of Congressional Development in the 1980s." *Parliamentary Affairs* 41 (1988): 236-246.

Center for Responsive Politics. *"Not for the Short Winded": Congressional Reform, 1961-1986*. Washington, D.C.: Center for Responsive Politics, 1986.

Congressional Quarterly. "Inside Congress." In *Congress and the Nation* 4, 743-794. Washington, D.C.: Congressional Quarterly, 1977.

Democratic Study Group. *Special Report: Reform in the House of Representatives*. No. 94-28. Washington, D.C.

Dodd, L. C. "The Rise of the Technocratic Congress: Congressional Reform in the 1970s." In *Remaking American Politics*, edited by R. A. Harris and S. M. Milkis, 89-111. Boulder, Colo: Westview Press, 1989.

Dodd, L. C., and B. I. Oppenheimer. "Maintaining Order in the House:

The Struggle for Institutional Equilibrium" In *Congress Reconsidered*, 5th ed., edited by L. C. Dodd and B. I. Oppenheimer, 41-66. Washington, D.C.: CQ Press, 1993.

Dumbrell, John. "Strengthening the Legislative Power of the Purse: The Origins of the 1974 Budgetary Reforms in the U.S. Congress." *Public Administration* 57 (1980): 479-496.

Havens, H. S. "Gramm-Rudman-Hollings: Origins and Implementation." *Public Budgeting and Finance* 6 (1986): 4-24.

Huntington, S. P. "Congressional Responses to the Twentieth Century." In *The Congress and America's Future*. 2d ed., edited by D. B. Truman, 6-38. Englewood Cliffs, N.J.: Prentice-Hall, 1973.

Kravitz, Walter. "The Advent of the Modern Congress: The Legislative Reorganization Act of 1970." *Legislative Studies Quarterly* 15 (1990): 375-399.

Lowe, D. E. "The Bolling Committee and the Politics of Reorganization." *Capitol Studies* 6 (1978): 39-61.

Ornstein, N. J. "The Democrats Reform Power in the House of Representatives, 1969-1975." In *America in the Seventies*, edited by Allen Sindler, 1-48. Boston: Little, Brown, 1976.

————. "The House and the Senate in a New Congress." In *The New Congress*, edited by T. E. Mann and N. J. Ornstein, 363-383. Washington, D.C.: American Enterprise Institute, 1981.

Ornstein, N. J., R. L. Peabody, and D. W. Rohde. "The U.S. Senate in an Era of Change." In *Congress Reconsidered*. 5th ed., edited by L. C. Dodd and B. I. Oppenheimer, 13-40. Washington, D.C.: CQ Press, 1993.

Patterson, S. C. "The Semi-sovereign Congress." In *The New American Political System*, edited by A. King, 127-177. Washington, D.C.: American Enterprise Institute, 1978.

Polsby, N. W. "Tracking Changes in the U. S. Senate." *Political Science & Politics* 22 (1989): 789-793.

Shaw, Malcolm. "Congress in the 1970s: A Decade of Reform." *Parliamentary Affairs* 34 (1981): 253-290.

Sheppard, B. D. *Rethinking Congressional Reform: The Reform Roots of the Special Interest Congress*. Cambridge, Mass.: Schenkman Books, 1985.

Sinclair, Barbara. *The Transformation of the U.S. Senate*. Baltimore: Johns Hopkins University Press, 1989.

Sundquist, J. L. *The Decline and Resurgence of Congress*. Washington, D.C.: Brookings Institution, 1981.

Collections

Davidson, R. H., ed. *The Postreform Congress*. New York: St. Martin's Press, 1992.

de Grazia, Alfred, coordinator. *Congress: The First Branch of Government.* Washington, D.C.: American Enterprise Institute, 1966.

Hertzke, A. D., and R. M. Peters, Jr., eds. *The Atomistic Congress: An Interpretation of Congressional Change.* Armonk, N.Y.: M. E. Sharpe, 1992.

Ornstein, N. J., ed. *Congress in Change: Evolution and Reform.* New York: Praeger, 1975.

Rieselbach, L. N. *Congressional Reform: The Policy Impact.* Lexington, Mass.: Lexington Books, 1978.

_____. ed. "Symposium on Legislative Reform." *Policy Studies Journal* 5 (1977): 394-497.

Welch, Susan, and J. G. Peters, eds. *Legislative Reform and Public Policy.* New York: Praeger, 1977.

Congressional Documents

U.S. Congress. *Hearings Before the Joint Committee on the Organization of Congress: Committee Structure.* Washington, D.C. Government Printing Office, 1993.

_____. *Hearings Before the Joint Committee on the Organization of Congress: Support Agencies.* Washington, D.C.: Government Printing Office, 1993.

U.S. Congress. House. Select Committee on Committees. *Hearings on the Subject of Committee Organization in the House.* 3 vols. Washington, D.C.: Government Printing Office, 1973.

_____. Commission on Administrative Review. *Final Report.* 2 vols. Washington, D.C.: Government Printing Office, 1977.

_____. Select Committee on Committees. *Final Report.* Washington, D.C.: Government Printing Office, 1980.

U.S. Congress. Senate. Commission on the Operation of the Senate. *Toward a Modern Senate: Final Report.* Washington, D.C.: Government Printing Office, 1976.

_____. Study Group on Senate Practices and Procedures. *Report of the Study Group on Senate Practices and Procedures to the Committee on Rules and Administration.* Washington, D.C.: Government Printing Office, 1984.

_____. Temporary Select Committee to Study the Senate Committee System. *Final Report.* Washington, D.C.: Government Printing Office, 1984.

Structural Change and Reform

Political Parties

Crook, S. B., and J. R. Hibbing. "Congressional Reform and Party Discipline: The Effects of Changes in the Seniority System on Party Loyalty in the U.S. House of Representatives." *British Journal of Political Science* 15 (1985): 207-226.

Davidson, R. H. "Congressional Leaders as Agents of Change." In *Understanding Congressional Leadership*, edited by F. H. Mackaman, 135-156. Washington, D.C.: CQ Press, 1981.

_____. "The New Centralization on Capitol Hill." *Review of Politics* 10 (1988): 345-364.

_____. "Multiple Referral of Legislation in the U.S. Senate." *Legislative Studies Quarterly* 14 (1989): 375-392.

Deering, C. J., and S. S. Smith. "Majority Party Leadership and the New House Subcommittee System." In *Understanding Congressional Leadership*, edited by F. H. Mackaman, 261-292. Washington, D.C.: CQ Press, 1981.

Jones, C. O. "Can Our Parties Survive Our Politics?" In *The Role of the Legislature in Western Democracies*, edited by N. J. Ornstein, 20-36. Washington, D.C.: American Enterprise Institute, 1981.

_____. "House Leadership in an Age of Reform." In *Understanding Congressional Leadership*, edited by F. H. Mackaman, 117-134. Washington, D.C.: CQ Press, 1981.

Oppenheimer, B. I. "The Changing Relationship between House Leadership and the Committee on Rules." In *Understanding Congressional Leadership*, edited by F. H. Mackaman, 207-226. Washington, D.C.: CQ Press, 1981.

Ornstein, N. J., and D. W. Rohde. "Political Parties and Congressional Reform." In *Parties and Elections in an Anti-Party Age*, edited by Jeff Fishel, 280-294. Bloomington: Indiana University Press, 1978.

Peabody, R. L. *Leadership in Congress: Stability, Succession, and Change.* Boston: Little, Brown, 1976.

Rohde, D. W. *Parties and Leaders in the Postreform House.* Chicago: University of Chicago Press, 1991.

Sinclair, Barbara. "The Speaker's Task Force in the Post-Reform House of Representatives." *American Political Science Review* 75 (1980): 397-410.

_____. "The Emergence of Strong Leadership in the 1980s House of Representatives." *Journal of Politics* 54 (1992): 657-684.

Smith, S. S. "Forces of Change in Senate Party Leadership and Organization." In *Congress Reconsidered.* 5th ed., edited by L. C. Dodd and B. I. Oppenheimer, 259-290. Washington, D.C.: CQ Press, 1993.

Waldman, Sidney. "Majority Leadership in the House of Representatives." *Political Science Quarterly* 95 (1980): 373-393.

Committees

Bach, Stanley. "Committee and Subcommittee Change in the House of Representatives." Paper presented to the annual meeting of the American Political Science Association, 1984.

Davidson, R. H. "Two Avenues of Change: House and Senate Committee Reorganization." In *Congress Reconsidered*. 2d ed., edited by L. C. Dodd and B. I. Oppenheimer, 107-133. Washington, D.C.: CQ Press, 1981.

Davidson, R. H., and W. J. Oleszek. *Congress against Itself.* Bloomington: Indiana University Press, 1977.

Deering, C. J. "Subcommittee Government in the U.S. House: An Analysis of Bill Management." *Legislative Studies Quarterly*, 7 (1982): 533-546.

Fenno, R. F., Jr. *Congressmen in Committees.* Boston: Little, Brown, 1973.

Haeberle, S. H. "The Institutionalization of the Subcommittee in the U.S. House of Representatives." *Journal of Politics* 40 (1978): 1054-1065.

Hall, R. L., and C. L. Evans. "The Power of Subcommittees." *Journal of Politics* 52 (1990): 335-355.

Ornstein, N. J. "Causes and Consequences of Congressional Change: Subcommittee Reforms in the House of Representatives, 1970-1973." In *Congress in Change: Evolution and Reform*, edited by N. J. Ornstein, 88-114. New York: Praeger, 1975.

Ornstein, N. J., and D. W. Rohde. "Seniority and Future Power in Congress." In *Congress in Change: Evolution and Reform*, edited by N. J. Ornstein, 72-87. New York: Praeger, 1975.

Parris, J. H. "The Senate Reorganizes Its Committees, 1977." *Political Science Quarterly* 94 (1979): 319-337.

Rieselbach, L. N., and J. K. Unekis. "Ousting the Oligarchs: Assessing the Consequences of Reform and Change on Four House Committees." *Congress & the Presidency* 9 (1981-1982): 83-117.

Rudder, C. E. "Committee Reform and the Revenue Process." In *Congress Reconsidered*, edited by L. C. Dodd and B. I. Oppenheimer, 117-139. New York: Praeger, 1977.

Smith, S. S., and C. J. Deering. *Committees in Congress.* Washington, D.C.: CQ Press, 1984.

Smith, S. S., and B. A. Ray. "The Impact of Congressional Reform: House Democratic Committee Assignments." *Congress & the Presidency* 10 (1983): 219-240.

Stanga, J. E., Jr., and D. N. Farnsworth. "Seniority and Democratic Reforms in the House of Representatives: Committees and Subcommittees." In *Legislative Reform: The Policy Impact,* edited by L. N. Rieselbach, 35-47. Lexington, Mass.: Lexington Books, 1978.

Strahan, Randall. *New Ways and Means: Reform and Change in a Congressional Committee.* Chapel Hill: University of North Carolina Press, 1990.

Unekis, J. K. "The Impact of Congressional Reform on Decision-Making in the Standing Committees of the House of Representatives." *Congressional Studies* 7 (1980): 53-62.

Unekis, J. K., and L. N. Rieselbach. "Congressional Committee Leadership: Continuity and Change, 1971-1978." *Legislative Studies Quarterly* 8 (1983): 251-270.

———. *Congressional Committee Politics: Continuity and Change.* New York: Praeger, 1984.

Staff and Information Resources

Frantzich, S. E. *Computers in Congress: The Politics of Information.* Beverly Hills, Calif.: Sage, 1982.

Hammond, S. W. "Congressional Change and Reform: Staffing the Congress." In *Legislative Reform: The Policy Impact,* edited by L. N. Rieselbach, 183-193. Lexington, Mass.: Lexington Books, 1978.

Jones, C. O. "Why Congress Can't Do Policy Analysis (or Words to That Effect)." *Policy Analysis* 2 (1976): 215-264.

Malbin, M. J. *Unelected Representatives: Congressional Staff and the Future of Representative Government.* New York: Basic Books, 1980.

Schick, Allen. "The Supply and Demand for Analysis on Capitol Hill." *Policy Analysis* 2 (1976): 215-234.

Worthley, J. A. "Legislative Information Systems: A Review and Analysis of Recent Experience." *Western Political Quarterly* 30 (1977): 418-430.

Rules and Informal Norms

Bach, Stanley. "The Nature of Congressional Rules." *Journal of Law & Politics* 5 (1989): 725-757.

Bach, Stanley, and S. S. Smith. *Managing Uncertainty in the House of Representatives: Adaptation and Innovation in Special Rules.* Washington, D.C.: Brookings Institution, 1988.

Loomis, B. A., and Jeff Fishel. "New Members in a Changing Congress: Norms, Actions, and Satisfaction." *Congressional Studies* 8 (1981): 81-94.

Oleszek, W. J. *Congressional Procedures and the Policy Process.* 3d ed. Washington, D.C.: CQ Press, 1989.

Oppenheimer, B. I. "Changing Time Constraints on Congress: Historical Perspectives on the Use of Cloture." In *Congress Reconsidered.* 3d ed., edited by L. C. Dodd and B. I. Oppenheimer, 393-413. Washington, D.C.: CQ Press, 1985.

Ornstein, N. J., and D. W. Rohde. "The Strategy of Reform: Recorded Teller Voting in the House of Representatives." Paper presented to the annual meeting of the Midwest Political Science Association, 1974.

Renfrow, P. D. "The Senate Filibuster System, 1917-1979: Changes and Consequences." Paper presented to the annual meeting of the Southern Political Science Association, 1980.

Rohde, D. W., N. J. Ornstein, and R. L. Peabody. "Political Change and Legislative Norms in the United States Senate, 1957-1974." In *Studies of Congress,* edited by G. R. Parker, 147-188. Washington, D.C.: CQ Press, 1985.

Schneier, E. V. "Norms and Folkways in Congress: How Much Has Actually Changed?" *Congress & the Presidency* 15 (1988): 117-138. See also D. W. Rohde. "Studying Congressional Norms: Concepts and Evidence." Ibid., 139-145.

Smith, S. S. *Call to Order: Floor Politics in the House and Senate.* Washington, D.C.: Brookings Institution, 1989.

Wolanin, T. R. "A View from the Trench: Reforming Congressional Procedures." In *The United States Congress: Proceedings of the Thomas P. O'Neill, Jr., Symposium,* edited by Dennis Hale, 209-228. Chestnut Hill, Mass.: Boston College, 1982.

Uslaner, Eric. "Comity in Context." *British Journal of Political Science* 21 (1991): 45-77.

Change, Reform, and the Legislative Environment

Redistricting, Elections, Turnover

Alexander, H. E. *Financing Politics: Money, Elections, and Political Reform.* 3d ed. Washington, D.C.: CQ Press, 1984.

Benjamin, Gerald, and M. J. Malbin, eds. *Limiting Legislative Terms.* Washington, D.C.: CQ Press, 1992.

Bullock, C. S. III. "Redistricting and Congressional Stability, 1962-1972." *Journal of Politics* 37 (1975): 569-575.

Butler, David, and Bruce Cain. *Congressional Redistricting: Comparative and Theoretical Perspectives.* New York: Macmillan, 1992.

Fenno, R. F., Jr. "If, as Ralph Nader Says, Congress Is 'the Broken

Branch,' How Come We Love Our Congressmen So Much?" In *Congress in Change: Evolution and Reform*, edited by N. J. Ornstein, 277-287. New York: Praeger, 1975.

Ferejohn, J. A. "On the Decline of Competition in Congressional Elections." *American Political Science Review* 71 (1977): 166-176.

Fiorina, M. P. *Congress: Keystone of the Washington Establishment*. 2d ed. New Haven, Conn.: Yale University Press, 1989.

Jacobson, G. C. "The Marginals Never Vanished: Incumbency and Competition in Elections to the U.S. House of Representatives, 1952-1982." *American Journal of Political Science* 31 (1987): 126-141. See also M. Bauer and J. Hibbing, "Which Incumbents Lose in House Elections: A Response to Jacobson's 'The Marginals Never Vanished'." Ibid., 33 (1989): 262-271.

———. "The Effects of Campaign Spending in House Elections: New Evidence for Old Arguments." *American Journal of Political Science* 32 (1990): 334-362. See also D. P. Green and J. S. Krasno. "Rebuttal to Jacobson's 'New Evidence for Old Arguments'." Ibid., 363-372.

Magleby, D. B., and C. J. Nelson. *The Money Chase: Congressional Campaign Finance Reform*. Washington, D.C.: Brookings Institution, 1990.

Mann, T. E., and R. E. Wolfinger. "Candidates and Parties in Congressional Elections." *American Political Science Review* 74 (1980): 617-632.

Nugent, M. L., and J. R. Johannes, eds. *Money, Elections, and Democracy: Reforming Congressional Campaign Finance*. Boulder, Colo.: Westview Press, 1990.

Parker, G. R., and R. H. Davidson. "Why Do Americans Love Their Congressmen So Much More Than Their Congress?" *Legislative Studies Quarterly* 4 (1979): 53-61.

Petracca, M. P., and P. A. Smith. "How Frequent Is Frequent Enough? An Appraisal of the Four-Year Term for House Members." *Congress & the Presidency* 17 (1990): 45-66.

Schwab, L. M. *The Impact of Congressional Reapportionment and Redistricting*. Lanham, Md.: University Press of America, 1988.

Sorauf, F. J. *Inside Campaign Finance: Myths and Realities*. New Haven, Conn.: Yale University Press, 1992.

Legislative-Executive Relations

Aberbach, J. D. *Keeping a Watchful Eye: The Politics of Congressional Oversight*. Washington, D.C.: Brookings Institution, 1990.

Cooper, Joseph. "Postscript on the Congressional Veto: Is There Life after Chadha?" *Political Science Quarterly* 98 (1983): 427-429.

Davidson, R. H. "Breaking Up Those 'Cozy Triangles': An Impossible Dream?" In *Legislative Reform and Public Policy*, edited by Susan

Welch and J. G. Peters, 30-53. New York: Praeger, 1977.

Davis, E. L. "Legislative Reform and the Decline of Presidential Influence on Capitol Hill." *British Journal of Political Science* 9 (1979): 465-479.

Dodd, L. C., and R. L. Schott. *Congress and the Administrative State.* New York: Wiley, 1979.

Fisher, Louis. "War Powers: The Need for Collective Judgment." In *Divided Democracy: Cooperation and Conflict between the President and Congress,* edited by J. A. Thurber, 199-217. Washington, D.C.: CQ Press, 1991.

Franck, T. M., and Edward Weisband. *Foreign Policy by Congress.* New York: Oxford University Press, 1979.

Franklin, D. P. "Why the Legislative Veto Isn't Dead." *Presidential Studies Quarterly* 16 (1986): 491-501.

_____. "War Powers in the Modern Context." *Congress & the Presidency* 14 (1987): 77-92.

Gilmour, J. B. *Reconcilable Differences? Congress, the Budget Process, and the Deficit.* Berkeley: University of California Press, 1990.

Kaiser, F. M. "Congressional Control of Executive Actions in the Aftermath of the *Chadha* Decision." *Administrative Law Review* 36 (1984): 239-276.

LeLoup, L. T. "Budgeting in the U.S. Senate: Old Ways of Doing New Things." Paper presented to the annual meeting of the Midwest Political Science Association, 1979.

_____. "Process versus Policy: The U.S. House Budget Committee." *Legislative Studies Quarterly* 4 (1979): 227-254.

Ogul, M. S., and B. A. Rockman. "Overseeing Oversight: New Departures and Old Problems." *Legislative Studies Quarterly* 15 (1990): 5-24.

Schick, Allen. *Congress and Money: Budgeting, Spending, and Taxing.* Washington, D.C.: Urban Institute, 1980.

_____. *The Capacity to Budget.* Washington, D.C.: Urban Institute, 1990.

Shuman, H. E. *Politics and the Budget: The Struggle between the President and Congress.* 2d ed. Englewood Cliffs, N.J.: Prentice-Hall, 1988.

White, J., and Aaron Wildavsky. *The Deficit and the Public Interest: The Search for Responsible Budgeting in the 1980s.* Berkeley: University of California Press, 1989.

Wildavsky, Aaron. *The Politics of the Budgetary Process.* 4th ed. Boston: Little, Brown, 1984.

_____. *The New Politics of the Budgetary Process.* 2d ed. New York: HarperCollins, 1992.

Zeidenstein, H. G. "The Reassertion of Congressional Power: New Curbs on the President." *Political Science Quarterly* 93 (1978): 393-409.

Public Scrutiny: Ethics

Beard, Edmund, and Stephen Horn. *Congressional Ethics: The View from the House.* Washington, D.C.: Brookings Institution, 1975.

Bullock, C. S. III. "Congress in the Sunshine." In *Legislative Reform: The Policy Impact,* edited by L. N. Rieselbach, 209-221. Lexington, Mass.: Lexington Books, 1978.

Congressional Quarterly. *Congressional Ethics: History, Facts, and Controversy.* Washington D.C.: Congressional Quarterly, 1992.

Hastings Center. *The Ethics of Legislative Life: A Report by the Hastings Center.* Hastings-on-Hudson, N.Y.: Hastings Center Institute of Society, Ethics, and the Life Sciences, 1985.

Jennings, Bruce, and David Callihan, eds. *Representation and Responsibility: Exploring Legislative Ethics.* New York: Plenum Press, 1985.

Thompson, D. F. *Political Ethics and Public Office.* Cambridge, Mass.: Harvard University Press, 1987.

Twentieth Century Fund. *Openly Arrived At: Report of the Twentieth Century Fund Task Force on Broadcasting and the Legislature.* New York: Twentieth Century Fund, 1974.

The Impact of Change and Reform on Public Policy

Asher, H. B., and H. F. Weisberg. "Voting Change in Congress: Some Dynamic Perspectives on an Evolutionary Process." *American Journal of Political Science* 2 (1978): 391-425.

Berg, John. "The Effects of Seniority Reform on Three House Committees." In *Legislative Reform: The Policy Impact,* edited by L. N. Rieselbach, 49-59. Lexington, Mass.: Lexington Books, 1978.

Dodd, L. C. "Congress, the Presidency, and the Cycles of Power." In *The Post-Imperial Presidency,* edited by V. Davis, 71-99. New Brunswick, N.J.: Transaction Books, 1980.

———. "Congress, the Constitution, and the Crisis of Legitimation." In *Congress Reconsidered.* 2d ed., edited by L. C. Dodd and B. I. Oppenheimer, 21-53. Washington, D.C.: CQ Press, 1981.

———. "A Theory of Congressional Cycles: Solving the Puzzle of Change." In *Policy Change in Congress,* edited by G. C. Wright, Jr., L. N. Rieselbach, and L. C. Dodd. New York: Agathon Press, 1986.

Hahm, S. D., M. S. Kamlet, D. C. Mowery, and Tsai-Tsu Su. "The Influence of the Gramm-Rudman-Hollings Act on Federal Budgetary Outcomes, 1986-1989." *Journal of Policy Analysis and Management* 11 (1992): 207-234.

Hammond, S. W., and L. I. Langbein. "The Impact of Complexity and Reform on Congressional Committee Output." *Political Behavior* 4

(1982): 237-263.

Huddleston, M. W. "Training Lobsters to Fly: Assessing the Impacts of the 1974 Congressional Budget Reform." Paper presented to the annual meeting of the Midwest Political Science Association, 1979.

Johnson, L. K. "Legislative Reform of Intelligence Policy." *Polity* 17 (1985): 549-573.

Kaiser, F. M. "Congressional Change and Foreign Policy: The House Committee on International Relations." In *Legislative Reform: The Policy Impact*, edited by L. N. Rieselbach, 61-71. Lexington, Mass.: Lexington Books, 1978.

LeLoup, L. T., B. L. Graham, and Stacey Barwick. "Deficit Politics and Constitutional Government: The Impact of Gramm-Rudman- Hollings." *Public Budgeting and Finance* 7 (1987): 83-103.

Malbin, M. J. "The Bolling Committee Revisited: Energy Oversight on an Investigative Subcommittee." Paper presented to the annual meeting of the American Political Science Association, 1978.

Oppenheimer, B. I. "Policy Implications of Rules Committee Reforms." In *Legislative Reform: The Policy Impact*, edited by L. N. Rieselbach, 91-104. Lexington, Mass.: Lexington Books, 1978.

_____. "Policy Effects of U.S. House Reform: Decentralization and the Capacity to Resolve Energy Issues." *Legislative Studies Quarterly* 5 (1980): 5-30.

Ornstein, N. J., and D. W. Rohde. "Shifting Forces, Changing Rules, and Political Outcomes: The Impact of Congressional Change on Four House Committees." In *New Perspectives on the House of Representatives*. 3d ed., edited by R. L. Peabody and N. W. Polsby, 186-269. Chicago: Rand McNally, 1977.

Price, D. E. "The Impact of Reform: The House Subcommittee on Oversight and Investigations." In *Legislative Reform: The Policy Impact*, edited by L. N. Rieselbach, 133-157. Lexington, Mass.: Lexington Books, 1978.

Quirk, P. J. "Evaluating Congressional Reform: Deregulation Revisited." *Journal of Policy Analysis and Management* 10 (1991): 407-425.

Rieselbach, L. N. "Congressional Reform: Some Policy Implications." *Policy Studies Journal* 4 (1975): 180-188.

Rudder, C. E. "The Policy Impact of Reform of the Committee on Ways and Means." In *Legislative Reform: The Policy Impact*, edited by L. N. Rieselbach, 73-89. Lexington, Mass.: Lexington Books, 1978.

Smith, S. S., and C. J. Deering. *Committees in Congress*. 2d ed. Washington, D.C.: CQ Press, 1990.

Thurber, J. A. "The Impact of Budget Reform on Presidential and Congressional Governance." In *Divided Democracy: Cooperation and Conflict between the President and Congress*, edited by J. A. Thurber, 145-170. Washington, D.C.: CQ Press, 1991.

Thurber, J. A., and S. L. Durst. "The 1990 Budget Enforcement Act: The Decline of Congressional Accountability." In *Congress Reconsidered.* 5th ed., edited by L. C. Dodd and B. I. Oppenheimer, 375-397. Washington, D.C.: CQ Press, 1993.

Young, Garry, and Joseph Cooper. "Multiple Referral and the Transformation of House Decision Making." In *Congress Reconsidered.* 5th ed., edited by L. C. Dodd and B. I. Oppenheimer, 211-234. Washington, D.C.: CQ Press, 1993.

Index